Studies in World History

DR. JAMES STOBAUGH

Vol. 1

Creation Through
the Age of Discovery
{4004 BC to AD 1500}

HISTORY GEOGRAPHY ECONOMICS GOVERNMENT

GEOGRAPHY

ECONOMICS RELIGION GOVERNMENT HISTORY

ECONOMICS

Jr. High
STUDENT

First printing: March 2014

Master Books®, P.O. Box 726, Green Forest, AR 72638

Master Books® is a division of the New Leaf Publishing Group, Inc.

ISBN: 978-0-89051-784-0

Library of Congress Number: 2014931472

Cover by Diana Bogartus

Unless otherwise noted, Scripture quotations are from the New King James Version of the Bible.

Please consider requesting that a copy of this volume be purchased by your local library system.

Printed in the United States of America

Please visit our website for other great titles:
www.masterbooks.net

For information regarding author interviews,
please contact the publicity department at (870) 438-5288

Master Books®
A Division of New Leaf Publishing Group
www.masterbooks.net

Table of Contents

Studies in World History: Creation to the Age of Discovery

"Unicorn" seal from the Indus valley civilization, 1500 BC., India. (PD)

Youth pouring wine, ca. 480 BC (PD).

Table of Contents (cont.)

Roman aquaduct

Hunters

The conquistadors enter Tenochtitlan by Margaret Coxhead, 1909 (PD).

Preface

Studying history, at its essence, is studying the truth of the ages. And if we discover this truth, the wisdom of the ages, maybe we will live some of it out today. Aristotle wrote, "If you would understand anything, observe its beginning and its development." History understands truth's beginning and its development. The discovery of that beginning, of its development, is ours.

I did not say, "We are on a quest for the truth." We most certainly are not. We already know that Jesus Christ is the Way, the Truth, and the Life. Rather, we are going to look at history and grasp its application to our lives, to our nation, and to our world.

History, to us, is not merely theory. History, as we see it unfold, is clean and objective. In her book *On Looking into the Abyss: Untimely Thoughts on Culture and Society*, Gertrude Himmelfarb warns us that the "abyss is the abyss of meaninglessness."[1] The interpreter takes precedence over the thing interpreted, and any interpretation goes. The most obvious aim of such a creed is to weaken our hold on reality, chiefly by denying that there is any reality for us to get hold of. Its most probable effect, if we were to take it seriously, would be to induce feelings of despair and dread. This view invites the tyranny of the subjective — anything goes so long as it does not hurt anyone and is believed sincerely.

Contemporary Americans are dedicated to the pleasure principle. They yearn to be considered creative and imaginative, casting off the chains of mere causality and chronology. They conceive of history as a form of fiction — postmodernist fiction, to be sure — what one of them has called "a historiographic metafiction."

The British author G.K. Chesterton writes, "The madman's explanation of a thing is always complete, and often in a purely rational sense satisfactory."[2] While I agree that absolute objectivity has yet to be attained, it is not the same for absolute truth. In any event, the idea of objectivity as a guiding principle is too valuable to be abandoned. Without it, the pursuit of knowledge is indeed hopelessly lost. As Aristotle argues in his seminal work, *Nicomachean Ethics*, ". . . the great majority of mankind is agreed about this; for both the multitude and persons of refinement speak of it as Happiness, and conceive 'the good life' or 'doing well' to be the same thing as 'being happy.' But what constitutes happiness is a matter of dispute; and the popular account of it is not the same as that given by the philosophers."

Objectivity is as elusive as happiness, but truth is real. Are people better at making observations, discoveries, and decisions if they remain neutral and impartial? Only if they pursue truth.

---

1 Gertrude Himmelfarb, *On Looking into the Abyss: Untimely Thoughts on Culture and Society* (New York: Knopf, 2004).
2 G.K. Chesterton, *Orthodoxy*, Chapter II, http://gutenberg.org (p. 93).

Scientists know that absolute objectivity has yet to be attained. But ask poets. In *The Poetic Imagination*, theologian Walter Bruggemann writes, "to address the issue of a truth greatly reduced requires us to be poets that speak against a prose world. . . By prose I refer to a world that is organized in settled formulae. . . By poetry I mean language that moves, that jumps at the right moment, which breaks open old worlds with surprise, abrasion and pace. Poetic speech is the only proclamation worth doing in a situation of reductionism."

Knowledge in history will be pursued, but only those who love and find truth will attain it. Are people better at making observations, discoveries, and decisions if they remain neutral and impartial? Absolutely not. Jesus Christ is the Way, the Truth, and the Life!

Today, however, the individual, and by implication, society, compartmentalizes knowledge. The compartmentalization of knowledge and the dissolution of epistemic coherence is a concern for Christians. If knowledge is subjective, then truth will be the next victim. There will no longer be a redemptive narrative for millions of post-modern Americans whose subjectivity has stampeded any semblance of metaphysical objectivity from the barn. This social studies text, indeed all this author's writings, are an attempt to reclaim the rock solid truth that Jesus Christ is Lord of all, and the true history of mankind is our acceptance or rejection of that truth.

The loss of a continuous, historically true, biblical narrative in American society has

been disastrous. Post-modernism breaks the subject into moments of subjectivity that do not cohere into an identity. Quite literally, separating the whole into parts means there is no whole.

What does post-modernism really mean? It means that millions of Americans will not know who they are. Their subjective interpretations of who they are — roughly based on perceived needs and desires — will not suffice to create a coherent whole. Like Oedipus in Sophocles' *Oedipus Rex*, Americans will rail against the fates while standing squarely in the path of inevitable destruction and not knowing what is happening.

This book is a response to that need to awaken a desire for the truth found only in God's Word and in history that He guides by His almighty hand of grace; history that began for humanity in the Garden of Eden:

> And the Lord God formed man of the dust of the ground, and breathed into his nostrils the breath of life; and man became a living soul. And the Lord God planted a garden eastward in Eden; and there he put the man whom he had formed. And out of the ground made the Lord God to grow every tree that is pleasant to the sight, and good for food; the tree of life also in the midst of the garden, and the tree of knowledge of good and evil (Gen. 2:7–9 KJV).

Using Your Student Textbook

How this course has been developed

1. Chapters: This course has 34 chapters (representing 34 weeks of study).

2. Lessons: Each chapter has five lessons, taking approximately 20 to 30 minutes each. There will be a short reading followed by discussion questions. Some questions require a specific answer from the text, while others are more open-ended, leading students to think "outside the box."

3. Weekly exams: The Teacher Guide includes two optional exams for the chapter.

4. Student responsibility: Responsibility to complete this course is on the student. Students are to complete the readings every day, handing their responses in to a parent or teacher for evaluation. This course was designed for students to practice independent learning.

5. Grading: Students turn in assignments to a parent or teacher weekly.

Throughout this book are the following components:

1. First thoughts: Background on the historical period.

2. Discussion questions: Questions based generally on Bloom's Taxonomy.

3. Concepts: Terms, concepts, and theories to be learned that are bolded for emphasis. Most are listed on the first page of the chapter.

4. History makers: A person or persons who clearly changed the course of history.

5. Historical debate: An examination of historical theories surrounding a period or topic.

What the student will need:

1. Notepad: For writing assignments.

2. Pen/pencil: For answers and essays.

3. The Teacher Guide with daily lessons and information for weekly exams and/or to record daily assignments.

Chapter 1

The Fertile Crescent: Nomads to Farmers

First Thoughts

Around the time of the Great Flood (2347 B.C.), mankind stopped merely herding sheep and guarding cattle, and settled into small farming communities. The first place this settlement occurred was in the Tigris and Euphrates River Valley. This development marked the genesis of culture, or that which separates human beings from other species. Art, literature, science, and mathematics emerged from these agrarian communities. Before long, with improved agrarian methods (e.g., the invention of the plow) and improved transportation, cities, like Babylon, were formed. Great masses of people could live in these relatively comfortable and safe places. Farmers provided food, craftsmen provided goods, and priests provided succor to the soul. Agricultural societies, by their nature, were also more cognizant of time. They formed the "week," the first artificial division of time that was not based on natural phenomenon (e.g., the month was based on phases of the moon). With basic needs met, mankind began to look to the cosmos to find answers about critical things like birth and death, fate and peace. Only the Hebrews, neighbors to the southwest, really found the answer, but that did not stop Mesopotamian sages from searching.

Chapter Learning Objectives

Chapter 1 explores the emergence of human communities in the Mesopotamia region before and after the Great Flood.

As a result of this chapter you should be able to:

1. Trace the rise of civilization in Mesopotamia.

2. Analyze the importance of agrarian communities.

3. Observe the emergence of aberrant religions.

4. Understand the importance of geography on economics.

CONCEPTS

Civilization

Antediluvian

Mesopotamia

Tigris and Euphrates Rivers

Sumer

Babylon

Hammurabi Code

Rule of Law

Agrarian Societies

The Concept of Time

Nomadic Societies

Monotheism

Polytheism

Marduk

History: The Fertile Crescent

Antediluvian topography refers to the geography and natural land forms before the Flood.

The LORD God made garments of skin for Adam and his wife and clothed them. And the LORD God said, "The man has now become like one of us, knowing good and evil. He must not be allowed to reach out his hand and take also from the tree of life and eat, and live forever." So the LORD God banished him from the Garden of Eden to work the ground from which he had been taken. After he drove the man out, he placed on the east side of the Garden of Eden cherubim and a flaming sword flashing back and forth to guard the way to the tree of life (Gen. 3:21–24).

No one is certain about where the Garden of Eden was located, but many historians believe it was in the land between the Tigris and Euphrates rivers, called Mesopotamia.

Where was the Garden of Eden and where did Adam and Eve live their lives after the Fall? This question has plagued generations of historians and theologians. No one knows. We will probably never know because the Flood destroyed all antediluvian topography.

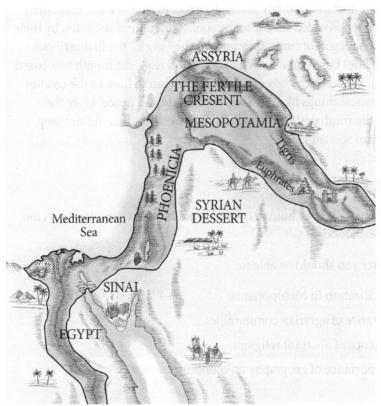

Nonetheless, our story begins in the Mesopotamian crescent, where the Tigris and Euphrates rivers join. There were many different civilizations that lived in and conquered the Mesopotamian region: Sumer, Assyria, Babylon, and Persia. We will merely explore the region generally.

Somewhere, perhaps in the fertile agricultural utopia between these two rivers, after Adam and Eve were driven from the Garden, their descendants herded sheep and made their living. Soon, though, they built houses from reeds or mud-brick and grouped in villages where they tended their crops. Additionally, they built barns called granaries to store their grain, and began developing a token system to record trade and accounts. In short, they created a **civilization**. For reasons still not well understood, the civilization of Southern Mesopotamia underwent a sudden growth and change, centered

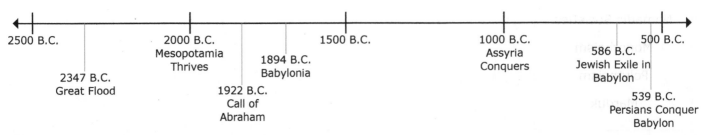

2500 B.C.

2347 B.C.
Great Flood

2000 B.C.
Mesopotamia
Thrives

1922 B.C.
Call of
Abraham

1894 B.C.
Babylonia

1500 B.C.

1000 B.C.
Assyria
Conquers

586 B.C.
Jewish Exile in
Babylon

539 B.C.
Persians Conquer
Babylon

500 B.C.

in the cities of Ur and Uruk. Perhaps the Great Flood caused these changes. People gathered into fewer, but larger, locations. The plow, the potter's wheel, and the introduction of bronze were invented. In this same period came the beginnings of writing and arithmetic. The name of this early civilization was Sumer.

Discussion Questions

Read Genesis chapter 1 and contemplate how God took a barren void and filled it with life, preparing Earth to be the homeplace of humanity. What astonishes you most about God's special relationship with people from the very beginning?

A detail of the Psalter World Map, 1265 A.D., featuring the Garden of Eden; many medieval maps used placement of the city of Jerusalem and other details like the Garden of Eden, Tower of Babel, or Noah's Ark to reveal a biblical connection to the geography of a world created by God.

Geography: A River Civilization

One of the people groups populating Mesopotamia was the Babylonians. Babylonians, like most ancient people, did not think much about what existed beyond the horizon. Inhabitants of Mesopotamia could reach the ocean in almost any direction in which they traveled — the Caspian Sea, the Black Sea, the Mediterranean Sea, or the Persian Gulf. Therefore, in a sense, they felt hedged in. Accordingly, the oldest map of the world that has been found is one accompanying a cuneiform inscription, representing the plain of Mesopotamia with the Euphrates flowing through it and the whole surrounded by two concentric circles, named *briny waters*. Outside of these circles were seven detached islets, possibly representing the seven zones or climates into which the world was divided according to the ideas of the Babylonians.[1]

The most important city in Mesopotamia was Babylon. Babylon rested on a level plain with the Tigris and Euphrates flowing right through it. Mountains surrounded the east and north sides of the plain, the Zagros chain and Kurdistan, and the Syrian and Arabian deserts guarded the west and the south. In short, it was an ideal place for a civilization to thrive.

In the summertime, the climate was hot and dry, but the winter was cold and wet. Average temperatures in Mesopotamia ranged from higher than 48°C (118.4°F) in July and August to below freezing in January. Inevitably, in the spring, the Tigris and Euphrates Rivers flooded great portions of the plain. That was a good thing. In ancient times, proper control of water enabled man to produce abundant crops, mostly barley and wheat, and the same water provided abundant grazing land in the rich meadows for livestock.

> The **Babylonian civilization** was urban in character, although based on agriculture. The country consisted of a dozen cities surrounded by agricultural settlements. At the head of the political structure was the king.

1 Joseph Jacobs, *The Story of Geographical Discovery: How the World Became Known* www.gutenberg.org, p. 19.

The success of the Mesopotamian civilizations was due to proper water management and resulting plentiful food supplies.

Because Babylon was situated on the river Euphrates, and all of Mesopotamia had access to river traffic, it was an ideal place for river trade. Mesopotamians could trade up the river to Syria and beyond and could act as a staging post with the cities of Sumer to the south. When Babylon became important, people would have wanted to live there because of the economic benefits it offered. It was the city, of course, in which Daniel and Esther lived. Babylon would have also given a greater degree of security to its inhabitants. Mesopotamia — Babylon in particular — was not easily conquered. Protected by inhospitable mountains and deserts, it was a determined foe that only those who would weather those obstacles could conquer.

Map of the world. c. 6th century BC. British Museum (CCA-SA2.5).

Discussion Questions

Can you identify the following map locations?

Babylon

Euphrates

Tigris

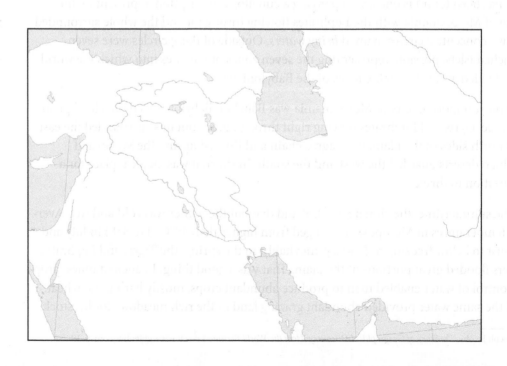

Government: Rule of Law

The rule of law is a legal maxim stating that governmental decisions should be made by applying written laws with minimal discretion in their application. Rule of law has a great deal of influence on the legal system and its relationship with political powers and individuals. This maxim was implemented in Babylon through the Code of Hammurabi.

The Code of Hammurabi is one of the oldest deciphered writings of significant length in the world. King Hammurabi, the sixth Babylonian king, enacted the code. It consists of 282 laws, with scaled punishments, adjusting "an eye for an eye, a tooth for a tooth" according to concerned parties' social status.

Nearly one-half of the Code deals with matters of contract, establishing, for example, the wages to be paid to laborers. The rest of the Code addresses social behavior.

The Code of Hammurabi is significant because it allowed men, women, slaves, and all others to read and understand the laws that governed their lives in Babylon. Laws of other civilizations were not written down, and thus could be manipulated to suit the rulers dictating them. The Code is particular to its time. For instance, it demands a trial by judges. It also advances laudable goals in society, like peace and security. In the words of Hammurabi: "Let any oppressed man who has a cause come into the presence of my statue as king of justice, and have the inscription on my stele read out, and hear my precious words, that my stele may make the case clear to him; may he understand his cause, and may his heart be set at ease!"[2]

Mesopotamia did not have a central national government until Babylon conquered all neighboring cities. The region mostly consisted of highly controlled city-states, in which priests and councils of male nobles ruled. This changed later when the city-states grew to unmanageable proportions and a king, called a suzerain, took over.

> The notion of a **king**, or **suzerain**, was a relatively late development in Mesopotamian history. Certainly nothing like it existed in the Sumer regime. It appeared during the Babylonian reign. Ironically, nomadic societies preferred a more democratic government ruled by groups of elders.

Code of Hammurabi, Louvre Museum, (CCA-SA3.0).

Discussion Question

Societies can have two types of laws: written and unwritten. Make a list of the written laws of your home or school and a list of the unwritten laws. For example, lying is a written law code violation, whereas playing soccer before finishing your homework might be a violation of an unwritten law.

> The Sumerian King List is revealed on a handful of ancient artifacts and manuscripts. The kings include pre-flood kings, those who reigned before the global deluge related to the biblical account of Noah.

---

2 C. H. W. Johns, MA, *The Oldest Code of Laws in the World*, #282. www.gutenberg.org

Lesson 4

Economy:
The Development of the Concept of Time

Nomadic people are communities of people who move from one place to another rather than settling permanently in one location. Nomadic cultures are hunter-gatherers or pastoral nomads. Abraham was a nomad.

An economy consists of the economic system of a nation or other political entity. An economy includes labor, capital (money), and land resources. It also includes the manufacturing, trade, and consumption of goods and services. Goods and services are exchanged according to demand and supply between participants by barter or a money exchange with a credit value accepted within the contracted groups.

The economy involves all aspects of a society: history and social organization, as well as its geography and natural resources. These factors give context to a developing economy and set the conditions and parameters in which an economy functions.

Much of what we think of as human history inevitably revolves around agriculture. It was mostly farmers who built cities, wrote books, and developed culture. Sometime before the Great Flood, Mesopotamia evolved into an agrarian society (a society of farmers).

Farmers developed a concept of time, a concept of "the week." The week, in contrast to the concept of a "month" (which is based on the stages of the moon), was based on God's creation as outlined in Genesis. Thus, weeks were started or stopped by religious events, market days, and other non-agrarian events.

Ruins in the town of Ur, Southern Iraq (CCA-SA 2.0).

Agriculture spawned ancillary economies such as cottage industries (small entities that produced products in their homes) and a religious class. Agriculture and improved transportation enabled cities separated from adjacent farms to emerge. Agricultural societies were usually very religious and were very focused on male leadership.

Hanging Gardens of Babylon - 16th century engraving by Dutch artist Martin Heemskerck (PD-US, PD-Art).

Farming communities had much higher birth and survival rates than nomadic, herding communities. When farming began in earnest, the world's population mushroomed to between 60 and 70 million people.[3]

Nonetheless, agriculture (or farming) brought some problems. Namely, as people lived sedentary lives in close proximity to one another, diseases and plagues had available hosts to infect and terrorize. Cities struggled with normal problems that large, closely packed, contiguous housing communities always face: how to deal with the social and physical needs of its people. Sewage, garbage control, and water acquisition all became concerns. In fact, wealthy Babylonians, because of these issues, moved outside the city and created the first suburb.

Mesopotamia was primarily an agrarian community after the Great Flood. In the arid but fertile river valleys, agriculture was possible only with irrigation, a fact that had a profound effect on the Mesopotamian civilizations. The need for irrigation meant that Mesopotamians built their cities along the Tigris and Euphrates and the branches of these rivers. Major cities, such as Ur and Uruk, took root on tributaries of the Euphrates, while others, notably Lagash, were built on branches of the Tigris. The rivers provided the benefits of fish, organic fertilizer, weaving reeds, and clay for building bricks. There is no doubt that Mesopotamia supported a thriving economy for most of its history and still does today.

From *Compilation of the Chronicles and Histories of the Bretons* by Pierre Le Baud, a 15th century chaplain in France. Images include the death of Abel, Noah's Ark, and Tower of Babel.

In summary, the Mesopotamian economy moved beyond subsistent farming. It appears to have been the first society to do so. For the first time in history, a civilization reached such a stage of prosperity and excess that it could afford to indulge itself in luxuries.

Discussion Questions

Psalm 126 is an agrarian song. King David, or an Israelite farmer who is talking about both the joy and the sadness of planting time, writes it.

> When the LORD restored the fortunes of Zion, we were like those who dreamed. Our mouths were filled with laughter, our tongues with songs of joy. Then it was said among the nations, "The LORD has done great things for them." The LORD has done great things for us, and we are filled with joy. Restore our fortunes, LORD, like streams in the Negev. Those who sow with tears will reap with songs of joy. Those who go out weeping, carrying seed to sow, will return with songs of joy, carrying sheaves with them. (NIV)

Who is the primary speaker in this verse? What is his vocation? What is his relationship with God?

---

3   Peter N. Stearns, *World History in Brief* (New York: Pearson Publishing Co., 2010), p. 13–14.

The farmer saved seed grain through the winter. He often had to watch family members starve—but he dared not use the seed grain. If he did, there would be no crops the next year and all would starve. What observation and conclusion does he draw from this long winter of sacrifice?

What application can you make to your own life?

Lesson 5

Religion: Polytheism

Monotheism is the belief in one God.
Polytheism is the belief in several gods.

From the beginning, Adam and Eve knew God, His grace and power revealed clearly to them. When they were driven from the Garden because of their sin, they and many of their ancestors continued to follow *YAHWEH* (Hebrew word for Almighty God) — the one and the only God. However, many forgot this and followed other gods. They abandoned **monotheism** for **polytheism**.

Like so many pagan religions of antiquity, the Mesopotamian religion had its roots in the worship of nature. Quite literally, Mesopotamians, particularly the Sumerians, created images of nature in approximate form. This was an attempt to appease, if not control, the forces of nature.

A paradise as created by God during the creation week is at the heart of the biblical account of the Garden of Eden.

16

Early man paid particular attention to their dead. They hoped that the cessation of human life was not the final answer. Religion explained the unexplainable to its people. It provided needed succor in time of stress and grief. Because religion invested so much in humanity, it was the source from which writing, reading, and art emerged. In short, there could be no culture without religion.[4]

The Sumerians regarded the universe as consisting of two realms, heaven and earth. Earth was a flat disk surrounded by a hollow space. This was enclosed by a solid surface which they believed was made of tin. Between earth and heaven was a substance known as **lil**, which means "breath." The cosmos adhered to established rules. Mesopotamians enjoyed an ordered universe.

The world below was known as the nether world. The Sumerians believed that the dead descended into the nether world, also known as the underworld. A person could enter the nether world from a special entrance, but could not leave unless a substitute was found to take one's place in the world below. The nether world was ruled by two gods: Nergal and Ereshkigal. After descending into the nether world, a soul had to cross a river with the aid of a boatman who ferried them across. They then con-

4   Todd Carney, *Cliffs AP World History* (New York: Wiley Publishing, 2010), p. 20.

fronted Utu, who judged their soul. If the judgment was positive, the soul would live a life of happiness. Nonetheless, Sumerians generally believed that life in the nether world (hell) was dismal. No one really wanted to go there.

The gods of Sumer were immortal, but human in form and demeanor. They could be hurt, and no one wanted to be the one who hurt them.

Each god adhered to a set of rules of divine authority known as *me*. They ensured that each god was able to keep the cosmos functioning according to a master plan. Thus it behooved Sumerians to appease the gods.

Sumerians had hundreds of gods. Many gods had spouses and children, and the more powerful gods had lesser gods as servants. Yes, the gods were organized into a caste system, or hierarchy, a sort of "pecking order" where the more important gods/goddesses ruled the lesser gods. The four most important deities were An, Enlil, Enki, and Ninhursag. These were the four creator deities who created all of the other gods. An was initially the head of the pantheon, though he was eventually seceded by Enlil. Enlil is seen as the most important god. He is known as "the king of heaven and earth," "the father of the gods," and "the king of all the gods." Enlil developed the broad designs for the universe. However, it was Enki who further developed and carried out his plans. Ninhursag was regarded as the mother of all living beings.

Austen Henry Layard's "Monuments of Nineveh, Second Series," London, J. Murray, 1853 (CCA-SA3.0).

Image of the war-god Nergal by Ernst Wallis et al, 1875 (PD-US).

Sumerians, like all ancient people, believed that their role in the universe was to serve the gods. To this end, the ancient Sumerians devoted much of their time to ensuring their favor with the gods through worship, prayer, and sacrifice. Generally speaking, though, the gods were mischievous and unpredictable in their responses. There was no concept of a loving, personal God that the Hebrews knew so well.

The temple was the center of worship. Each city usually had a large temple dedicated to its favorite god or goddess and might also have small shrines dedicated to other gods. Daily sacrifices of animals and foods were made. Anything would do (e.g., wine, milk, and meats); it was the thought that counted. Additionally, special occasions called for spectacular festivities that would sometimes last for days.

The most famous Mesopotamian god, the one most Hebrew captives would have learned about in their captivity, was Marduk, the son of Enki. He was without a doubt the most important and most powerful of the Mesopotamian gods. In Babylonian legend, Marduk destroyed all other gods, particularly evil Tiamat, and became the head god. This was the closest that Mesopotamian worshipers came to believing in one god (monotheism).

Discussion Question

Contrast the God of the Old Testament with the gods that the Mesopotamians served.

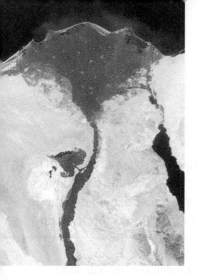

Chapter 2

A River Runs North: Nile

First Thoughts

If we were asked to name the most interesting country in the world, I suppose most people would say Israel — not because there is anything in the geography so very noteworthy, as it isn't very large and a good portion is desert, but because of all the great things that have happened there, and above all because it was the birthplace of Christ. But after Israel, Egypt would be my choice. For one thing, it is linked to the story of Joseph in the Old Testament, and Moses brought Israel out of Egypt into the Promised Land. Egypt is a wondrous land. Powerful pharaohs, exotic plants, deadly snakes, and mighty pyramids all populate our imaginations.

One historian explains, "The pyramids, for instance, those huge piles that are still the wonder of the world, were far older than any building now standing in Europe, before Joseph was sold to be a slave in Potiphar's house. Hundreds upon hundreds of years before anyone had ever heard of the Greeks and the Romans, there were great kings reigning in Egypt, sending out their armies to conquer Syria and the Soudan, and their ships to explore the unknown southern seas, and wise men were writing books which we can still read." When America was a wild, unknown island, inhabited only by natives, Egypt was a great and highly civilized country, full of great cities with elaborate palaces and temples.[1]

Chapter Learning Objectives

Chapter 2 reveals the mystery that was Egypt. Suddenly, the land of the pharaohs, the land of the Exodus, comes alive.

As a result of this chapter you should be able to:

1. Evaluate the effect of Egyptian political stability on its development as a world power.

2. Analyze the impact of the Nile River geography on the development of Egypt.

3. Understand the role of the pharaohs.

4. Contrast Egyptian views of women with those of Judaism and Christianity.

---

1 James Baikie, *Peeps at Many Lands: Ancient Egypt* (London, UK: Black, 1916), p. 1.

Lesson 1

History: The Fertile River Valley

Timeline

2347 B. C.
The Great Flood

2250–1750 B. C.
The Old Kingdom

1750–1500 B. C.
The Middle Kingdom

1500–332 B. C.
The New Kingdom

Historian James Breasted stated, "The art of Egypt was so ripe and so far advanced that it is surprising to find any student of early culture proposing that the crude contemporary art of the early Babylonians is the product of a civilization earlier than that of the Nile."[2] Perhaps, but many other historians disagree. If this was true, it was mostly, if not completely destroyed by the Great Flood.

Nonetheless, Egypt, whose civilization emerged along the rich delta of the Nile River, was one of the ideological, social, and historical heavyweights of the ancient world. Most secular historians divide Egyptian history into three periods: The Old Kingdom (2250–1750 B.C.), The Middle Kingdom (1750–1500 BC), and The New Kingdom (1500–332 B.C.).

The Old Kingdom, arising after the Great Flood, developed a strong national government for the first in history. Egypt was ruled from Memphis, a city on the Nile. Relatively free from invasion, the Old Kingdom was able to flourish. Kings supervised vast public works, which included the pyramids at Giza.

The Middle Kingdom was not so quiet. There were several civil wars. King Mentuhotep II united the kingdom again but moved the capital to Thebes.

In about 1700 B.C., some major trouble arose. A group of nobles led a revolt against the king. Weakened by internal strife, the Hykos from Syria conquered Egypt. This is one of the first examples in history where a numerically inferior but technologically advanced nation was able to conquer a numerically superior nation. The Hykos had chariots; the Egyptians did not.

The Pyramids of Chéfren and Mycérinus at Gizeh, Pascal Sébah, c1860-1890 (PD-US).

After a relatively short reign, the Hykos were defeated by Egyptian King Ahmose. Ironically, King Ahmose drove the Hykos from Egypt with his own superior horse-drawn chariots. King Ahmose was the first pharaoh. Pharaohs were fairly serious rulers who saw themselves as gods on earth and demanded absolute obedience.

It was in the New Kingdom era, probably during the reign of Ramses II, that Moses took his people from Egypt to the Promised Land. Ramses III, one of the sons of Ramses II (who was born after the Exodus), lost several wars in neighboring Syria. Egypt became vulnerable to attack, and was eventually conquered by Alexander the Great in 332 B.C.

2 www.brainyquote.com/quotes

Discussion Question

Historian Jason Thompson, in his book *A History of Egypt*, argues that few, if any, other countries have as many threads of continuity running through their entire historical experience as does Egypt.[3] Speculate what effect this common history and stability has had on Egyptian history.

Geography: Between Red Land and Black Land

The Nile River **Delta** (the land around the mouth of the Nile River) is a great place to start a civilization. The river flows north, is 4,160 miles long, and empties into the Mediterranean Sea. The good thing is that across all 4,000-plus miles, the river gathers rich, African soil that it deposits along the banks of northern Egypt. Because of the favorable climate and rich Nile sediment, cities (e.g., Memphis and Thebes) were created fairly quickly in Egyptian ancient history.

Another positive advantage of Egypt was its natural geographical defenses. Bordered by the inhospitable Libyan Desert on the west, the wide Red Sea and arid Arabian Desert on the east, the Mediterranean Sea on the north, and the vast African subcontinent on the south, Egypt was rarely invaded by enemy forces.

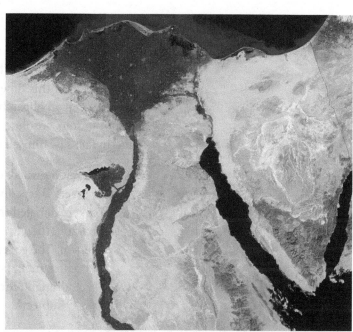

The ancient Egyptians spoke of Egypt as containing two types of land — the "black land" and the "red land." The "black land" was the fertile land on the banks of the Nile. Most people lived here. The ancient Egyptians used this land for growing their crops.

The "red land" was the barren desert that protected Egypt on two sides. These deserts separated ancient Egypt from neighboring countries and invading armies. They also provided the ancient Egyptians with a source for precious metals and semi precious stones. It is no wonder that Egypt used iron and other hard metals in weaponry before other ancient peoples.

The dark area down the center of the image is the Egyptian "black land", which is dark, rich soil fed by the Nile (NASA/GSFC).

As intimated, Egypt is divided into four main parts: the Nile Valley, the Arabian Desert, the Libyan Desert, and the Sinai. About 95 percent of Egypt is desert land. The Sahara Desert covers more than two-thirds of Egypt. The other deserts are the Libyan Desert, the Arabian Desert, and the Nubian Desert.

---

3 Jason Thompson, *A History of Egypt* (New York: Knopf, 2009).

Egypt is 50 feet below sea level. Some important cities are Cairo (the capital), Giza, Memphis, Thebes, and Alexandria. The highest point in Egypt is Jabal Katrina, which is 8,668 feet high. The lowest point is Qattara Depression, which is 436 feet below sea level.

There are five important oases in Egypt, and they are all located in the Libyan Desert. They are the Farafirah, Bahriah, Dakhilia, Kharijah, and the Siwah oases. The area of Egypt is 386,662 square miles, or about three times the size of New Mexico. The distance from east to west is 770 miles and from north to south is 675 miles.

There are only two seasons: winter (December through March), and summer (April through November). The average temperature in the winter is between 55° and 70°F. The average temperature in the summer is between 80° and 90°F. In the summer the temperature is sometimes 110°F.[4]

Discussion Question

The Nile River Civilization (Egypt) is a land of contrasts. That is especially true as far as the geography goes. Explain.

Lesson 3

Government: Pharaoh

Ramses II in Luxor Temple (CCA-SA3.0).

The pharaoh, meaning "big house," was a new kind of ruler. Nothing like it existed in the world at this time. The pharaoh did not create an **oligarchy** (rule by a group), even an oligarchy where he was the head ruler. The pharaoh was a true **despot** (a solo, absolute, omnipotent ruler). He shared leadership with no man, and in fact saw himself as a god.

The pharaoh owned all of Egypt — all animals, mines, people, and even the Nile River. The people gave the pharaoh portions of their crops in taxes. Workers donated their labor, and artists created art for the pharaoh. The pharaoh, then, was not merely powerful; he was also an extremely wealthy person. The government built storehouses to hold grain that was given as tax payment (see the story of Joseph in Genesis). During times of severe draught, the pharaoh would sell some of this grain to his hungry subjects.

It was not that the pharaoh did not have nobles and advisors to help him rule. The Egyptian state developed some sophisticated social, political, and religious systems. There were several classes of people. At the top, below the pharaoh of course, were the royal

4 http://www.ancientegypt.co.uk/geography/home.html.

families, nobles, and priests. Next were the merchants (businessmen), artisans (craftsmen), scribes (learned men who copied manuscripts), and tax collectors. Very close to the bottom were the farmers on whose back the economy rested. At the very bottom were slaves, mostly collected from the conquered people brought back from successful campaigns.

Discussion Question

What distinct advantages does a pharaoh-type government bring to a growing, thriving state/empire? What disadvantages?

Ramses II and the Exodus

Ramses II was the greatest, most celebrated, and most powerful pharaoh of the Egyptian Empire. Moses was Ramses' adopted brother. Moses is an Egyptian name meaning "one who is born." It uses the same root as Ramses.

Ramses II led several military expeditions into the Levant, reasserting Egyptian control over Canaan. It is possible that Moses participated in some of these early campaigns. He also led expeditions to the south, into Nubia. At age 14, Ramses was appointed prince regent by his father Seti I. He ruled Egypt for 66 years and two months.

The early part of his reign was focused on building cities, temples, and monuments. He established the city of Pi-Ramses in the Nile Delta as his new capital and as the main base for his campaigns in Syria. This city was built on the remains of the city of Avaris, the capital of the Hyksos when they took over, and was the location of the main Temple of Set. He is also known as Ozymandias in the Greek sources, from a transliteration into Greek of a part of Ramses' throne name.

Ramses II's temple of Beit el-Wali in Northern Nubia, Oriental Institute, University of Chicago (CCA-SA3.0).

23

The Destruction of Pharaoh's Army, illustration from the 1890 Holman Bible (PD-US).

The Hebrews had come 450 years before when Joseph brought his starving family to live with him in Egypt. Eventually, the Egyptians saw the Hebrews as a threat and forced them to work as slaves.

In an attempt to reduce their numbers, newborn Israelite babies were drowned in the river Nile. In order to escape death, Moses' mother placed baby Moses in a basket and set him adrift on the river Nile. The infant Moses was rescued by the pharaoh's daughter and brought up in the palace as a royal prince and brother to Ramses II.

As an adult, Moses reacted against the unfair treatment of his own people and killed an Egyptian guard. Moses was then forced to flee from the wrath of pharaoh. He was sent into the Arabian Desert and eventually wandered to Midian. He married Zipporah, the daughter of the priest of Midian, and worked as a shepherd for 40 years. One day, when he was in the desert, Moses heard the voice of God speaking to him through a bush, which burned but was not consumed. God told Moses to set His people free.

When Moses returned, his brother, Ramses II, was pharaoh. At first, the pharaoh refused to let the Israelites leave, and then God unleashed ten plagues on the Egyptians. It was the tenth plague — the plague of the firstborn — that eventually persuaded the pharaoh to let them go. The pharaoh then changed his mind, and sent his army in pursuit of the Israelites. Six hundred chariots pursued them, but famously, the waters of the Red Sea parted; the Israelites walked through, then the waters returned and destroyed the pharaoh's army.

Discussion Question

Retell the Exodus story from the perspective of Ramses II.

The Great Temple of Ramses II (PD-US).

Egyptian Culture

Culture is the set of shared attitudes, values, goals, and practices that characterizes a nation, organization, or group. Culture is that part of society that determines how people live, and includes the economy, science, and religion.

The Egyptian economy, as one would expect, was more government-controlled than in Mesopotamia. As evident in later **totalitarian** (where life is completely controlled by the government) regimes, the Egyptian government — more specifically the pharaoh — controlled all aspects of the economy. In the case of Egypt, this system of government may actually have been good. For one thing, an economy that was ruled by one person assured that irrigation control was manifestly evident every year. The pharaoh would appoint **monopolies** (the exclusive control of a trade or commodity by one individual or business entity) that would oversee all aspects of the irrigation process, which was vital to Egyptian prosperity, even survival.

A monopoly can be a precipitation agent for innovation and profits in the early stages of an industry. For instance, the monopoly AT&T had on the telephone in its early years assured a steady profit margin in the initial stages of expensive experimentation and innovation. Similarly, Egypt had one of the most successful and innovative irrigation systems in the ancient world. With a dependable, growing agricultural base, the pharaohs would build other aspects of their societies and economies.

As a society experiences prosperity, it inevitably develops the arts. Egyptian art was especially robust, colorful, and lively; Egyptian artists loved to decorate palaces and tombs with colorful images.

Likewise, science flourished. For instance, Egyptian mathematics produced the concept of a 24-hour day.

The most famous art form and scientific achievement was the pyramid. The largest pyramids required more than 100,000 workers. It is amazing that Egyptian workers, mostly paid laborers, rolled huge stones over logs and onto barges for transport to other river locations. Then, building long temporary ramps (like contemporary construction people create scaffolding), the workers would push these stones into place in precise, exact locations.

Egyptian religion was far more diverse than Mesopotamian religion, indeed, more than any religion, other than perhaps Hinduism. This is reflected in the fact that there are at least two creation myths (stories explaining a natural phenomenon). This is significant. No culture in the world, before the Nile Civilizations, nor after, has ever advanced two creation myths! Inevitably, the religious community effectively advances one theory. Not so with the diverse, mentally active ancient Egyptians.

The Keops pyramid (CCA-SA2.5).

The first creation myth states that, from the beginning of time, there was only the watery chaos, called Nu. Amon Ra, the sun god, rose up from the chaotic waters. Desiring a place to stand, he created a hill. But he was lonely so he produced a son and daughter. They had god kids and so forth until mankind appeared.

Another creation story argues that Amon Ra took the form of Khepri, the scarab god who was mostly credited as the great creative force of the universe. In a quote, Khepri tells us that in the beginning, nothing existed before him, not heaven or earth. He also says that everything came out of Amon Ra's mouth — that he rose from Nu, the watery abyss, which he also created, and then used the material in it to make everything in the universe. He created everything and was alone. Later, he decided to create more gods, so he breathed the god Shu (the god of air) and spit up the goddess Tefnut (the goddess of moisture).

After this, Khepri created animals and plates, while Shu and Tefnut became parents to Geb (earth) and Nut (sky). Then Geb and Nut gave birth to Osiris, Isis, Set, and Nephthys.[5]

For the beginning, the early Egyptian gods were combinations of animals and gods.

Beyond this there was no single, specific set of ancient Egyptian religious beliefs, but rather a set of generic ritual superstitions that folks followed. For instance, most everyone believed that people had to take a journey in the afterlife and that it was important for living family survivors to provide in the tomb what was needed for the journey. In the beginning, the afterlife was only a possibility for kings. They therefore needed to be mummified and given ample provisions and resources to enter the afterlife in style. Later, as Egyptian nobility emerged, they were also included in this select group.

Discussion Question

Egyptian civilization gave women, at least in the wealthier families, some power. Nefertiti, queen of Egypt, had considerable power and influence. Mesopotamia had no queens. However, Egyptian women were not generally valued. An ancient Egyptian scribe (scholar) noted, "Love your wife . . . but keep her at home and master her." Contrast this view with Jewish, and later, Christian, views of women.

5 Brandon Toropov and Father Luke Buckles, *World Religions* (New York: Penguin Group, 2004), p. 266–267.

Chapter 3

God's Precious Treasure: Prospering in a Hostile Place

First Thoughts

How fascinating it is that God chose a rather obscure people to be His chosen people; His precious treasure. The history of Israel begins with Abraham's call, "I will make you into a great nation" (Gen. 12:2). The name *Israel* (meaning either "one who fights victoriously with God" or "a prevailing prince with God") comes from the new name God gave Abraham's grandson Jacob, after Jacob withstood a spiritual struggle at Jabbok (Gen. 32:28).

Chapter Learning Objectives

Chapter 3 explores the history of Israel, the specialness of its people, and its impact on world history. We begin with a short history. Then we travel across the physical nation from the Negev to the Dead Sea. Then we examine the government, and then we finish with an inspiring, and to some, controversial, essay from a Jewish leader.

As a result of this chapter you should be able to:

1. Evaluate if Israel's claim to the present-day geographical land is a rightful claim.

2. Define "nomadic food gatherer" and contrast him with a farmer/agrarian.

3. Delineate the different aspects of Israeli geography.

4. Trace the evolution of government in Israel from the time of Adam's fall to the Roman Empire.

5. Analyze Rabbi Anteby's conclusions.

Overview

The people of Israel trace their origin to Abraham, who established the belief that there is only one God, the Creator of the universe. He did this in the midst of an alien, even hostile people. Abraham, his son Isaac and grandson Jacob, all lived in the Land of Canaan, Palestine, that later came to be known as Israel.

The name *Israel* derives from the name given to Jacob (Gen. 32:29). His 12 sons were the 12 tribes that later became the nation Israel.

Israel became a nation after its exodus from Egypt under the leadership of Moses. Soon after the **Exodus**, Moses transmitted to the people of this new emerging nation the Torah and the Ten Commandments (Exod. 20). After 40 years in the Sinai Desert, Moses led them to the land of Israel, cited in the Bible as the land promised by God to the descendants of the patriarchs Abraham, Isaac, and Jacob (Gen. 17:8).

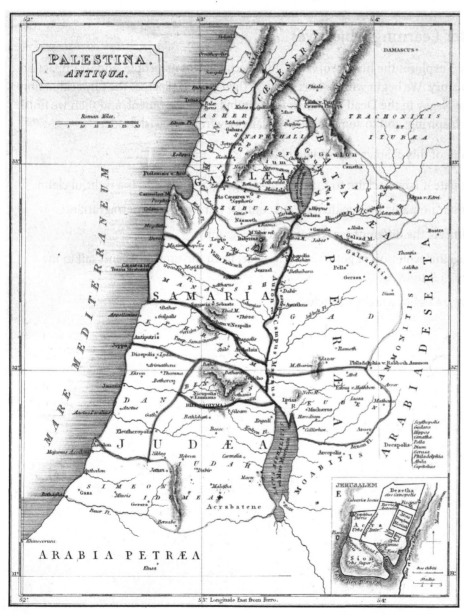

After Joshua and his people conquered **Canaan, the Promised Land**, Israel was officially a nation among nations. This period is called the "Period of the Kings," the most noteworthy being King David, who made Jerusalem the capital of Israel, and his son Solomon, who built the first temple in Jerusalem.

In 587 B.C., Babylonian Nebuchadnezzar's army captured Jerusalem, destroyed the temple, and exiled the Jews to Babylon. From this year onward, the region was ruled or controlled by several empires of the time: Babylonian, Persian, Greek Hellenistic, Roman and Byzantine Empires, Islamic and Christian crusaders, the Ottoman Empire, and the British Empire.

In 520–515 B.C., exiled Jews returned from Babylon and constructed the second temple. In 333 B.C., Macedonian Alexander the Great conquered the whole known world, including Israel. Macedonians ruled until the Romans arrived in 63 B.C.

Ancient map of Palestine.

In A.D. 70 there was a violent revolt that Rome subdued. Afterward, many Jewish people migrated to Europe and North Africa. In the **Diaspora** (Israelis scattered outside of the land of Israel), they continued their national culture and prayed to return to Israel. In the first half of the 20th century there were major waves of immigration of Jews back to Israel from Arab countries and from Europe. During World War II, the Nazi regime murdered about six million Jews, creating the great tragedy of the Holocaust. In 1948, the Jewish community in Israel, under the leadership of David Ben-Gurion, re-established sovereignty over their ancient homeland. The declaration of independence of the modern state of Israel was announced on the day that the last British forces left Israel — May 14, 1948.

Discussion Question

Despite the fact that the land was/is occupied by Islamic Palestinians, why does Israel claim the present-day geographical land on which it is established? Is it a rightful claim?

Israel is the only nation on earth that inhabits the same land, bears the same name, speaks the same language, and worships the same God that it did 3,000 years ago. You dig the soil and you find pottery from Davidic times, coins from Bar Kokhba, and 2,000-year-old scrolls written in a script remarkably like the one that today advertises ice cream at the corner candy store.

— Charles Krauthammer, *The Weekly Standard*, May 11, 1998.

Abraham: Nomadic Food Gatherer, Father of Judaism

No other people in the world claim a land because of divine right. Israel's claim is based on Abraham, who admittedly was not born there. Israel points to the promise made to Abraham (originally from the Babylonian city of Ur). Although the modern **Zionist** (pro-nationalist, pro-Israel homeland) movement was largely non religious, the idea of the "promised land" has had a powerful influence in creating and maintaining the modern State of Israel. Ironically and sadly, this same story also tells of the origin of another people, the offspring of Ishmael, the Islamic people. Both religions therefore trace their origins back to Abraham, and both hold the land of Israel sacred, though only the Jews claim it is exclusively their land.

Abraham migrated with his father Terah from Ur to Haran. After his father's death, God called Abraham to go to the land that he would show him where he would make of Abraham a great people. This land was called **Canaan**. Abraham went to Canaan with his wife Sarah and nephew Lot.

Abraham and Isaac depicted in "Lay Not Your Hand on the Child" from 1728, The Hague (PD-US).

29

Abraham fathered a son, Ishmael, through Sarah's servant Hagar. The birth of Ishmael did not fulfill God's promise of a child to Abraham and Sarah; therefore, the promise of a great nation remained unrealized. God reaffirmed His promise to give Abraham descendants as numerous as the stars in heaven, however, and Abraham continued to hope. Eventually, when Abraham was 100 years old, Sarah bore a son named Isaac.

God tested Abraham by commanding him to sacrifice Isaac on Mt. Moriah. As Abraham prepared to sacrifice the boy, God intervened and spared Isaac, and Abraham instead sacrificed a ram caught in the bushes. The New Testament portrays Abraham as an example of faith, affirming that the promises God made to Abraham extend to all who believe.

Abraham was a **nomadic food gatherer**, which means he moved from place to place drawing on the resources of the land to feed his vast herds and family. They normally did not create important aspects of civilization like writing, but they did provide trading contacts among other people groups and often had an impact far greater than their numbers imply. Abraham and his other nomadic friends preferred to live on the huge grassy planes and semi-arid lands of the Middle East. Seasons were not as pronounced in the Middle East as elsewhere; nonetheless, Abraham was forced to move from place to place to replenish food supplies. Abraham would normally have traveled the same route, so it was extraordinary and no doubt worrisome to family and friends when he launched out on his own toward Canaan (Gen. 12:1–2).

Abraham's life and economy was centered on animals, not on crops. Nomadic cultures like Abraham's inevitably valued courage and stamina. This was called **courage culture**. Warlike men normally dominated, and Abraham was himself a great warrior. Nomads depended a great deal on relatives and kin. Kinship was critical. It must have broken Abraham's heart when his nephew Lot left the family fold to move to the city. Large families were more the rule than the exception. The apparent barrenness of Sarah must also have been very painful to this couple.

Nomads often traded with agricultural communities, as Abraham traded with Abimelech. Nomads and their kin would often set up tribute payments with agricultural, settled societies.

Discussion Question

Define "nomadic food gatherer" and contrast him with a farmer/agrarian.

Dead Sea shipments being transported, between 1910 and 1920 (PD-US).

Lesson 3

Israel: Geography

Israel is 8,630 square miles, of which 8,367 square miles is land area. Israel is 290 miles in length and about 85 miles across at the widest point. The country is bordered by Lebanon to the north, Syria to the northeast, Jordan to the east, Egypt to the southwest, and the Mediterranean Sea to the west.

Its climate and geography approximate California, although California is double the size of Israel. Mountains and plains, fertile land, and desert are often minutes apart. The width of the country, from the Mediterranean Sea in the west to the Dead Sea in the east, can be crossed by car in about 90 minutes; and the trip from the far north to the southern tip takes about nine hours. It is clearly not a big country.

Israel may be divided into four geographical regions: three parallel strips running north to south and a large, mostly arid, zone in the southern half. The coastal plain runs parallel to the Mediterranean Sea and is composed of a sandy shoreline, bordered by stretches of fertile farmland extending up to 25 miles inland.

Several mountain ranges run the length of the country. In the northeast, the basalt landscapes of the Golan Heights overlook the Hula Valley. The hills of Galilee ascend to heights ranging from 1,600 to 4,000 feet above sea level. Small permanent streams and generous rainfall keep the area verdant all year round. Therefore, many residents of Galilee and the Golan are engaged in agriculture.

The Jezreel Valley, separating the hills of Galilee from those of Samaria, is Israel's richest agricultural area, cultivated by many **cooperative communities** called **kibbutzim**. A kibbutz (in Hebrew: "gathering, clustering") is a collective community in Israel that was traditionally based on agriculture.

The rolling hills of Israel concentrate the population mainly in small urban centers and large villages.

The Negev, comprising about half of Israel's land area, is sparsely inhabited, its population supported by an agricultural and industrial economy. Further south, the Negev becomes an arid zone characterized by low sandstone hills and plains, abounding with canyons and **wadis** (a ravine or valley dry except in a rainy season) in which winter rains often produce flash floods.

The Arava, Israel's savannah region, begins south of the Dead Sea and extends to the Gulf of Eilat, Israel's outlet to the Red Sea. **The Dead Sea**, the lowest point on earth at about 1,300 feet (400 m) below sea level, lies at the southern end of the Jordan Valley. Its waters, with the highest level of salinity and density in the world, are rich in other minerals.

Israel's climate ranges from temperate to tropical. Two distinct seasons predominate: a rainy winter period from November to May, and a dry summer season through the next six months.[1]

The Dead Sea is a salt lake bordering Jordan to the east and Israel and the West Bank to the west. Its surface and shores are the lowest elevation on the Earth's surface. Nothing can live in the lake, hence it is the "dead sea." It lies in the Jordan Rift Valley, and its main tributary is the Jordan River.

Modern map of Israel.

---

1 http://www.mfa.gov.il/MFA/Facts+About+Israel/Land/.

Discussion Question

Golda Meir, born in Kiev, Russia, became the fourth prime minister of Israel. She and her husband emigrated from the United States to Palestine as Zionists. When Israel won independence, Golda Meir was the only woman in the first Israeli cabinet. She was prime minister from 1969 to 1974. She once said, "Let me tell you something that we Israelis have against Moses. He took us 40 years through the desert in order to bring us to the one spot in the Middle East that has no oil!"[2] Perhaps, though oil was recently found in Israel! Israel has other geographical assets. What are they?

Lesson 4

Israel: Government

Statue of King David by Nicolas Cordier in the Borghese Chapel of the Basilica di Santa Maria Maggiore.

From the time of the Fall to about 1150 B.C., the Jewish people had no central leader. The leadership mostly fell to tribal leaders, called **patriarchs**. Notable among these are Noah, Abraham, Isaac, Jacob, and Joseph. These patriarchs were both leaders of their tribes and often ancillary people groups who paid tribute. Moses, the lawgiver, represented a new leader — whose role included judicial (law giving), legislative (law enactment), and executive (administration) roles. He was not a king, but he was close to it. Other leaders emerged, including military leaders such as Joshua.

In 1150 more new leaders arose: **judges**. A biblical judge was a ruler or a military leader, as well as someone who presided over legal hearings. He (except in the case of Deborah, judges were exclusively male) was both warrior leader and legal judge in matters of civil suits and litigation.

These leaders were not permanent. They served as long as a crisis existed, and departed when the crisis was over. Following the conquest of Canaan by Joshua until the formation of the first Kingdom of Israel, the Israelite tribes formed a loose **confederation** (an organized group of autonomous, loosely connected states or people groups).

Gradually, a growing priestly class asserted its influence. These prophets (e. g., Eli, Samuel) assumed leadership in Israel. This proved unsatisfactory to most Israelites, so eventually a king was anointed — the first being King Saul. The kings ruled through the Exile in Babylon and then the time of conquest by Macedonia (Alexander the Great) and Rome.

---

2 David Shear, "Could Israel Become Oil Production Leader?" in *Shalom Life*, http://www.ynetnews.com/articles/0,7340,L-4049471,00.html

Ironically, God preferred to be the one and only ruler of Israel. If His people had accepted His authority as a **benevolent totalitarian ruler** (someone in total control), Israel would have fared much better. Paul, in his writings, coined a new phrase for government. He said that Christians should be "willing slaves or servants" of God. In other words, Paul called believers to willingly accept the "bondage" of servitude to the Almighty God so that God could then free believers to be all that they could be in Christ (Gal. 5:1).

Discussion Question

Trace the evolution of government in Israel from the time of Adam's fall to the Roman Empire.

Israel: Religion

"A Contemporary Account of Judaism"

by Rabbi Max Anteby

The Bible tells us that the Jewish people have a patriarch by the name of Abraham. God made a promise to Abraham that his descendants would be an eternal nation. If you have been following this column or the other articles, videos, and audios on this website, you would know that we are, in fact, eternal. We have survived against unspeakable odds while nations and empires greater than us have disappeared off the face of the earth.

In this week's Bible portion, God makes an even more astounding claim. He tells Abraham that He will bless those who bless the Jewish people and curse those who curse us. We have been chosen by God to be His messenger and He is telling the world that He will go out of His way to protect us (as long as we don't forget to deliver His message).

Has this also come true? Let's take a look at a few examples:

The Star of David also known as the Shield of David.

In the Middle Ages, Spain boasted the most powerful navy in Europe. It controlled the trade routes and sent its explorers around the world. The 1300s were known as the Golden Age of Spain, not only for the Spanish but also especially for the Jews. In 1492, the Jews were expelled from Spain. When was the last time you heard of Spain as a world power?

In the early 1500s, shortly after the Inquisition, the king of Poland invited the Jews of Europe to come to his country to help build the economy. He issued a warning that anyone who harmed a Jew would have to answer personally to the king. Then came the Chmelnicki pogroms of 1648 and 1649, killing more than 350,000 Polish Jews. Poland has since been defeated in every war it has ever fought.

Germany was the most sophisticated, technologically advanced country in Europe in the 1700s and 1800s. As Jews became emancipated and more prominent members of society, German anti-Semitism eventually came to the forefront. By 1935, the Jews had become totally disenfranchised. Germany lost World War I, followed closely by World War II.

The Jews of America have had unprecedented rights and freedoms. America continues to be the number-one economy of the world. If we continue to give Americans reason to bless us, we have every reason to expect that God will continue to make good on His promise.

On a more personal level, the Bible gives us a way to bless each other. It is called the **Blessing of the Cohanim**. (The Cohanim today are the priestly class, direct descendents of Moses' brother Aaron, who was the first Jewish High Priest.) Every day during the recital of the morning prayers, the cantor (or, in the Sephardic synagogues, the Cohanim themselves) recites the following blessing from the Bible:

"The LORD bless you and keep you; the LORD make His face shine on you and be gracious to you; the LORD turn his face toward you and give you peace" (Num. 6:24–26).

What a powerful blessing to receive every day. It is also the blessing that parents give to their children on Friday nights. If your children are blessed, then you are surely blessed.[3]

Discussion Question

Do you agree with Rabbi Anteby's conclusions?

An ibex in Mitzpe Ramon, Israel.

3 Rabbi Max Anteby, "A Blessing on Your Head," http://SimpleToRemember.com

Chapter 4

Indus Valley: Religion and Culture are United

First Thoughts

While Rome was conquering Egypt and most of the Western world, South Asians, called the Guptas, enjoyed unprecedented peace and prosperity. The Indus River Valley spawned one of the most fruitful and enduring civilizations in world history.

Chapter Learning Objectives

We will discuss the daily life of several Indus civilizations. Next, we will observe the origination of the priest class, be amazed by the Gupta civilization, and muse over the development of the caste system!

As a result of this chapter you should be able to:

1. Ruminate upon the early government that emerged in nascent Indus civilizations.

2. Analyze the origination of the priest class.

3. Discuss the Golden Age of India.

4. Delineate the caste system of India.

5. Debate the location of the first world civilization.

Indus Valley Civilization

Mold of a seal, Indus Valley civilization, 1500 BC. State Museum, India.

In the northwestern parts of the Indian **subcontinent** (India is part of the Asia continent, but is really part of the South Asian subcontinent), there flourished a highly developed civilization. It derived its name from the main river of that region, **Harappan** or "Indus." At its peak, it stretched across the whole of northern India.

The cities were far more advanced than their counterparts in prehistoric Egypt, Mesopotamia, Israel, or anywhere else in western Asia. As in most other contemporary civilizations, agriculture was the backbone of the Indus economy. The people made extensive use of the wooden plows (borrowed from the Mesopotamians). Agriculture sustained the rudimentary urban center that emerged.

Barley and wheat were the main food crops. Barley was good to eat but was also the backbone of a flourishing alcohol industry, both to drink in beer and as a way to store valuable crops until they could be sold in the **marketplace**. Farmers would convert barley and hops into beer and transport it long distances to return a profit. The marketplace was a very interesting venue — an outdoor **retail** and **wholesale** destination where farmers and entrepreneurs sold their produce and wares. Marketplaces existed in all cultures, but in the Indus culture, these marketplace **outlets** — very similar to contemporary discount outlets — were mobbed by clever **entrepreneurs** and cautious buyers.

Meanwhile, for the first time, the cultivation of cotton appeared. Cotton apparel adorned the backs of beautiful Indus women and **Brahmin** (the wealthiest) men. There is also evidence of the domestication of cats, dogs, goats, sheep, and perhaps, the elephant. These, too, were sold in the marketplace.

Unlike other **city-states**, which were managed by kings, the Indus people were ruled by groups of merchants. They had commercial links with Afghanistan, Persia, Egypt, Mesopotamia, and the Samaritans. Trade was in the form of **barter**. There was a cleverly organized system of weights and measures. There is a striking contrast between the rest of the civilization and the Indus Valley in the way that it was managed. In

Bullock cart with driver, 2000 BC, Harappa, National Museum, New Delhi.

most civilizations the most impressive buildings were temples; in the Indus Valley the most impressive buildings were public, commercial buildings.

The people were very artistic and evidence can be found in the pottery, stone sculpture, and seal making. The pottery was made of well-fired clay, with painting in black pigment. People were **animistic** and worshiped natural forces like plants and animals. To ward off evil spirits, the people even used charms.

Discussion Question

What interesting new development occurred in early Indus civilizations?

Aryan Civilization Daily Life

The Vedic & Epics Periods, 1500–500 B.C.

By 1500 B.C., the Harappan civilization had faded away into a culture that was spreading throughout India with new ideas from the west.

According to the **Vedas**, a people calling themselves **Aryans** conquered the Harappan and destroyed their forts. Because of language similarities, these Aryans were particularly associated with the Iranians. The general consensus seems to be that this culture must have begun somewhere in the Russian **steppes** (flat, unforested grassland) and Central

> The Vedas are a large body of texts originating in ancient India. Composed in Vedic Sanskrit (a language), the texts are the oldest scriptures of Hinduism.

Asia about 2000 B.C., though some have put their origin in Lithuania because of similarities to that language. A branch of these speakers came to India under the name Aryans, which means "noble ones." Other branches spread into Greece and western Asia as Hittites, Kassites, and Mitanni.

The Aryans were, of course, **polytheists**. Their religion is the basis of much of contemporary **Hindu** theology.

A map of the Aryan-speaking peoples, 1000–500 BC (PD).

The Aryans also originated the contemporary practice of placing a red dot on all married females' foreheads. An Aryan bridegroom applied a spot of his blood on his bride's forehead in recognition of wedlock! Today, married Indian women may choose to wear this mark or not.

The Aryans were **nomadic food gatherers**. That is, they made their living by raising livestock. However, when they arrived in the Indus River Valley, they settled down. Nonetheless, while they embraced farming with vigor and ingenuity, they retained the fierce independent nomadic spirit. Accordingly, they had no government, grouped in **clans**, and were ruled by warrior chiefs called **rajas**. Therefore, their history involved constant war among competing clans. They created many stories, though, including perhaps the *Panchatantra* (a series of beast fable tales).

The Aryan beliefs and daily life are described in the four Vedas. The Vedas were composed of the *Rig, Sama, Yajur,* and *Atharva* Vedas. This is why the period from roughly 1500 B.C. to 1000 B.C. is called the Vedic Period. It is named after the Vedas.

A scene from the battle at Lanka as depicted in the *Ramayana*, British Library (PD-Art).

Around 1000 B.C., the Aryans created two literary epics. We know about daily life during this period from these famous epics, the *Ramayana* and the *Mahabharata*. These epics are stories about Aryan life, wars, and accomplishments. School children in India today know these stories very well. They're great stories! The *Ramayana* tells a story in which the (good) Aryan king Rama destroys the (evil) pre-Aryan king Ravana. The other epic, *Mahabharata*, talks of Aryan wars amongst themselves, where two clans, the Pandavas and the Kauravas, battle it out, and the Pandavas emerge victorious. This is why the period from roughly 1000 B.C. to 500 B.C. is called the Epics Period. It is named after these two great epics, the *Ramayana* and the *Mahabharata*.

How did the Aryans live? The position of chief of each tribe was hereditary. The chief made decisions after listening to a committee or perhaps even to the entire tribe. People had a voice, but the chief was the final word. There was no rule of law, any Hammurabi Code, or Ten Commandments.

Everyone lived in straw and wooden huts. Life focused around the central fireplace called the **yagna**. There is no indication that anyone thought of building a chimney.

Dinner time was social time. The tribe would gather around the central fireplace and share news. Those who tended the central fireplace also cooked for the rest of the tribe. The clan unit was sacrosanct, but meals were communal with other clans. The cooks, or **fire tenders,** were the go-betweens for different clans, and later, mediators between the gods and the people. As the fire tenders, or cooks, prepared communal meals, Aryans would gather and share their concerns and woes. These "counseling" sessions were critical to Aryan life. It comes as no surprise, then, that these fire tenders later formed the caste of priests.

Goblet from Navdatoli, Malwa, ca. 1300 BC (CCA-SA3.0).

What did they do when they were not working or fighting each other? The Aryans loved to gamble. They introduced the horse to ancient India and raced chariots. They played fighting games. They loved to tell stories. The ancient Aryans were proud and fierce as well as deeply religious. They believed in many gods and goddesses.

Boys were taught by a **guru** (a teacher). Even chiefs' sons had to obey the guru. All students followed a rigorous course of studies, which was imparted orally. Writing was done on bark and leaves, hence was perishable, so we have very few rock edicts to tell us what they studied or what they wrote.

The Aryan culture, in summary, introduced several South Asia contemporary cultural anomalies: the Vedas, the family clan, and the priesthood.

Discussion Question

How did Hindi priests originate?

Age of Empires

Daily Life 500 B.C.–A.D. 647

The next thousand years saw a great many kings and emperors. Some did wonderful things, like plant trees along the roads and build rest houses for travelers. Others started great public works programs.

The **Gupta Empire** existed at around the same time as the Roman Empire and dominated northern India. The Guptas developed a home guard and civil government. Villages were protected from raids by local **militia**. Each local militia (like the National Guard) had an arsenal of one elephant, one chariot, three armored cavalrymen, and five infantry soldiers. In times of war, all the militia groups were brought together to form the royal army! Thus, the Gupta Empire could muster a formidable military force at the drop of a hat and no military — including the Roman Empire — wanted to confront the Guptas.

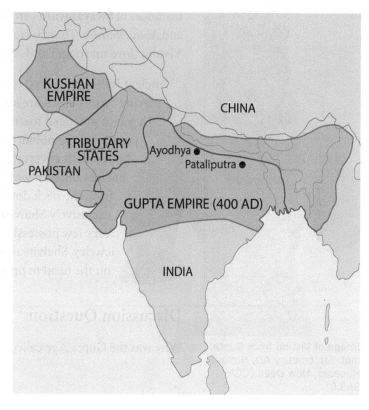

Historians call this the "Golden Age" of ancient India. They had religious freedom. They were given free medical care, which included simple surgery. Criminals were never put to death. Instead, they were fined for their crimes. Monetary rewards were given to writers, artists, and scholars to encourage them to produce wonderful work, and they did. Very few of the common people were educated, but the Gupta Empire had many universities. Students came from as far away as China to study at Gupta universities! As one Chinese visitor wrote, "Indian cities are prosperous and stretch far and wide. There are many guest houses for travelers. There are hospitals providing free

Queen Kumaradevi and King Chandragupta I on a coin of their son Samudragupta, 350-380 AD, in the British Museum (CCA-SA3.0).

medical service for the poor. The temples are majestic. People are free to choose their occupations. There are no restrictions on the movement of the people. Government officials and soldiers are paid their salaries regularly. People are not addicted to drinks. They shun violence. The administration provided by the Gupta rulers is fair and just."[1]

The Guptas introduced iron to their region, a very great advance in technology for that age. They believed the earth was a sphere and rotated around the sun; the Guptas were perhaps the first civilization to believe this. They also figured out that the solar year had 365.358 days.

What did they eat? The concept of breakfast did not exist. They ate a simple lunch around 11, a sweet drink at 4, and supper at dark.

In earlier times, meals were both vegetarian and non-vegetarian, depending upon religious beliefs. After the coming of **Buddhism, Jainism,** and other pacifist religions and reforms in Hinduism, vegetarian food (strictly excluding animal and fish meat) became the norm for as much as half of the population. In the Gupta Empire, they mostly ate vegetables, cereals, fruits, and breads, and drank milk. Older boys, who went to school, also lived at school.

In Gupta, India, the most popular form of marriage was called Swayamvara. In this type of marriage, potential grooms assembled at the bride's house and the bride selected her spouse. Love and romance were not involved, but this was the first culture where the potential wife had a say in her spouse!

Instances of **Swayamvara** ceremony are found in India's national epics, the *Ramayana* and *Mahabharata*. There were other types of marriage as well, such as **Gandharva Vivaha** (love marriage) and **Asura Viviha** (marriage by abduction).

Ancient Indians invented many of the games we play today, like chess, polo, and playing cards (which are said to have gone from India to other parts of our globe). They also practiced martial arts, wrestling, and fencing. Hunting was a favorite pastime of the nobility. Women wore **saris** (a single cloth wrapped around the body which covers the woman from head to toe). A **dhoti** is less modest. In ancient times, it was considered very important for women to be covered from the neck down to the feet. The southern half of India has been almost exclusively **Shaivite** for thousands of years. Shaivites typically have very, very few possessions. A Shaivite woman would not have worn much jewelry. Shaivite men typically wore only a loin cloth and perhaps a cloth on the head to protect from the sun, never jewelry.

Discussion Question

Why was the Gupta Age called the "Golden Age" of India?

Image of Vishnu from Gupta, mid. 5th century AD, National Museum, New Delhi (CCA-SA3.0).

---

1 A Short History Of Bengal by Tanmoy Bhattacharya
   A History of the Indian People by D. P. Singhal
   http://mukto-mona.net/new_site/mukto-mona/bengali_heritage/bengal_history.htm

Historical Essay

The Caste System

Society divisions, or **castes**, appeared with the Aryans. Castes were unchanging groups. A person born into one caste never changed castes or mixed with members of other castes. Caste members lived, ate, married, and worked with their own group.

Images of castes in India from 1837, Beinecke Rare Book & Manuscript Library, Yale University (PD-Art).

At the top of the caste system were the Brahmin — the priests, teachers, and judges. Next came the Kshatriya, the warrior caste. The Vaisya caste included the farmers and merchants, and the Sudras were craft workers and laborers.

The **untouchables** were the outcastes, or people beyond the caste system. Their jobs or habits involved "polluting activities" including:

- Any job that involved ending a life, such as fishing

- Killing or disposing of dead cattle or working with their hides

- Any contact with human emissions such as sweat, urine, or feces. This included occupational groups such as sweepers and manual laborers.

- People who ate meat. This category included most of the primitive Indian hill tribes.

Untouchables were often forbidden to enter temples, schools, and wells where higher castes drew water. In some parts of southern India, even the sight of untouchables was thought to be polluting. The untouchables were forced to sleep during the day and work at night. Many untouchables left their rigid social structure by converting to Islam, Buddhism, or Christianity.

The caste system has been illegal in India for more than 50 years, but it continues to shape people's lives. The Indian government has provided the *Harijan*, a term now popularly used in place of untouchable, with specific employment privileges, and granted them special representation in the Indian parliament. Despite such measures, the Harijan continue to have fewer educational and employment opportunities than Indians from higher castes.

Discussion Question

Who originated the caste system and which castes existed?

The Panchatantra

The *Panchatantra* is an ancient Indian collection of animal or beast fables told in verse and prose in a frame story format. The original Sanskrit work is attributed to Vishnu Sharma. Following is an example of one such fable.

The Foolish Crane and the Mongoose

A big banyan tree was home to a number of cranes in a forest. In the hollow of that tree lived a cobra, which used to feed on the young cranes that did not yet learn to fly. When the mother crane saw the cobra killing her offspring, she began crying. Seeing the sorrowing crane, a crab asked her what made her cry.

The crane told the crab, "Every day, the cobra living in this tree is killing my children. I am not able to contain my grief. Please show me some way to get rid of this cobra."

The crab then thought, "These cranes are our born enemies. I shall give her advice that is misleading and suicidal. That will see the end of all these cranes. Elders have always said that if you want to wipe out your enemy your words should be soft like butter and your heart like a stone."

Then the crab told the crane, "Uncle, strew pieces of meat from the mongoose's burrow to the hollow of the cobra. The mongoose will follow the trail of meat to the cobra burrow and will kill it."

The crane did as the crab advised her. The mongoose came following the meat trail and killed not only the cobra but also all the cranes on the tree. "That is why," the king's men said, "if you have a strategy, you must also know what the strategy would lead to. Papabuddhi considered only the crooked plan but not what would follow. He reaped the consequences."[2]

Discussion Question

Which Hindi cultural elements does the *Panchatantra* tale exhibit?

2 http://panchatantra.org/the-loss-of-friends/the-foolish-crane-and-the-mongoose-1.html.

Chapter 5

Ancient China: Technology Triumphs

First Thoughts

The ancient Chinese had learned to make bronze weapons and tools. These early Chinese set a pattern replicated throughout Chinese history: when faced with problems, they were quick to embrace new technology and use that knowledge to advance their civilization. In this case, they were likely making copper in pottery kilns, then experimented by adding tin, in this way creating bronze. The world had entered the Bronze Age, which started in China.

Chapter Learning Objectives

First we will explore life in ancient China. Next, we will see the emergence of the Chinese military, a formidable power in the Pacific world. We will then be amazed at the short but powerful years of Chinese exploration. Finally, we will explore the life of ancient Chinese women.

As a result of this chapter you should be able to:

1. Explore ancient Chinese life.
2. Study the ancient Chinese military.
3. Evaluate the impact of the Chinese Age of Exploration.
4. Describe life for ancient Chinese women.
5. Compare ancient China to contemporary America.

CONCEPTS

Typography

Yellow River

Class System

Oriental

Monarch

European Monarch

Clan

Infanticide

Confucius

Calligraphy

Mandarins

Conscripted

Feudal System

Zhing He

Galloping Horse Ships

Empress Wu

Xi Shi

Lesson 1

Chinese Geography

Chinese civilization developed in a vast area, one-third larger than the United States if including such places as Manchuria, Inner Mongolia, and Tibet. For centuries, China was almost completely isolated from other regions by mountains, deserts, and seas. This isolation helps explain the uniqueness of China's culture.

China's **topography** is a vast watershed drained by three river systems that begin together on the high Tibetan plateau and flow eastward to the Pacific.

Three mountain systems also rise in the west, becoming smaller and smaller as they slope eastward between the river systems. The **Yellow River** (Huang Ho) traverses the North China plain. In this area, the original homeland of Chinese culture, the climate is similar to that of France. The Yangtze River and its valley form the second river system. South of this valley lie the subtropical lands of South China, the home of ancient cultures that were destroyed or transformed by Chinese expansion from the north. Here the shorter rivers and valleys converging on present-day Canton formed the third major river system. China's history and culture thus grew along these three rivers.

This pattern of mountain ranges and river systems has, throughout China's history, created problems of political unity. At the same time, the great river valleys facilitated the spread of a homogeneous culture over a greater land area than any other civilization in the world.

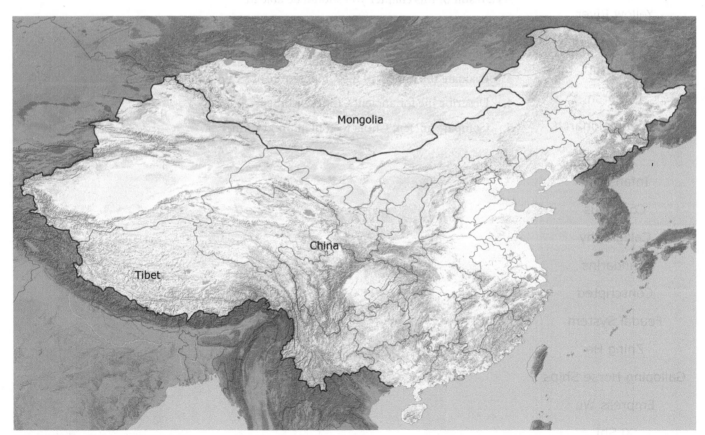

Map of Tibet, China, and Mongolia.

Egypt, Mesopotamia, and Israel all developed with a clear sense that they existed as a nation among nations; they had no sense of being isolated. In the case of Israel, the nation was constantly being conquered and subjugated by conquering armies — it could have stood a little isolation! In China, however, the huge mountain ranges, long wide rivers, endless plains and vast distances between hospitable regions caused the Chinese to develop separately from other civilizations. Surprisingly, isolated China was significantly more technologically advanced than the other nations. Why?

Lesson 2

Traditional Chinese Life

Like all ancient civilizations, traditional China had a very distinct **class system**. There was a very wealthy upper class as well as a poor peasant class, and each lived mostly separate from one another. Physically and culturally, Chinese social classes had almost no interaction.

Wealthy Chinese not only lived better than their lower class counterparts, they looked better too! In some cultures, such as Indian culture, clothing was about the same among all the classes. Not so in ancient China. In ancient China, it was very easy to tell who was rich. From head to toe, the wealthiest Chinese wore the finest silk clothes. Furthermore, members of the royal family and high-ranking officials wore jade and precious silver bracelets. In a culture where food was at a premium, the wealthy also ate more nutritious food. China's richest man, of course, was the emperor. The emperor lived in the Forbidden City, a complex of almost a thousand buildings.

Oriental monarchs were not like **European monarchs** in the sense that they lived lavish, extravagant lifestyles and intentionally separated themselves from the people. They claimed to be gods, or at any rate, direct representatives of the gods. The Chinese empress' palace was called the Palace of Terrestrial Tranquility, while the emperor's was known as the Palace of Celestial Purity. No one could

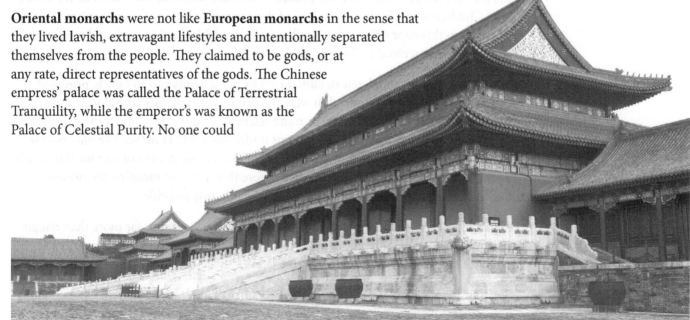

The Forbidden City, Bejing, China.

enter the Gate of Celestial Purity except the emperor. The empress, and other members of her entourage, lived in palaces behind the gate, but they couldn't enter or exit through the same gate as the emperor.

In Beijing in 1900 in the courtyard of a wealthy home (PD).

Another onerous practice emerged in Chinese society: the binding of young female feet. The practice of binding the feet of young girls with long strips of cloth began early in ancient China. Foot binding stopped the growth of the feet and was very painful. Tiny feet forced women to take small steps, a much-desired ancient Chinese feminine trait. This practice did not disappear until the 20th century.

While the rich experienced opulence and wealth unrivaled in Mesopotamia, India, or Egypt, the poor languished in equally obscene poverty. This was not the Gupti or Sumerian civilization. Few could read or write. Most were indentured slaves to wealthy landowners. Poor families sometimes sold their daughters to be servants to the rich. Even in good times, farmers kept little of their crops. Poverty and hunger were prevalent in ancient China.

In northern China, the poor ate wheat noodles (similar to our pasta), steamed bread, and bean curd (not unlike refried beans). In the south, rice was the main part of every diet. Meat was rare. The poor ate their food in small bowls. Along with their meals, they drank green tea. The rich ate vast amounts of any foods they wanted — rice, vegetables, and meats, usually pork or chicken.

The rich lived in large, roomy houses with beautiful courts and gardens. The poor lived in straw huts whose cracks were filled with mud and clay. In poor homes, a fire pit surrounded by stones, placed in the center of the house, served as a kitchen oven and trash pit. Technologically, ancient Chinese were unable or chose not to use a chimney. Many also built their houses partially underground to keep them warmer in the winter.

Poor women wore simple homespun wool garments in winter and cotton in summer. They never wore silk. Peasant men wore baggy pants made of hemp with a loose cotton shirt. Both men and women in the peasant class wore shoes made of straw or went barefoot. Children wore child-size versions of their parents' clothes. The **concept** of a "child" was alien to this poor culture that needed every available hand to work and to survive — children were perceived as "little adults."

In a culture that so completely dehumanized its participants and so poorly provided sustainable life, the family and **clan** were the primary social units. The elderly were revered and valued. As many as 100 or more relatives lived together under the rule of the oldest male. The goal was "five generations under one roof." However, the only people who lived this way were wealthy landowners. Poor families could not sustain 100 people in one place. Moreover, poor people died before they were 30, meaning the notion of having five generations alive at the same time was hardly possible.

Regardless of social strata, however, Chinese families valued sons far more than daughters. A husband could divorce his wife if she failed to give birth to sons. There is also evidence that female **infanticide** was practiced.

Relationships within families were extremely formal and static in ancient China. Family honor was valued a great deal as the family, particularly the younger generation, was expected to "know their place" in society and give the family name a good reputation.

Parents also expected their children to show unquestioning obedience. A father could legally kill his children if they disobeyed him and there is evidence that some did. Parents arranged marriages, with pairings decided when the children were infants. The notion of "romantic love" was completely absent from China until the end of the 20th century. Most brides and grooms did not see or know each other until the wedding day.

Only males went to formal schools. There they mostly memorized the teachings of the Chinese philosopher **Confucius**. They also learned **calligraphy** — ornate writing. Of course, only a minority of boys went to school. Most did not. Instead they worked in the fields from an early age, along with their parents.

In spite of the rigid class system, there was no caste system. In China the upper class were officials called **mandarins**. To become a mandarin, one had to pass certain exams. The exams were, in theory, open to almost all men. However, Chinese merchants were held in low esteem and rarely allowed to participate. Peasants were never allowed to take this test.

Discussion Question

Based upon the above reading alone (you do not have to consult other sources), why do you suppose that the difference among Chinese classes was more pronounced than that of other ancient civilizations?

Image of Confucius on paper (The Granger Collection, New York) circa 1770 (PD).

Lesson 3

Chinese Weapons

The Chinese military officer corps was an honorable occupation for the wealthy, but, generally, ordinary foot soldiers were **conscripted** poor farmers. Even in ancient times, Chinese armies were more technologically advanced than their enemies. For instance, Chinese armies utilized gunpowder and the compass centuries before others.

The first recorded battle in ancient China was the Battle of Banquan. The battle took place between the forces of Emperor Huang Di (also known as the Yellow Emperor) and the Shennong tribe. The significance of this battle is that many tribes in the surrounding areas united to form the Huaxia tribe.

A decorative bronze ax head, dated 13th to 11th century BC, Shang Dynasty (PD).

The Xia and the Shang dynasty were the initial dynasties of ancient China. During the rule of the Shang rulers, the military of ancient China was basically made up of chariot armies. The Shang dynasty was abolished by the Zhou dynasty, which led to the start of a new era of warfare in the military of ancient China. During this time, when the Shang

Yellow Emperor (PD).

The Battle of Banquan was fought by Huang di, the Yellow Emperor, and Yandi, the Flame Emperor. Huangdi, the Yellow Emperor, shortly afterward fought Ciyou, or Chi You, at the Battle of Zhuolu. Both battles were fought not long apart, and on nearby plains, and both involved the Yellow Emperor. The Battle of Banquan is credited for the formation of the Huaxia tribe, the basis of the Han Chinese civilization.

dynasty was declining, the **feudal system** was slowly coming into vogue. In a feudal regime, the nobility pledged loyalty to the emperor, and the peasants pledged loyalty to the nobility. In return for this felicity, the emperor and nobility provided protection for all involved.

The military of ancient China was organized into three divisions. The infantry was predominantly armed with sharp knives (not unlike the American Bowie knife), axes, and spears. The chariots usually carried the important and more skillful warriors, the feudal lords, officers, or even the emperor himself. The use of chariots declined gradually after the crossbows were introduced.

The era or period of the Warring States is often considered to be the last era of ancient China, as well as the beginning of the period known as the Imperial Period or the Period of Imperial China. Warfare drastically changed during the era of the Warring States. The importance of crossbows and distant combat using archery was realized and also implemented. The **concept** of siege warfare greatly increased during this time. In addition, mounted cavalry started evolving and was put into use during this period.

The military power of China expanded as the empire started growing. Martial arts, weapons, and military constructions like the Great Wall of China were developed during the imperial and the post-imperial periods and were an important part of the military history of China as the empire expanded.

Discussion Question

Chinese emperors were able to maintain order even when they had smaller numbers of troops than their opponents. How was this possible?

Lesson 4

Admiral Zheng He, Quanzhou Maritime Museum (CCA2.0).

Chinese Age of Exploration

Most people do not know that Chinese sailors were regularly exploring the eastern Pacific and Indian Ocean 400 years before Europeans reached the same areas. By A.D. 1050, Chinese navigators were using the float compass. In 1070, the Chinese developed dry docks. In the 1100s, Chinese junks reached the Persian Gulf and the Red Sea. In the 13th century, Chinese ships regularly sailed to India and occasionally to East Africa. But ironically, the first Chinese ship to round the Cape of Good Hope and arrive in Europe — a 160-foot-long, 750-ton teak junk that had journeyed to London from Hong Kong — didn't show up until 1848.

Why? Africa had things the Chinese wanted; Europe did not. Africa provided ivory, medicine, spices, exotic wood, and exotic wildlife. Beginning in A.D. 100, when the emperor was given a rhinoceros, the only gifts from the tributary states that really seemed to impress the Chinese emperor were animals. **Zheng He** brought back a lion, zebras, and an ostrich from Africa, but the biggest commotion was caused when a giraffe was delivered as a tribute from a ruler in Bengal in 1414.

The Chinese Age of Discovery lasted for 28 years (1405–1433), and consisted of seven voyages led by Zheng He. These were by far the largest expeditions the world would see for the next five centuries. Not until World War I did anything like them appear. To the Chinese these were like the first manned expeditions to the moon. The Chinese were unprepared for the wonders they would behold!

The largest expedition employed a crew of 30,000 men and a fleet of 317 ships, including a 444-foot-long teak-wood treasury ship with nine masts, the largest wooden ship ever made; 370-foot **"galloping horse ships,"** the fastest boats in the fleet; 280-foot supply ships; 240-foot troop transports; 180-foot battle junks; a billet ship; patrol boats; and 20 tankers to carry fresh water. The expedition was nothing less than a floating city that stretched across several miles. Compare this to Columbus' expedition consisting of three ships with 90 men, and the largest ship was 85 feet long.

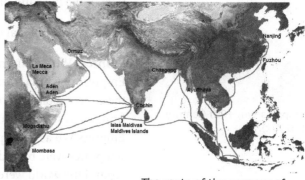

The route of the voyages of Zheng He's fleet, 1405–1433 (CCA-SA3.0).

During the seven expeditions, the treasure ships carried more than a million tons of Chinese silk, ceramics, and copper coins and traded them for tropical species, gemstones, fragrant woods, animals, textiles, and minerals. Among the things that the Chinese coveted most were medicinal herbs, incense, pepper, lumber, peanuts, birds' nests, African ivory, and Arabian horses. The Chinese were not interested in Europe, which only had wool and wine to offer — things the Chinese could produce for themselves.[1]

Discussion Question

Why were the Chinese uninterested in European trades?

Women in Ancient China

According to Confucius, women were not equal to men and were not worthy to receive an education. "A woman should look on her husband as if he were Heaven itself, and never weary of thinking how she may yield to him," Confucius' followers wrote.

By law — not custom — a Chinese woman had to obey her father and other male members in the family.

On the third day of her birth, a Chinese female was placed under the cot and given a piece of broken pottery to play with, and her birth was announced by giving an offering

---

1 http://www.chinaculture.org/.

Empress Wu, 18th Century (PD-Art).

Image of Xi Shi (PD-Art).

to her ancestors. Placing the baby child under the cot denoted that she was weak and that she should humble herself before men. The broken pottery meant she must be laborious, while giving an offering to the ancestors signified that one of her primary duties was to worship her elders. The young girl was not given a name; instead she was referred to as "Daughter Number 1," "Daughter Number 2," and so on.

After marriage, an ancient Chinese woman would serve her husband like a slave and could not even raise her voice. Men were allowed to have more than one wife. In contrast, if the husband of a young Chinese woman died, she was not allowed to remarry.

Historian Maya Pillai describes two famous women who lived in ancient China:

Empress Wu — Empress Wu challenged Confucius' rules when she became the Empress of China. During her reign, she elevated the position of women. For instance, the court scholars were asked to write biographies of famous women from China and from the rest of the world. Chinese Buddhism also attained its glory under the reign of Empress Wu as she replaced Daoism with Buddhism. Many Buddhist temples and cave sculptures were built during her period of rule. Furthermore, many gifted scholars from around the world were invited to China under Empress Wu's reign.

Xi Shi — This beauty queen was the daughter of a tea merchant in China. She became popular because she was responsible for the fall of the kingdom of Wu. Prince Fuchai of the State of Wu humiliated the King of Yue, Gou Jian. The king was then forced to serve the prince for several years before he was released from bondage. Upon his return, he asked his court to summon the most beautiful woman in his kingdom. The king approved of Xi Shi's beauty. Thereafter, she was taught royal etiquette and sent to entice the prince of Wu. The prince was enchanted by her beauty and spent most of his time with her, neglecting his responsibilities. In the meantime, King of Yue attacked the State of Wu and annexed it to his kingdom. Xi Shi disappeared from public life to lead a secluded life. She is one of the notable women of the ancient Chinese culture, who is remembered even today.[2]

Discussion Question

What humiliating practices were inflicted on ancient Chinese women?

---

2 Maya Pillai, "Women in the Ancient Chinese Culture,"
  http://www.buzzle.com/articles/women-in-the-ancient-chinese-culture.html.

Chapter 6

Mongol Hordes: Nomads by Choice

First Thoughts

In one generation, the Mongols conquered all of the land between the Pacific Ocean and the Danube River. China was once again united under a single ruler. Russia was separated from the rest of Europe, but was no longer a divided feudalistic society. Although the Mongols killed many and destroyed much, they also brought stability.

Chapter Learning Objectives

Chapter 6 begins with a short history of the Mongol civilization, with special emphasis on the Khan dynasty. After conquering China and all of Asia, the Mongols failed to hold on to their empire beyond one generation. The Mongols were the only nomadic food gatherers who were able to build such an empire. However, their independent, clannish spirit doomed the Mongol Empire to an early demise.

As a result of this chapter you should be able to:

1. Assess the value of Genghis Khan as a leader.

2. Understand why the Mongol Empire collapsed after only one generation.

3. Evaluate the limitations of Mongol military prowess.

4. Understand why the Mongols purposely chose a nomadic lifestyle when it was unnecessary.

5. Analyze why Mongols were so successful in their campaigns.

6. Evaluate why the Mongol Confederations destroyed the Mongol Empire.

CONCEPTS

Empire

Mongol

Tatars

Khan

Genghis Khan

Kublai Khan

Marco Polo

Composite Bow

Steppes

Domesticated Animals

Consumer-Driven Society

Labor Intensive

Confederation

Overview

Perhaps no **empire** in history has risen so quickly as that of the Mongols. In less than one generation — about 80 years — a band of warriors comprised of a few ferocious fighters grew to an empire that encompassed everything from the Pacific Ocean to the Danube River. This story is one of the most interesting ones in history, and ultimately it was the Mongols themselves who were their own worst enemy.

Sometime in the 12th century, various **Mongol** tribes roamed the steppes of Mongolia. The Mongols, a nomadic food-gathering people, emerged as the most powerful tribe in history. They first defeated neighboring nomads and forced a portion of northern China to pay tribute. This was not to last. In 1160, the neighboring tribe of Tatars decimated the Mongol Kingdom. At that time, it looked like the Mongols would depart from the world stage forever.

> The **Tatars** were a powerful, numerous tribe in central Asia.

The leader of the Mongols was Yesugei, who was a descendant of a **Khan** (chieftain). In 1167, Yesguei and his wife had a son named Temujin, the one who would become **Genghis Khan**. When Temujin was nine years old, Tatar chiefs poisoned his father.

Temujin and his family (seven people in total) moved to the most desolate areas of the steppes. When Temujin was 16, the Merkid Tribe attacked his family and captured his wife. With help from neighboring Mongol tribes, Temujin recovered his wife. Temujin then took control over most of the Mongol clans.

By 1204, Temujin had subjugated all who opposed him; he defeated the Tatars and all neighboring nomadic tribes.

In 1206, Temujin held a great **Khuriltai** (assembly) on the banks of the Onon River. There, he took the title Genghis Khan. Genghis Khan created a military superstructure that conquered all of Asia. The population was divided into units responsible for maintaining a certain amount of warriors ready at any given time, thus overriding previous tribal organizations. Furthermore, he decreed many specific laws and created an efficient administrative hierarchy. Genghis Khan created the most advanced government of any nation up to that time. He was planning to conquer China next.

Statue of Genghis Khan from the 14th century, Mongolia.

Discussion Question

Perhaps no empire was so dependent upon a personality or historical figure as the Mongol Empire was dependent upon Genghis Kahn. Why was he such a successful Mongol leader?

Kublai Khan

Probably there was no greater Mongol leader than the grandson of Genghis Khan, **Kublai Khan**.

The conquest of the Chinese Empire began during the reign of Genghis Khan. Kublai Khan finished the conquest of China in A.D. 1279. By then, the Mongols controlled most of Asia.

Unlike his grandfather, Kublai Khan retreated from the harsh life of being a nomad and adopted the extravagant life of a Chinese emperor. As Kublai Khan got more into the Chinese way of life, the Mongol government followed his lead. While the Mongols conquered the Chinese, in more important ways, the Chinese conquered the Mongols. The Mongols adopted everything Chinese and became more "Chinese" than Mongol.

Mongol Empire reaches its largest extent, about 1300 AD.

Kublai moved the Mongol Imperial capital from Karakorum to modern-day Beijing. The new capital at Beijing was named Ta-tu. The Mongol Empire experienced another dramatic change, although in a different way. Defying the style of previous conquests, Kublai launched two naval invasions of Japan in 1274 and 1281. Both of these were ill-fated. Kublai also launched a series of campaigns into southern Asia. In Burma, the Mongols were victorious, but eventually abandoned the campaign. In Vietnam, a temporary Mongol victory turned into defeat. A naval expedition to Java was unsuccessful as well, with the Mongols being forced to withdraw. The Mongols made headway in Russia and even conquered portions of Europe, though neither victory was permanent, and the Mongols were not able to stay in either area very long. The Mongols, it seemed, were the victim of their own success that came too quickly.

Despite the few military fiascos spearheaded by Kublai, there is no doubt that Kublai Khan's reign was the zenith of Mongol rule as a whole. The Mongol dominion stretched from China to Mesopotamia to the Danube to the Persian Gulf — a size five times that of Alexander's empire. Although much of the land suffered great destruction during the conquests, the more organized Mongol government that followed gradually made this up. Economic activity thus flourished and trade spread throughout the gigantic empire. Despite the formation of the Khanates in the other sections of the empire, the authorities of the great Khan Kublai were recognized in all corners of the empire. Kublai enjoyed his position as one of the powerful rulers of all time, the emperor of an empire that ruled most of the known world. The famed Italian traveler **Marco Polo** described Kublai as the "greatest lord there will ever be."

A painting of Shizu, better known as Kublai Khan, 1294 (PD-Art).

While Kublai Khan was still recognized as the ruler of the Mongol Empire, he himself did not seem to be interested with the rest of the empire outside of central China. The Mongols thus lost unity and no longer acted as a unified government. When Kublai

Khan died in 1294, there would be no more "Great Khan of the Mongols." The death of Kublai Khan meant the end of the Mongol Empire. This is somewhat ironic, as the Mongol Empire ended immediately after its golden age.

Discussion Question

Why did the Mongol Empire collapse after only one generation?

Lesson 3

Mongol Army

The Mongol army was probably the most disciplined, well-led, and effective fighting force that ever existed until well into the 19th century. Mongols were masters of horsemanship and were deadly with their **composite bow**. Unlike Roman legionnaires or hoplites who had to be trained in camps or academies, nomadic warriors were already skilled warriors. These warriors were well known for their horse archers, being able to hit targets accurately while galloping on the horse. But the Mongol army was not merely a steppe army. Foot soldiers were no match for Mongol horsemen.

Genghis Khan organized his army with a commander for every series of ten units elected by the troops. No military drills were practiced, but military tactics were thoroughly rehearsed; each warrior was expected to know precisely what to do from the signals of the commanders, which were initiated in flaming arrows, drums, and banners. The Mongol horde was extremely disciplined. The commanders rode with their men in front, not in the back. They experienced all the same hardships as their men. The combination of skill, discipline, tactics, and some of the most brilliant commanders in history assured the Mongols victory after victory. Enemies were not merely defeated; they were utterly vanquished — slaughtered.

A confrontation between mounted archers, 14th century (PD-Art).

The Mongol army was the last army to win mostly with cavalry. The mobile Mongols dictated the positional flow of the battle, particularly feigned retreats, which could easily fool an enemy into a foolish charge that would inevitably result in a Mongol countercharge.

Utilizing skill and daring, with technology borrowed from the Chinese, the Mongols were the scourge of Asia.

Discussion Question

During the early years of World War II, through superior leadership and equipment, the German army was able to obtain one victory after another. The German Panzer tank, for instance, was superior to the American Sherman tank. Nonetheless, the Americans ultimately won the war and the Mongols lost control of China. Why were the Mongols' superior tactics, personnel, and technology able to bring initial victory but unable to sustain long-term control of conquered territories?

Life in the Steppes

Life in the steppes was like other nomadic experience. The critical difference was the domestication of horses. Early Mesopotamian figurines showing equine animals pulling a cart most likely record the domestication of donkeys, not horses. Only a few horse bones have been identified at early sites, and they attest to the fact that Mesopotamians liked to eat — not ride — horses.

Like so many nomadic food gatherers, feeding domesticated herds made it necessary to pursue a migratory way of life because animals kept together for protection and control consumed the grass faster than it could grow. The interesting thing is that civilizations before and after the Great Flood evolved from nomadic societies into agrarian societies. This was not the case in the central Asian steppes.

In all probability, the steppe nomadic dwellers preferred the nomadic way of life and continued to live that way. Other groups continued to be nomads — the Arabian people group for instance — but it was not by choice. Their harsh environment demanded it. The steppe encouraged farm life, and some groups chose this, but not the Mongols.

They embraced a permanent nomadic lifestyle, ironically, for the simple reason that they had learned to live largely on animal milk and milk products, thus tapping a new food source and, in effect, discovering a new ecological niche by displacing male lambs, calves, and colts from their mothers' teats. Lactating animals had to be tamed to allow human beings to milk them by hand, and human populations also had to adjust physiologically by continuing as adults to secrete the enzymes children need to digest their mother's milk.

There was another distinct advantage to steppe life. Hundreds of **domesticated animals** could be managed by a few people; thus, there were a huge number of Mongol warriors left to protect their own people from, and later conquer, other hostile people groups. The Dakota Sioux in North America utilized the same advantage and dominated most of the Northern Plains.

A Kazakh home in Mongolia with carts, and a horse on a field, 1885–1886 (LOC).

Every few days or weeks the group had to move to a new location where the herbage had not yet been eaten. But in the vast steppes this was no problem. Therefore, only portable goods were of much value to nomads, though of course their animals allowed them to transport heavier loads than human strength alone could support. The Mongols were certainly no **consumer-driven society**!

Dependence on animals meant that relatively few human beings could make a living from the vast expanse of the steppe. This gave what Europeans called "the Mongol hordes" a distinct advantage.

Discussion Question

Why did the Mongols choose a nomadic lifestyle when it was unnecessary?

Lesson 5

The Rise of Confederations

There were distinct advantages for steppe dwellers to avoid forming large groups. Dispersal across the steppe to maximize milk and meat production made a lot of sense. In fact, that was initially the case. A few clans gathered to participate in tasks that were **labor intensive** (required lots of work). For example, during hog slaughter time, families would gather to share the workload and enjoy the fellowship.

Eventually, clans grew larger and stronger and engaged in war-like undertakings against other communities. The Khan Clan was one of these groups and became, without a doubt, the most famous clan in history. The head of the Khan clan, then, literally became the emperor of China.

Kazakh men on horses in north Kazakhstan, 1885–1886 (LOC).

Along the way, the Khan leader could develop a series of autonomous, tribal allies called a **confederation** (union of divergent people groups united for a central purpose). On the other hand, tribes and tribal confederations were always liable to break apart if the constituent groups felt aggrieved or merely distrusted the leader's luck or military skill. This was one of the reasons that the Mongols were not able to sustain a presence in conquered territories.

Control of nomadic people — any control — held the danger of undermining the entire spontaneity of nomadic life. Nomadic customs and institutions thus superimposed fragile political structures on the migratory herding of small kinship groups.

Discussion Question

Why did the Mongol confederations eventually destroy Mongol hegemony (political control) over Asia?

Chapter 7

Early Japan: Identity Crisis

First Thoughts

Settled by migrants from Asia, mostly China, after the Great Flood, Japan has seen the rise and fall of emperors, rule by samurai warriors, isolation from the outside world, expansion over most of Asia, defeat, and victory. Other than a few violent decades of the 20th century, Japan has been viewed as a voice of pacifism and restraint on the international stage.

Chapter Learning Objectives

Chapter 7 explores the history of Japan, its people, its government, its economy, and its social structure. Japan has struggled from its beginning with isolationism, a constant lure in the midst of world turmoil. Regardless, its people have prospered with agricultural surpluses and political stability.

As a result of this chapter you should be able to:

1. Assess Japan's contributions to world history.
2. Understand why Japan resisted expanding its empire until the 19th century.
3. Analyze the impact to a nation and a society when it practices deficit spending.
4. Discern why Japan consciously rejected a new technology.
5. Evaluate the impact of isolationism on Japanese history.

Lesson 1

Overview

The Samurai Code demanded immense commitment from its adherents. Samurai were fierce warriors and fearless leaders but they were also poets and scholars.

Japan, like Great Britain, is an **island nation**. It is part of Asia, but at the same time, Japan has consciously cultivated an entirely different destiny. Japan has thus suffered from a type of national identity crisis. On one hand, it is first cousin to China and her Asian neighbors. On the other hand, Japan became the most industrialized and "European" Asian nation of the 20th century.

The history of Japan encompasses the history of the islands of Japan and the Japanese people, spanning the ancient history of the region to the modern history of Japan as a nation state.

The main cultural and religious influences came from China. The first permanent capital was founded at Nara in A.D. 710, which is rather late compared to other ancient civilizations. From the beginning, religion and culture were interconnected. Accordingly, Japan became a center of Buddhist art, religion, and culture.

Samurai on horse back, 16th century.

The **Emperor** (Tokugawa) became an important leader about A.D. 700, but until 1868 (with few exceptions) had high prestige but little power. By 1550, political power was divided into several hundred local units, controlled by local **daimyō** (lords), each with his own samurai warriors. Tokugawa Ieyasu came to power in 1600, gave land to his supporters, and set up his **bakufu** (military government) at modern Tokyo. The **Tokugawa period** was prosperous and peaceful, but Japan deliberately terminated the Christian missions and cut off almost all contact with the outside world. In the 1860s, the **Meiji period** of leadership systematically transformed an isolated, underdeveloped island country into a world power that closely followed Western models. The military was very powerful and effective, and it moved into China starting in 1931 but was defeated in World War II.

Occupied by the United States, Japan was transformed into a peaceful and democratic nation. It has since become a world economic powerhouse, especially in automobiles and electronics.

Discussion Question

In some ways Japan has gained its identity from what it is not, rather than what it is. It sought to separate itself from all of Asia and to set its destiny in a unique direction, yet this was impossible. Starting in A.D. 600, Japan copied everything Chinese. Languages, art, religion — all were copied from China. What unique worldviews did Japan contribute to world history?

Government

Until the emperor emerged as a powerful figure in the seventh century A.D., Japan was governed by local nobles and lords. Even after the emergence of the emperor, however, local military generals called **shoguns** generally governed without much opposition. The emperor was merely a figurehead.

Local autonomy increased isolation and discouraged expansion. While other nations, for example China, ruled by a strong **tertiary leader** were expanding throughout their continental mass, Japan showed no signs of wanting an empire beyond its own island. However, Japanese industrialization on a European model, with its insatiable need for natural resources that were not available on the Japanese homeland, forced Japan to expand its empire — but not until the 20th century.

During the **Asuka** period (538 to 710), Japan gradually became a clearly centralized state, gaining a national identity, defining and applying a code of governing laws, such as the **Taika Reforms** and **Taihō Code**. During the same period, the Japanese also developed strong economic ties with the **Korean Peninsula**.

Buddhism was introduced to Japan in 538 by Koreans, for whom Japan continued to provide military support. In Japan, Buddhism was promoted largely by the ruling class for their own purposes. Accordingly, in the early stages, Buddhism was not a popular religion with the common people of Japan. On the other hand, atheistic Buddhism, with its emphasis on discipline and sacrifice, was heavily promoted by a ruling class inclined to like everything Chinese and foreign.

With a few notable exceptions, emperors were men. Prince Shōtoku came to power in Japan as heir to the throne of Empress Suiko in 594. Empress Suiko had come to the throne as the niece of the previous emperor, Sujun (588–593), who was assassinated in 593. Empress Suiko had also been married to a prior emperor, Bidatsu (572–585), but she was the first female ruler of Japan for hundreds of years.

Japan then experienced almost six centuries of peace until the Chinese attempted to invade it in 1274 and 1281.

The Chinese invasions of Japan of 1274 and 1281 were major military efforts undertaken by Kublai Khan to conquer the Japanese islands after a successful Chinese invasion of Korea. The Japanese were able to thwart the efforts of a vastly superior Chinese force. They were successful in part because the Chinese lost up to 75 percent of their troops and supplies both times on the ocean as a result of major storms. The invasions are referred to in many works of fiction, and are the earliest events for which the word **kamikaze**, or "divine wind," is widely used. With the exception of the occupation of Japan at the end of World War II, these failed invasion attempts are the closest Japan has come to being conquered by a foreign power in the last 2,500 years.

Discussion Question

Unlike most ancient empires, Japan resisted expanding its empire until the 19th century. Why?

> The **Taika Reforms** mandated a series of reforms that established the *ritsuryo* system of social, fiscal, and administrative mechanisms of the seventh to tenth centuries. *Ritsu* was a code of penal laws, while *ry* was an administrative code. Combined, the two terms came to describe a fairly radical judicial system.

Prince Shotoku, painted by Kogan Zenji, 1800 (PD-Art).

Lesson 3

Japanese Economy

Elderly Japanese woman in rice paddy carrying basket on her back, Yokohama 1918 (LOC).

Japanese feudalism and its origins emerged in the seventh century because of a need to control renegade shogun officials and the samurai. The emperor and his government established feudal ties with lords, treating them as **vassals**, creating mutually beneficial allies that made all involved more powerful.[1]

Feudalism worked especially well in Japan because Japan was agrarian from the beginning. Given the size of Japan, and other factors (e.g., the reliance on the sea) Japan never went through a nomadic food-gatherer phase. About 80 percent of the people were rice farmers; rice was the staple of the Japanese diet. Rice production increased steadily, but the population remained stable. Thus, with increased supply and steady demand, Japanese families grew healthy and wealthy at the same time. Like most ancient civilizations, the ability to irrigate crops was important. Improved technology helped farmers control the all-important flow of irrigation to their paddies. This increased harvests and prosperity.

To this author, all rice seems the same. But that is not the case. For starters, different types of rice have different tastes and textures. Basmati rice was used in Indus cooking, and the Chinese used short-grained rice. Typical Japanese rice is not like any of these. Although common people often used to eat brown rice or millet, both of which are much healthier, wealthier Japanese preferred polished, but less nutritious, white rice. So, ironically, in Japan, the poor typically had a healthier diet than the rich!

Large-scale so-called rice markets developed. Other **merchants** joined. In the cities and towns, **guilds** (associations of craftsmen) of merchants and **artisans** (workers in skilled trades) met the growing demand for goods and services. The merchants, while holding a low status in Japanese society, prospered, especially those with support from local shoguns. Merchants invented **credit** instruments to transfer money, **currency** came into common use, and the strengthening credit market encouraged **entrepreneurship** (innovative small businesses).

The market on Odawaracho at Nihonbashi in Edo. Woodcut print, 1796–1801 (LOC).

The samurai, who were forbidden to engage in farming or business but allowed to borrow money, borrowed too much. In fact, one of the first **deficit**-plagued societies emerged. A growing governing class was, for the first time in history, spending more than it was producing or collecting; a rising, dangerous deficit occurred. This inevitably led to a draconian taxing of the middle class and poor, which spawned several riots.

The nation had to deal somehow with samurai impoverishment and treasury deficits. The financial troubles of the samurai deteriorated their loyalties to their shogun, and the growing deficit threatened the whole system of government.

---

1 Peter Stearns, *World History in Documents* (New York: New York Press, 2008), p. 107.

One solution was reactionary — with prohibitions on spending for luxuries. Other solutions were modernizing, with the goal of increasing agrarian productivity. Whatever intervention occurred was, by any standard, unpopular and inefficient. Until Japanese society stopped spending more than it had, there was to be no prosperity.

Discussion Question

Why was Japan one of the first civilizations to experience a deficit economy? What was the outcome? What was the solution?

Social Structure

Japanese society had an elaborate social structure in which people knew their place and level of prestige. At the top were the emperor and the court nobility, invincible in prestige but weak in power and resources. Next came the **bushi** of shogun, daimyo, and layers of feudal lords whose rank was indicated by their closeness to the emperor. They had power. The **daimyo** comprised about 250 local lords of local **han**, with annual outputs of 50,000 or more bushels of rice. The upper strata lived in extravagant dwellings.

Then came the 400,000 samurai in numerous grades and degrees. A few samurai were eligible for high office; most were foot soldiers with minor duties. The samurai were affiliated with senior lords in a well-established chain of command. The shogun had 17,000 samurai; the daimyo each had hundreds. Most lived in modest homes near their lord's headquarters, and lived off of rents and stipends. Together these high-status groups comprised Japan's ruling class, making up about 6 percent of the total population.

Lower orders divided into two main segments — first, the peasants which made up 80 percent of the population. They were illiterate and poor.

Also near the bottom of the prestige scale, but much higher up in terms of income and lifestyle, were the merchants and artisans of the towns and cities. They had no political power, and even rich merchants found it difficult to rise in the world in a society in which place and standing were fixed at birth, but they became increasingly wealthy as Japan expanded her markets and economy.

The Wooden Flute and the Potted Tree by Okumura Masanobu, c. 1710. (PD)

Literacy was highly valued. Woodblock printing had been standard for centuries. After 1500, Japanese printers experimented with movable type but reverted to the wood blocks. It is one of the few examples where a civilization rejected an advance in technology to retain something it valued.

Discussion Question

An advance in technology, in most civilizations, is enthusiastically embraced, no matter the consequences. This does not always bring laudable results. The single-family automobile, for instance, popular for the first time in the 1920s, increased mobility but also increased illegitimate births and deaths among juveniles (due to traffic accidents). The Japanese actually said no to one technological advance. What was it? Why?

Lesson 5

Sakoku: Isolationism as a Political Policy

Throughout its history, Japan struggled with isolationism, or **sakoku**. As the island nation grew more and more prosperous, no thanks to outside forces (or so the shoguns felt), the more suspicious the leadership grew toward outsiders.

Since Buddhist China was forever trying to conquer Japan, during the early part of the 17th century the shogunate suspected that foreign traders and missionaries were actually forerunners of a military conquest by European powers. Surprisingly, Christianity had spread in Japan, especially among peasants, and shoguns were alarmed. To them, Christianity had a national feeling, and it was not Japanese in origin or in culture. This led to a revolt by persecuted peasants and Christians in 1637 known as the **Shimabara** Rebellion, which saw Christians facing a massive samurai army. The rebellion was crushed with high casualties on both sides.

All foreign traders, missionaries, and visitors, with the exception of the Dutch and Chinese merchants who were restricted to Nagasaki Bay, were expelled. This dark time lasted for more than 200 years.

Perry's expedition to Japan, 1855 (LOC).

In 1844, William II of the Netherlands sent a message urging Japan to open its doors, which was rejected by the Japanese. Sakoku was ended when, on July 8, 1853, **Commodore Matthew Perry** of the United States Navy steamed into Yokohama Bay with four warships. Bristling with gunports open, Perry laconically requested that Japan open to trade with the West.

The following year Perry returned with seven ships and established formal diplomatic relations between Japan and the United States. Within five years, Japan had signed similar treaties with other Western countries.

Discussion Question

The Japanese practiced one of the earliest examples of isolationism. What advantages and disadvantages does this policy bring?

Chapter 8

Ancient Religion: To Tame the Savageness of Man

First Thoughts

For as I [Paul] walked around and looked carefully at your objects of worship, I even found an altar with this inscription: TO AN UNKNOWN GOD. So you are ignorant of the very thing you worship — and this is what I am going to proclaim to you (Acts 17:23).

Scholars argue that organized religion emerged as a means of providing social and economic stability by explaining natural, often unexplainable behavior. Religion also, to borrow the words of the Greek dramatist Aeschylus, emerged "to tame the savageness of man." Unfortunately, all religions — except Judaism and Christianity — found or created an "unknown god" who never really provided the right answers to life's dilemmas. One final word: This course is not on a search for the truth. On the contrary, Jesus Christ is the Way, the Truth, and the Life (John 14:6).

Chapter Learning Objectives

Chapter 8 explores several religions that flourished at one time or another in the ancient world.

As a result of this chapter you should be able to:

1. Contrast Christianity and Zoroastrianism.

2. Understand Confucianism and how it can be a religion.

3. Comprehend the meaning of "salvation" in Buddhism.

4. Synthesize thoughts about Taoism and understand why Christians have a problem with this religion.

5. Evaluate Hinduism.

Zoroastrianism

Zoroastrianism was founded by **Zarathushtra** in ancient Persia; it competed with Judaism and the Egyptian worship of Amon Ra as a monotheistic religion. It was once the main religion of the Persian Empire, but has since been reduced in numbers to fewer than 200,000 adherents today. Zoroastrianism seems strange now, but at its height, it was a major competitor to Judaism and Christianity. Surprisingly, Zoroastrianism shares the same beliefs as Judaism, Christianity, and Islam concerning God and Satan, eternal judgment, heaven and hell, the virgin birth, slaughter of the innocents, Resurrection, and the Final Judgment.

In Zoroastrianism, the creator **Ahura Mazda** is all-good, and no evil originates from him. Furthermore, in Zoroastrianism, good and evil have distinct sources, with evil trying to destroy good. Zoroastrianism can therefore be called a dualistic religion, with a clear **concept** of good and evil. Mazda, though, is not **omniscient** or **omnipotent** like the Judeo-Christian God, but he is all — completely — good. Our God is both good and in complete control of the universe. In our faith, God is not dueling with Satan; rather, God is the Lord of heaven and hell. All He has to do is think that Satan is destroyed and he is destroyed! Mazda, however, is fighting — even now — with Satan.

Like Christianity and other major religions, Zoroastrianism has sacred scriptures. Their most important texts are those of the **Avesta**, of which a significant portion has been lost, and mostly only the **liturgies** (orders of worship) have survived. Zoroastrianism scripture is inspiring, but not inspired! It is not the inerrant, infallible Word of God like our Bible!

Relief of Ardeshir II; from left to right: Mithra, Shapur II, Ahura Mazda, c. 650 (PD).

Zoroastrianism followers worship in temples with priests. But the priests do not perform any **expiation** (sacrifice) for sins. This is curious since Zoroastrianism espouses a moral system. Followers must not marry outside the faith, for instance. But Zoroastrianism offers no satisfactory way for redemption.

Finally, there is no **conversion**. Followers are either born into the faith or experience an unsolicited revelation. But adherents are forbidden to share their faith with others.

By the time Christ came to live among us, Zoroastrianism was more or less an ancient religion. However, during its heyday it was one of the most powerful and influential religions of the Middle East.[1]

Discussion Question

Contrast Christianity and Zoroastrianism.

---

1 www.zoroastrianism.com.

Confucianism

Confucianism is both a religion and a philosophy. It is a Chinese ethical and philosophical system developed from the teachings of the Chinese philosopher Confucius in about 450 B.C. Confucianism became the official state ideology of China until it was replaced by the **Three Principles of the People** ideology during the establishment of the Republic of China, and then Maoist communism after the Republic of China was replaced by the People's Republic of China in mainland China. In a sense, Confucianism was the state religion of China until communism (also a religion and a philosophy) replaced Confucianism.

The core of Confucianism is **humanism**, the notion that humans are at the center of the universe — not God. Confucianism, then (like Buddhism) is really a form of **atheism**.

Confucius is said to have believed that human beings could acquire a sort of **utopia** or utopian society through adherence to a series of wise sayings or **aphorisms**. Many, including this author, feel that Confucius believed no so such thing. The notion that his writings would be a religion or even a philosophical worldview would have been laughable to Confucius.

Nonetheless, Confucianism focuses on the cultivation of **virtue** and **ethics**. Again, in Confucianism there is no **concept** of a personal god.

Cultures and countries strongly influenced by Confucianism include mainland China, Taiwan, Korea, Japan, and Vietnam, as well as various territories settled predominantly by Chinese people, such as Singapore. Although Confucian ideas prevail in these areas, few people outside of academia identify themselves as Confucian, and instead see Confucian ethics as a complementary guideline for other ideologies.[2]

Discussion Question

How can a religion not believe in any God?

Illustration from "Life and Works of Confucius", by Prospero Intorcetta, 1687 (PD).

---

2 www.travelchinaguide.com/intro/religion/confucianism.

Lesson 3

Buddhism

Four Main Teachings of Buddhism

1. All things are impermanent, including living things.

2. We are forever "clinging" to things, each other, and ourselves, in a mistaken effort at permanence.

3. Nirvana is our goal — letting go of clinging, hatred, and ignorance, and the full acceptance of imperfection, impermanence, and interconnectedness.

4. And then there is the path, the middle way, which is understood as meaning the middle way between such competing philosophies as materialism and idealism, or hedonism and asceticism.

Buddhism is a religion and philosophy encompassing a variety of traditions, beliefs, and practices, largely based on teachings attributed to **Siddhartha Gautama**, commonly known as the Buddha. The Buddha lived and taught in the eastern part of India between the 6th and 4th centuries B.C. He is neither a god nor a savior. He is an enlightened teacher who shared his insights to help end ignorance.

Buddhist schools vary on the exact nature of the path to liberation. Normally, Buddhism advances the development of mindfulness and practice of **meditation**, cultivation of higher wisdom and discernment, and study of sacred writings.

Discussion Question

To Buddhism, which is a sort of atheism, "salvation" comes through a heightened, increased degree of knowledge. Why is such a view completely unacceptable to Christians?

One of the earliest known representations of the Buddha, first to second century (PD).

Lesson 4

Taoism

The Chinese character *dao* in Taoism.

Taoism (also spelled **Daoism**) refers to a philosophical or religious tradition in which the basic **concept** is to establish harmony with the Tao, which is the origin of everything that exists. The word "Tao" means "nature," as in the nature of all things as well as the natural world.

Taoist propriety and ethics emphasize the **Three Jewels of the Tao**: compassion, moderation, and humility. Taoist thought generally focuses on nature, the relationship between humanity and the cosmos, health and longevity, and **wu wei** (action through inaction).

Reverence for ancestor spirits is common in Taoism. While there is no savior or ubiquitous metaphysical god, there are said to be eight immortals — and more. **Laozi** was the founder of Taoism, but countless are the numbers of hermits and wandering Taoist sages whose levels of realization were known only to themselves — and perhaps also to their equally anonymous teachers!

Discussion Question

Taoism is very popular among "back to nature" movements who celebrate "natural" life unencumbered by the structures of society. This sounds nice, but why would Christians have a problem with this religion?

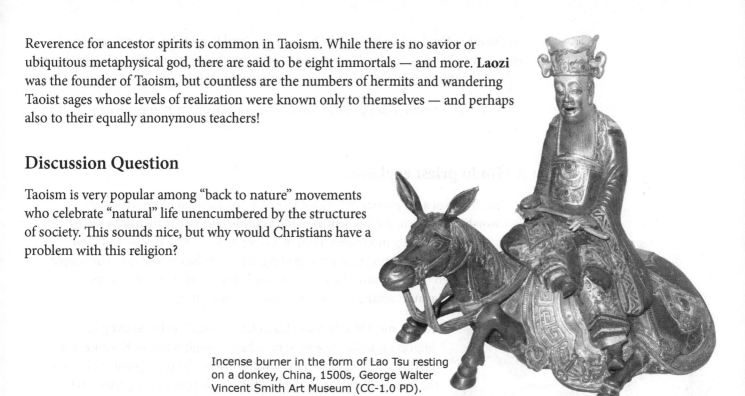

Incense burner in the form of Lao Tsu resting on a donkey, China, 1500s, George Walter Vincent Smith Art Museum (CC-1.0 PD).

Lesson 5

Hinduism

Hinduism is the predominant and indigenous religious tradition of India. Hinduism is "the eternal law — the eternal law that sustains." Hinduism is formed of diverse traditions and has no single founder. Among its direct roots is the historical Vedic religion; therefore, Hinduism is very ancient. Classic Hinduism promotes four different goals. Like other aspects of Hinduism, the goals are split between those emphasized by the "life is good" perspective (similar to the Platonic view popular in Western culture) and by those emphasized by the "life is bad" perspective. The three life-affirming goals are **Dharma** (virtue), **Artha** (success), and **Kama** (pleasure), while the life-negating goal is that of **moksha** (release).

Hinduism has a moral code of sorts. There are three goals of life.

Dharma is the practice of virtue. The primary virtue is to fulfill the duties assigned to one's caste. **Artha** is the working for and achieving of success, in terms of both wealth and power; under Artha the disciple is asked to work hard. **Kama** is pleasure, usually understood as aesthetic pleasure of all kinds.

The Thanjavur Brihadeeswara Temple, also known as the Big Temple, built in 1010 (CCA-3.0).

On the other hand, when bad things happen, the goal is **moksha**. It is the striving for release from life. To achieve this, a person must turn their back on life and strive to live without the things that normally are thought to make up life.

In Hinduism, worship takes place in three different places: the home, a temple, and/or a shrine.

A Hindu priest explains:

The home of a religiously observant Hindu is the location of two types of worship. At dawn, the householder and his wife rise, purify themselves with a bath — usually in a temple pool or a river if one is available — and then make an offering to the fire-god **Agni** in their household fire. The couple then turns towards the rising sun and says a prayer to the sun-god **Savatar**, asking for blessing and understanding.

Second, most Hindu households have a small shrine to the gods important to that house. It may have a small statue of **Krishna** or a picture of **Shiva** or **Durga**. If the householder has a **guru**, a photo of the guru will appear, to remind the worshipper of the guru's teachings. This shrine will be the focus of household **puja**, e.g., worship. Offerings of food or drink may be laid before the statues and prayers may be said, and so on.

A nearby temple to a god or goddess is usually the focus of regular puja. While a local temple may do for everyday worship, a grander, cathedral-like temple may be visited on special occasions. Offerings of meals, money, flowers, etc. may be brought by the devotee. Once the god has taken his part of the sacrifice, the devotee may share in some of the now-blessed food (called **Prasad**).

Within the temple, the god or goddess will be treated as royalty — living royalty to be exact. The statue will be bathed and dressed, sometimes with sumptuous clothes for "holding court," other times with pajamas for sleeping. Meals and other gifts will be regularly given. During the gods' or goddess' festival, the statue will be paraded through the streets. While some of this may seem silly to Western sensibilities, these actions help the worshippers view the divine being as immediately present. A mere statue does not need any special care, a statue revealing the divine presence does.

Small shrines to Hindu gods and goddesses, both major and minor, stand on road sides in the country and on the streets in cities. They may be permanently fixed and unattended, or on a cart and moved around by an attendant. During the day, as people pass by, they may stop, offer a short prayer, and perhaps leave a small offering in gratitude for some blessing.[3]

Shiva as the Lord of Dance, between circa 950 and circa 1000, Los Angeles County Museum of Art (PD).

Discussion Question

While I was visiting India in 1987, I wrote an article on Hinduism where I stated, "The Hindus have three million gods but not one savior." What did I mean?

---

3 Surendranath Dasgupta, *A History of Indian Philosophy*, Vol. 1 (www.gutenberg.org).
   Also see http://www.uwyo.edu/religionet/er/hinduism/htime.htm.

Chapter 9

Greece: Made Gentle the Life of Man

First Thoughts

Sophocles, an ancient Greek dramatist, described Greek Athenian civilization as a place that "made gentle the life of man." In the days of Abraham and Isaac, Greece was inhabited by a savage race called the Hellenes. They lived in the forests, or in caves hollowed out of the mountainside, and hunted with stone-tipped arrows and spears. They ate raw meat, berries, and the roots that they dug up with sharp stones or even with their hands. From this crude beginning emerged the most sophisticated and advanced civilization of the ancient world!

Chapter Learning Objectives

Chapter 9 discusses the history of Greece. We will see that the Minoans, from Crete, slowly, but completely, dominated this mountainous peninsula. We will see that Greek civilization, because of geography, concentrated along the oceans and rivers. Along the way we will review the great battles and sagas that emerge from Greek civilization. Finally, we will be inspired by the first and only significant democracy in 2,000 years of human history.

As a result of this chapter you should be able to:

1. Analyze the Minoans.
2. Understand what effect the geography had on the political development of Greece.
3. Discuss the effect of exaggeration and embellishment upon historical event.
4. Compare examples in warfare or other arenas (e.g., sports, to the heroic stand of the 300).
5. Evaluate why, in spite of the fact that democracy seemed to work so well for Athens during the Age of Pericles, it took so long — 2,000 years — for it to reappear in a nation.

History

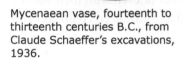

Although Greece (or **Hellas**) is only half as large as the state of New York, it is the most important nation in the ancient world. It is situated in the southern part of Europe, cut off by a chain of high mountains that form a great wall on the north. It is surrounded on nearly all sides by the Mediterranean Sea. In fact, no part of the country is 40 miles from the sea or 10 miles from the hills. In a sense, then, Greeks developed more or less isolated from the rest of the world.

After the Great Flood, the **Hellenes**, a group of nomadic food gatherers, lived among the mountains and hills of central and northern Greece. Eventually, an island people, the **Minoans**, from **Crete**, colonized Greece. The Hellenes merged with the Minoans.

Mycenaean vase, fourteenth to thirteenth centuries B.C., from Claude Schaeffer's excavations, 1936.

The Minoans were a very sophisticated culture and had opened trade with the Phoenicians and other people groups in the region. This led to an exchange of culture and ideas which not only became established as part of Minoan culture but spread to influence cultures, religion, and government all over the **Aegean** islands and mainland Greece. Thus, from the beginning, Greek culture was freely interacting with neighboring cultures and both influenced and was influenced by other cultures. In fact, Minoa was the first people group to develop a **merchant marine** fleet that facilitated trade all over the known world.

This state of affairs continued until around 1500 B.C. when the destruction of Crete occurred due to the eruption of the volcano of Santorini. The mainland Minoans, who now called themselves **Mycenaeans**, became the most developed and industrious Mediterranean civilization.

Athens and other city-states, like Pylos, Tiryns, Thebes, Iolkos, and Sparta were established. These so-called city-states, isolated by geographical barriers, emerged all over Greece. These cities were individual nations; there was no "Greek" consciousness. These city-states were ruled by a military class for about 400 years. In about 1200 B.C., the **Dorian** tribes from the north invaded Greece. They came and went but Greek Mycenaeans' culture was essentially over. A new Greece was slowly forming.

There was a long period of cultural and economic stagnation, which lasted from around 1150 to 900 B.C. This dark age, however, ended with the emergence of the Greek renaissance. The Greek city-states thrived, and Homer wrote the *Iliad* and the *Odyssey*.

The Greek city-states began to colonize and open up their dominance, establishing colonies in North Africa to the south, the Black Sea to the north, and Spain to the west.

This was the start of what has come to be known as the **Classical period**. By the fifth and fourth centuries B.C., Athens dominated both politically and culturally in what is called the **Golden Age of Pericles**, only to lose this dominance at the end of the **Peloponnesian War** in 404 B.C.

"Agamemnon Mask" of gold found in Tomb V in Mycenae, National Archaeological Museum, Athens (CCA-SA3.0).

The fourth century B.C. saw the development of Macedonians as a new force in the Greek world. **Philip II**, king of Macedonia, and his son **Alexander** conquered all of Greece.

Discussion Question

Who were the Minoans and what were their distinctive characteristics?

Geography

Greece is the southern portion of a great **peninsula** of Europe, enclosed on three sides by the Mediterranean Sea. It is bounded on the north by the **Cambunian Mountains**, which separate it from Macedonia. Its greatest length is not more than 250 miles, and its greatest width is only 180 miles. Its surface is considerably less than that of Portugal. This small area is singularly unimpressive, but the Greeks had a huge impact on the Western world nonetheless.

The two northerly provinces are separated by **Mount Pindus**. There is only one convenient way to reach central Greece: the narrow pass of **Thermopylae**, between the sea and a range of mountains. Central Greece is connected to the southern peninsula by a narrow **isthmus** (a narrow strip of land that joins two larger areas of land) on which stood the city of **Corinth**. So narrow is this isthmus that locals regarded the peninsula as an island and gave it the name **Peloponnesus**.

Greece is surrounded by many islands, the most important of which was **Euboea**. Not too far away, to the southeast, was Crete.

Map of Greece and surrounding region.

Greece founded a great number of **colonies**. There were so many Greek colonies that the Mediterranean became a kind of Greek, specifically Athenian, lake. Many colonies were only too happy to come under the enlightened Greek economic and political system. But a Greek colony was always considered politically independent of the mother-city and emancipated from its control. Almost every colonial Greek city was built upon the seacoast, and the site usually selected contained a hill sufficiently lofty to form an **acropolis** (the ancient citadel of Athens in Greece that was the religious focus of the city. It contains the remains of several classical temples, including the Parthenon).

Discussion Question

What effect did the geography have on the political development of Greece?

Lesson 3

The Trojan Wars

Mykonos vase found at Mykonos, Greece depicting one of the earliest known renditions of the Trojan Horse, 670 BC (CCA-SA2.0).

Homer chronicles the Trojan War in his book *Iliad*.

Around 1200 B.C., the Spartan king **Menelaus**, husband of beautiful **Helen**, entertained his Trojan guest, **Paris**. However, when Menelaus left Sparta to go to a funeral, Paris abducted Helen (who perhaps went willingly).

Menelaus sought revenge. He called for Greek warriors to join him in a siege/attack on the **City of Troy**, a Greek colony city, to regain his wife. The first nine years of the war consisted of both war in Troy and war against the neighboring regions.

The Greeks won many important battles, but the Greeks could not break down the walls of Troy. Still seeking to gain entrance into Troy, clever Odysseus ordered a large **wooden horse** to be built. Its insides were to be hollow so that soldiers could hide within it.

The Trojans celebrated what they thought was their victory and dragged the wooden horse into Troy. That night, after most of Troy was asleep or in a drunken stupor, Greek warriors descended from the horse and slaughtered the Trojans.

Aeneas, a Trojan prince, managed to escape the destruction of Troy, and Virgil's *Aeneid* tells of his flight from Troy.[1]

Discussion Question

Both Troy and the Battle of Troy existed. However, over the years legends have been added to this historical event. Give an example from your own life where a true event, through exaggeration and embellishment, became something more than the actual event.

Troy was a city located in northwest Turkey. A new city called Ilium was founded on the site in the reign of the Roman Emperor Augustus. In 1868, Heinrich Schliemann, a wealthy German businessman and archaeologist, began excavating in the area. These excavations revealed several cities built in succession, one of which was Troy.

1 http://www.stanford.edu/~plomio/history.html.

Battle of Thermopylae: 300 Spartans

The **Battle of Thermopylae** in 480 B.C. was fought between an alliance of Greek city-states led by **King Leonidas** of Sparta and **King Xerxes** of Persia, the husband of Esther. At the battle of **Marathon**, 490 B.C., Darius, Xerxes' father, had been turned back in a conquest attempt. Xerxes, with a much greater army, intended to finish what his father began.

To counter Xerxes' move, the Athenian general **Themistocles** had proposed that the allied Greeks block the advance of the Persian army at the pass of Thermopylae and simultaneously block the Persian navy at the **Straits of Artemisium**.

A Greek force of approximately 7,000 men marched north to block the pass in the summer of 480 B.C. The Persian army, composed of about a million men, arrived at Thermopylae and confronted the Greeks. During two full days of battle, the small Greek force led by King Leonidas I of Sparta blocked the only road by which the massive Persian army could pass. After the second day of battle, a local resident betrayed the Greeks by revealing a small path that led behind the Greek lines. Aware that his force was being outflanked, Leonidas dismissed the Greek army, and, wishing to delay the Persians as long as possible, remained with 300 Spartans so that Themistocles could prepare an adequate response. They were wiped out.

Persian warriors, Pergamon Museum/Vorderasiatisches Museum, c.4 BC (CCA2.0).

Now the Greeks had to withdraw farther south to Salamis. This was a difficult decision because it meant that Athens would fall to the Persians. The Persians captured the evacuated Athens. Meanwhile, the Greek fleet attacked and defeated the invaders at the **Battle of Salamis** in late 480 B.C. With no navy to supply his troops, and not wishing to be trapped on the Greek peninsula, Xerxes withdrew with most of his army; this

Detail of monument to Leonidas I at Thermopylae, (CC-CA3.0).

was a strategic retreat. He left a sizeable force to complete the conquest of Greece. The following year, however, saw a Greek army decisively defeat the Persians at the **Battle of Plataea**, thereby ending the Persian invasion.

Discussion Question

Both ancient and modern writers have used the Battle of Thermopylae as an example of the power of a patriotic army defending native soil. The performance of the defenders at the battle of Thermopylae is also used as an example of the advantages of training, equipment, and good use of terrain as force multipliers and has become a symbol of courage against overwhelming odds. What other examples in warfare or other arenas (e.g., sports) can you offer in comparison to the heroic stand of the 300?

Lesson 5

Golden Age of Pericles

Pericles (495–429 B.C.) was Athens' most famous leader during the city's **Golden Age** — specifically, the time between the **Persian** and **Peloponnesian Wars**. He was descended from a powerful Athenian family.

Pericles had such a profound influence on Athenian society that historian **Thucydides** called him "the first citizen of Athens." Pericles turned the **Delian League** (a group of Greek states under the leadership of Athens) into an Athenian empire and led his countrymen during the first two years of the Peloponnesian War.

Pericles promoted the arts and literature; this is a chief reason Athens holds the reputation of being the educational and cultural center of the ancient Greek world. He started an ambitious project that generated most of the surviving structures of the **Acropolis** (including the **Parthenon**). Furthermore, Pericles encouraged Athenian **democracy** to such an extent that no nation would reach its democratic standard until the 20th century.

Other Greek cities set up democracies, and although most followed an Athenian model, none were as known, or as effective, as that of Athens. Their system was not a democracy as we know it today. Citizens did not elect representatives to vote on their behalf, but voted on legislation and executive bills in their own right. Participation was by no means universal, to be sure, but participants were able to vote regardless of economic class and participated on a scale that was truly revolutionary.

Bust of Pericles bearing the inscription "Pericles, son of Xanthippus, Athenian." Marble Roman copy after a Greek original from ca. 430 BC (PD).

The reign of Pericles was cut short by the Peloponnesian War, which devastated Athens. The Peloponnesian War — 431 to 404 B.C. — was fought by Athens and its empire against the **Peloponnesian League** led by Sparta. Sparta launched repeated, unsuccessful invasions of Attica (the province in which Athens lies), while Athens took advantage of its naval supremacy to raid the coast of the **Peloponnese Peninsula** (where Sparta lay). Athens essentially won the first part of this war.

In 415 B.C., Athens dispatched a massive expeditionary force to attack Syracuse in Sicily. The attack failed disastrously with the destruction of the entire force. This ushered in the final phase of the war. In this phase, Sparta, now receiving assistance from Persia, supported rebellions in Athens' colonies and ultimately destroyed Athens' once invincible fleet. Athens surrendered the following year.

Bronze shield from the Spartans at the victory of Pylos in 425 BC, ancient Agora Museum in Athens, around 510 BC (Picture by Giovanni Dall'Orto).

Discussion Question

In spite of the fact that democracy seemed to work so well for Athens during the Age of Pericles, why did it take so long — 2,000 years — for it to reappear as a nation state?

The Acropolis of Athens and other notable ancient buildings surrounding the site.

The Olympic Games were open to all persons who could prove their Hellenic blood, and the games were frequented by spectators from all parts of the Grecian world. They were celebrated at Olympia, on the banks of the Alpheus, in the territory of Elis. When the Greeks at a later time began to use the Olympic contest as a chronological era, this year was regarded as the first Olympiad. It was celebrated at the end of every four years, and the interval which elapsed between each celebration was called an Olympiad. During the month in which it was celebrated, all hostilities were suspended throughout Greece. The games comprised various trials of strength and skill, such as wrestling, boxing, the Pancratium (boxing and wrestling combined), and the complicated Pentathlum (including jumping, running, the quoit, the javelin, and wrestling), but no combats with any kind of weapons. There were also horse races and chariot races; and the chariot race, with four full-grown horses, became one of the most popular and celebrated of all the matches.

The only prize given to the conqueror was a garland of wild olive; but this was valued as one of the dearest distinctions in life. Such a person was considered to have conferred everlasting glory upon his family and his country, and he was rewarded by his fellow citizens with distinguished honors.

Hoplitodromos (armoured race) with some tripods as winning prizes, ca. 550 BC (CCA-SA3.0).

The Parthenon in Athens, Greece.

Chapter 10

Greek Drama: Art is Life

First Thoughts

"The special characteristic of the Greeks was their power to see the world clearly and at the same time [see it] as beautiful," scholar Edith Hamilton explains.[1] Greek culture transcended time and location. Greece culture had an enormous influence on the culture of many countries, particularly in the areas of sculpture and theater. In the West, the art of the Roman Empire was largely derived from Greek models. In the East, Alexander the Great's conquests initiated several centuries of exchange between Greek, Central Asian, and Indian cultures, resulting in Greco-Buddhist art, with ramifications as far as Japan. Following the Renaissance in Europe, the humanist aesthetic and high technical standards of Greek art inspired generations of European artists. Well into the 19th century, the classical tradition derived from Greece dominated the art of the Western world. Almost every subsequent civilization — including Asian civilizations — has duplicated some aspect of Greek culture.

Chapter Learning Objectives

First, we will discuss the origin of Greek drama and explore why it was so religious. Next, we will look closely at one playwright, Euripides. Finally, we will examine the history of Greek sculpture.

As a result of this chapter you will be able to:

1. Discuss how Greek drama remains religious.

2. Compare and contrast Greek and American drama.

3. Evaluate the impact of Euripides on history.

4. Analyze the three periods of Greek sculpture.

5. Predict the future of American culture.

---

1 Edith Hamilton, *The Greek Way* (New York, London: W.W. Norton & Co., 1958), chapter 7.

Greek Art

Heracles and Athena, 480–470 BC, Vulci (PD).

Art, more than any other cultural form, reflected the true character of Greek civilization. The Greek conceived his world in physical terms — that is to say, physical beauty was everything. The spirit, or **pathos**, was secondary and unimportant. Sculptures and paintings on vases were anatomically realistic figures because the Greeks worshiped the body. This explains 1 Corinthians 15, where Paul warned the Greek converts not to reject the Resurrection out of fear that the returning body forms would be deteriorated.

The art of ancient Greece has exercised an enormous influence on the culture of many countries all over the world, particularly in the areas of sculpture and architecture. In the West, the art of the **Roman Empire** was largely derived from Greek models. In the East, Alexander the Great brought Greek culture into the Middle East and the subcontinent of South Asia. This melding of cultures resulted in Greco-Buddhist art, with ramifications as far as Japan. Following the **Renaissance** in Europe, the humanist subject matter and the high technical standards of Greek art inspired generations. Well into the 19th century, the classical tradition derived from Greece dominated the art of the Western world.

Art and music in the history of our own country passed through phases: folk, realism, and modern. The art of ancient Greece is divided into four periods: the **Geometric**, **Archaic**, **Classical**, and **Hellenistic**. The Geometric Age is usually dated from about 1000 B.C., although in reality little is known about art in Greece during the preceding 200 years (traditionally known as the **Greek Dark Ages**). The period of the seventh century B.C. witnessed the slow development of the Archaic style as exemplified by the black-figure style of vase painting. The onset of the Persian Wars (480 to 448 B.C.) is usually taken as the dividing line between the Archaic and the Classical periods, and the reign of Alexander the Great (336 to 323 B.C.) is taken as separating the Classical from the Hellenistic periods.

In reality, there really was no sharp demarcation from one period to another. Art styles developed at different rates in different parts of Greece.

Discussion Question

Greek art symbolized humanism — the glorification of man as the most important creature in the universe. The Greeks were the first — and only — ancient culture to be so humanistic. In fact, this pervasive humanism would not return to world history for 3,600 years (with the advent of the Renaissance). Why did the Greeks glorify the human body and why was such a view unpopular in culture? Do not consult any other source. Based on the above discussion, hypothesize as to why this is true.

Statue of Artemis Bendis, from the third century BC, Metropolitan Museum of Art (CCA2.5).

Small Roman replica of the Athena Parthenos by Phidias, third century (PD).

Greek Drama

General Discussion

Drama began in the Greek world as a form of religious ritual; it was quite literally part of Greek religious liturgy. Before long, however, drama in classical Athens became entertaining. Nonetheless, its religious character and **didactic**/moral lesson was never absent. Dramas inevitably offered the following themes: the power of **fate**, the allure of the material world, and an exploration of human emotion.

Origins of Athenian tragedy and comedy are obscure. The basic background is the existence, perhaps for centuries, of a chorus with a leader singing a song about some legendary hero. Then the leader, instead of singing about the hero, began to impersonate him. These early Greek plays were like **Roger and Hammerstein's Broadway plays** (e.g., *Oklahoma*) that told a story in song and dialogue. So imagine, an actor comes on stage and sings and acts out a tragic story.

Three types of drama were composed in Athens: **tragedy**, **comedy**, and **satyr plays**, all of which were present during the **Greek Enlightenment** (450–400 B.C.). The Greeks distinguished between tragedy and comedy in two ways. The first, the **Aristotelian tradition (in Poetics)**, defined tragedy as a drama which concerns better-than-average people who suffer the tragedy of an unhappy fate. Greek playwrights were hopelessly corny and loved to evoke a tear-filled emotional response in the audience.

Comedy was a "low art" and was written in colloquial language to entertain lower-class people. There was nothing fancy about the diction in Greek comedy.

Tragedies were part of a religious festival to **Dionysus**. On each of three days, three tragedies and a **satyr play** were presented by the same poet. "Tragedy is an achievement peculiarly Greek," scholar Edith Hamilton writes. "It concerns the entire people . . . who felt the appeal of the tragic to such a degree that they would gather thirty thousand strong to see a performance."[2]

Like modern tragedies, the plot of a Greek tragedy usually followed a known storyline, something that would resonate with the audience. Just as American moviegoers expect the same storyline in a western — good guy saves the farm from unscrupulous rich rancher — Greek playwrights chose a similar cultural **motif** (or theme). Normally, Greek dramas begin with a prologue by one or two actors, then the chorus enters and sings its first song, then a number of "acts" follow, separated by choral refrains. The actors also sometimes sing as well as engage in dialogue with each other. Tragedies have sad endings; comedies have happy endings.

The Greek Enlightenment occurred in Athens during the fourth century B.C. It was a time of great political and artistic progress in the Western world.

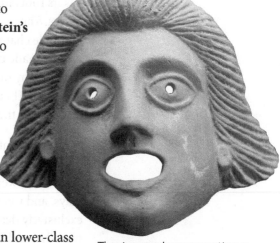

Theater mask representing a youth, first century B.C.

Aeschylus, Sophocles, and Euripides are arguably the greatest Greek dramatists.

Discussion Question

In what way does Greek drama remain religious?

---

2 Ibid.

Greek Drama

Production

Attending a tragedy or comedy in fifth-century B.C. Athens was in many ways a different experience than attending a play in the United States today. Greek plays were performed in an outdoor theater, used masks, and were almost always performed by a chorus and three actors (no matter how many speaking characters there were in the play, only three actors were used; the actors would go backstage after playing one character, switch masks and costumes, and reappear as another character).

Greek masks continue to hold our fascination. So much of the history of modern theater has its roots in ancient Greece, and much of Greek theater is associated with these masks. The use of masks was also helpful when an actor had to play more than one role. A simple change of masks was all one needed to switch characters. The masks were usually made of wood, cloth, or leather, and were as creative as the people who made them. Many of the masks were decorated with hair, either human or animal, to complete the effect. There was only a small hole drilled where the pupil of the eye would be for the actor to see through.

Again, as mentioned previously, Greek plays were performed as part of religious festivals in honor of the god **Dionysus**, and unless later revived, were performed only once. Plays were funded by the **polis**, were always presented in competition with other plays, and were voted either the first, second, or third (last) place. Tragedies almost exclusively dealt with stories from the mythic past (there was no "contemporary" tragedy), and comedies dealt almost exclusively with contemporary figures and problems. No one wanted to see ancient comedies or present tragedies. The former was too archaic; the latter was too painful. Greek playwrights tried to distance their audience from the harsh realities of tragedy and brought very close to home the earthy, humorous aspect of everyday life.

The theater of the later fifth century B.C. consisted of a large circular orchestra for the chorus, surrounded by the audience; on the other side was a low stage offering easy communication with the orchestra. There was, of course, no sound equipment, so this was very necessary. Behind the stage was some kind of building where actors could hide. The chorus could enter the orchestra from either side. The chorus (from 12 to 15

Theater in Epidaurus, 4th century BC.

people) sang and danced; their leader might engage informally in dialogue with the actors — there were no actresses.

Furthermore, Greek tragedies and comedies were always performed in outdoor theaters and occurred in the daytime.

Discussion Question

Compare and contrast Greek and American drama.

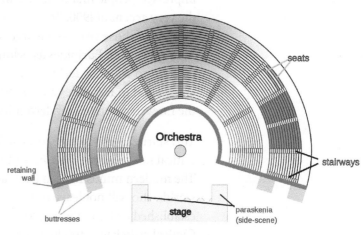

ANCIENT GREEK THEATRE

Euripides: Greek Poet

From *The Greek Way* by Edith Hamilton[3]

Euripides was "with all his faults the most tragic of the poets," said Aristotle, supreme among critics, whose claim to ever pronounce the final verdict has only of late been called into question. Aristotle's judgment here is a factor in the latter-day attitude toward him: the great critic was wrong. He confused sadness and tragedy. Euripides is the saddest of the poets, and for that very reason not the most tragic. He is a very great tragedian, beyond all question one of the world's four greatest, all of whom have that strange power to so present the spectacle of pain that we are lifted to what we truly call the height of tragedy.

Euripides can indeed walk "those heights exalted," but the dark depths of pain are what he knows best. He is considered to be the poet of the world's grief. He feels, as no other writer has felt, the pitifulness of human life, as of children suffering helplessly what they do not know and can never understand. No poet's ear has ever been as sensitively attuned as his to the still, sad music of humanity — a strain little heeded by that world of long ago. And together with that, he alone of the entire classic world so deeply felt something even more unheeded — the sense of the value of each individual human being. It is an amazing phenomenon. Out of the pages written more than twenty-three hundred years ago sound the two notes which we feel are dominant in our world today: sympathy with suffering and the conviction of the worth of everyone alive. A poet of the antique world speaks to us, and we hear what seems peculiarly our own.

Bust of Euripides, Roman copy after a Greek original from ca. 330 BC.

There is an order of mind which is perpetually modern. All those possessed of it are akin, no matter how great the lapse of time that separates them. When Professor Murray's translations made Euripides popular in the early years of this century, what

---

3 Hamilton, *The Greek Way.*

impressed people first of all was his astonishing modernity: he seemed to be speaking the very accent of l900. Today another generation who has little care for the brightest stars of those years — George Meredith, Henry James, any or all of the great later Victorians, read Euripides as belonging to them; so the younger generation in 400 B.C. felt, and so will they feel in many a century to come. Those in the vanguard of their time always find in Euripides an expression of their own spirit. He is the great exponent of the forever-recurring modern mind.

This spirit, always in the world and always the same, is primarily a destructive spirit, critical not creative. "The life without criticism," Plato says, "is not worthy to be lived." The modern minds in each generation are the critics who preserve us from a petrifying world, who will not leave us to walk undisturbed in the ways of our fathers. The established order is always wrong to them. But there is criticism and criticism. Cynical criticism is totally opposed to the temper of the modern mind. The wise king, who looked upon all the works that his hands had wrought and on all the work that he had labored to do, and beheld that all was vanity and vexation of spirit, was not a modern mind. To read Ecclesiastes is to feel, "This is what men have always thought at times and will always think." It never carries the conviction, "This, just this is modern. It is the new note of today." The same is true of Voltaire, that other wisest man and greatest critic, whose mighty pen shook the old unhappy things of his day until their foundations gave way. He is not a modern mind. His attitude, given in brief by his "Je ne sais pas ce que c'est que la vie Èternelle, mais celle-ci est une mauvaise plaisanterie" [I don't know about the eternal life, but this one here is a bad joke] is of another order. His is the critical intellect, directed upon human affairs but quite separated from "the human heart all ages live by," and that is a separation the modern-minded know nothing of.

Above all, they care for human life and human things and can never stand aloof from them. They suffer for mankind, and what preoccupies them is the problem of pain. They are peculiarly sensitized to "the giant agony of the world." What they see as needless misery around them and what they envisage as needless misery to come is intolerable to them. The world to them is made up of individuals, each with a terrible power to suffer, and the poignant pity of their own hearts precludes them from any philosophy in the face of this awful sum of pain and any capacity to detach themselves from it. They behold, first and foremost, that most sorrowful thing on earth, injustice, and they are driven by it to a passion of revolt. Convention, so often a mask for injustice, they will have none of. In their pursuit of justice at any cost they tear away veils that hide hateful things; they call into question all pleasant and comfortable things. They are not those who take "all life as their province." What is good in the age they live in they do not regard; their eyes are fixed upon what is wrong. And yet they never despair. They are rebels, fighters. They will never accept defeat. It is this fact that gives them their profound influence, the fact that they who see so deep into wrong and misery and feel them so intolerable, never conclude the defeat of the mind of man.

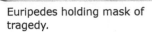

Euripedes holding mask of tragedy.

Euripedes was, the stories that have come down about him say, an unhappy man. He withdrew from the world and lived the life of a recluse in his library; "gloomy, unsmiling, averse to society," duns an ancient description of him. A misanthrope, they said, who preferred books to men. Never was a judgment less true. He fled from the world of men because he cared for men too much. He could not bear the poignant pity of his own heart. His life had fallen on unhappy times. As final defeat drew ever nearer, Athens grew terrified, fierce, and cruel. And Euripides had a double burden to carry —

the sensitivity of a great poet and the aching pity of a modern mind. How could such a one stand to come into contact with what his city had learned to tolerate and to commend? He had been fitted to do one thing alone to help her: he could so write as to show the hideousness of cruelty and men's fierce passions, and the piteousness of suffering, weak, and wicked human beings, and move men thereby to the compassion which they were learning to forget.

On these two scores it is easy to explain what at first sight seems puzzling, his great unpopularity in his lifetime and his unexampled popularity shortly after his death. Only five of his plays were awarded a first prize, whereas Sophocles gained more than twenty. Furthermore, Aristophanes has good words for Aeschylus and higher praise for Sophocles but nothing is too bad for him to say about Euripides. The modern mind is never popular in its own day. People hate being made to think, above all, upon fundamental problems. Sophocles touched with the radiant glory of sublime poetry the figures of the ancient gods, and the Athenians went home from his plays with the pleasing conviction that old things were right. But Euripides was the arch-heretic, miserably disturbing, never willing to leave a man comfortably ensconced in his favorite convictions and prejudices. Prizes were not for such as him. And yet, very soon after his death, the verdict swung far to the other side and extraordinary tales of the way he was loved by all manner of men have come down to us.

The dogmatisms of each age wear out. Statements of absolute truth grow thin, show gaps, and are discarded. The heterodoxy of one generation is the orthodoxy of the next. The ultimate critique of pure reason is that its results do not endure. Euripides' assaults upon the superstructure of religion were forgotten; what men remembered and came to him for was the pitying understanding of their own suffering selves in a strange world of pain, and the courage to tear down old wrongs and never give up seeking for new things that should be good. And generation after generation since have placed him securely with those very few great artists — those who feel the giant agony of the world, and more, like slaves to poor humanity, labor for mortal good. . . .

Discussion Question

According to Hamilton, why was Euripides unpopular with Athenian viewers?

Greek Sculpture

Sculpture is one of the most ancient and also one of the most enduring forms of art. Nearly all cultures have left sculptural art history, but the 500 years of Greek culture iares remarkable. Greek sculptors created beautiful works of art — not anthropomorphic blobs of dry clay!

Athena, Roman copy after a Greek original of the late fifth century BC, Capitoline Museums (PD).

Never in any other civilization has the art form developed as rapidly and as **aesthetically** beautifully as was seen in ancient Greece. The first Greek sculptors carved small statuettes, but within a few decades sculptures had increased in size and quality. The prosperous city of Athens served as the sculptural hub of the entire Greek civilization. There, the art form was nurtured by the wealthy city. Athenian governments and patrons paid vast sums of money for sculptures. Greek artists, quite literally, were the wealthiest people in the city. Never before, and never again, would a civilization so extravagantly reward its artists.

Monumental sculptures produced by Athens were made possible by this influx of monetary support that the Greeks devoted to sculpture. Few other cultures have ever enjoyed the large-scale production of sculpture. The method for casting bronze sculptures transformed Western sculpture forms forever.

There are three main periods of Greek sculpture: Archaic, Classical, and Hellenistic. The Greeks had plenty of marble, which was what they used most in their sculptures. Bronze was also used, mostly in their artistic work of humans. Many sculptural pieces were so beautiful that the Romans made copies or duplications of the original works. In fact, Western civilizations for 2,000 years have made copies!

The Archaic period was the earliest period in Greek sculpture and started around 600 B.C. and lasted until 480 B.C. These works have a stiff and ridged appearance similar to that of the typical Egyptian sculpture.

The second period, the Classical period, was between the Archaic and Hellenistic times. The Classical period exhibits a more realistic and sometimes idealistic portrayal of the human figure. Many sculpture figures had robes. The robes gave the sculpture the idea of movement and realism in an effort by the artist to show humans more realistically.

The third period, the Hellenistic period, started a little before 300 B.C. These works idealized the individual and in a way attempted to capture the idea of youth and strength in their design. The works no longer emphasized the human body — Greek sculpture wanted to go much further into the human soul and psyche.

One final note: Greeks portrayed the gods in a very similar fashion as they did regular humans. There were no distinctions of size or body make up in their sculpture which would suggest that the gods where greater or more powerful than the humans. This lack of distinction is also similar in Greek stories, where the gods are shown to have very human characteristics, both good and bad.

Discussion Question

What were the three periods of Greek sculpture and what distinguished each period?

Bronze figure of a male worshipper wearing an Egyptian crown and shenti, made in Cyprus about 550 BC, from the sanctuary of Apollo at Idalion.

Chapter 11

Alexander the Great: Descended from Hercules

First thoughts

The Roman historian Plutarch was sure that Alexander the Great had descended from the mythical figure Hercules. Hercules — half god, half man, more powerful than any living man — nonetheless tragically destroyed his own family and died young himself. There is, in the life of Alexander of Macedonia, Alexander the Great, both triumph and tragedy. Alexander the Great died when he was 32 years old. What is amazing is that he did not begin his military conquests until he was 20. In 12 years, Alexander the Great conquered the known world. He left a lasting imprint on this world and deserved, no doubt, the appellation, "great."

Chapter Learning Objectives

We will discuss Alexander's life and see if it hinted at the great things that will come later. Next, we will discuss how Alexander conquered the world and then administrated his empire. We will analyze what Hellenism is, as well as its legacy in world history. Next, we will read a historical essay that argues that Alexander was not as great as many claim. Finally, we will speculate upon what a real history maker is.

As a result of this chapter you should be able to:

1. Describe Alexander's childhood and how/if this childhood gave a hint of what was to come.

2. Explain how Alexander administrated his empire.

3. Analyze what was Alexander's most important legacy.

4. Summarize Professor Worthington's argument.

5. Evaluate what a real history maker is.

CONCEPTS

Byzantium

Darius III

Tyre

Gaugamela

Persepolis

Hellenistic

Alexandria

Ptolemy

Pharos Island

Septuagint

Octavian

Clement

Origen

Alexander the Great (356-323 B.C.)

Alexander Comes to Power

Alexander was born in Pella, the Macedonian capital, at about the time his father, Philip II, became king of Macedonia. Philip II's expansion of the kingdom was the crucible that formed Alexander's boyhood.

From the beginning he was both a ruthless warrior and skilled military tactician. At age 16, he was left in charge of Macedonia while his father campaigned in the east against Byzantium (present-day Constantinople). During his father's absence, he crushed a rebellion. At age 16, Alexander had his first conquest.

Philip's campaign in 340 against **Byzantium** provoked the Greek city-states Athens and Thebes (in northern Greece) into taking the field against the Macedonians. The two sides met in 338 at Chaeronaea. Later tradition credits the 18-year-old Alexander with leading a cavalry charge that decided the outcome of the battle, yet there is no historical evidence for this. Nonetheless, the prince certainly fought at Chaeronaea, and the day ended with a conclusive win for the Macedonians.

This victory enabled Philip to present himself as the leader of all the Greek states. His position was formally acknowledged at a congress in Corinth in 337. One of the resolutions of the League of Corinth was to launch a war against Persia, with Philip as commander of the confederate forces. In the following spring (336), an advance guard of ten thousand troops set off eastward. But that same summer, at a feast to celebrate the wedding of his daughter, Philip was murdered by one of his courtiers. The League immediately elected his son, Alexander, in his place as commander. But this degree of unity was short-lived. The Thebans rebelled against the League. Alexander stormed Thebes in 335 B.C., killing six thousand. He then put into effect a stern judgement by the council of the League. Theban territory was thus divided between its neighbors, and the surviving Thebans were enslaved.

Portrait of Alexander the Great from the second to first century B.C., British Museum (CCA-SA2.0).

This concerted effort enabled Alexander to leave Macedonia under the control of a regent, with reasonable confidence that Greece would remain calm during what might prove to be a prolonged absence.[1]

Discussion Question

Describe Alexander's childhood and how/if this childhood gave a hint of what was to come.

---

1 http://www.historyworld.net/wrldhis/PlainTextHistories.asp?historyid=aa02.

Military Campaigns

In the spring of 334 B.C., 22-year-old Alexander marched east with some five thousand cavalry and thirty thousand infantry troops. His destination was Greece's perennial enemy, Persia. Alexander, tutored by reading the *Iliad* by Aristotle, visited the ruins of Troy along the way.

A short distance to the east of Troy, a Persian army waited for the Macedonians. There, King Alexander fought his first battle. The battle was fought at the Granicus River, with Alexander leading a cavalry charge through the water, and the Persians were routed. Many of their troops were Greek mercenaries, thousands of whom were executed. Two thousand were sent back to Macedonia in chains to provide valuable slave labor.

Within a year, Alexander defeated an army led by the Persian emperor, **Darius III**. He captured the emperor's mother, wife, and children but treated them well.

Within a mere 18 months, Alexander had essentially removed the Persians from Turkey where they had ruled for two thousand years. Alexander then moved south along the coast through present-day Syria, Lebanon, and Israel. The ports here were the home bases of the Persian fleet in the Mediterranean. By occupying them he crippled the fleet to deprive it of support from the Empire. Most of the Phoenician (coastal) towns opened their gates to him. The exception is the greatest of them all, **Tyre**, which he captured after seven months.

By autumn of 332, Alexander conquered Egypt. He spent the winter in Egypt. For the first time the soldier Alexander now had to become the administrator Alexander — of an expanding empire. He chose to establish outposts of Greek culture.

Believing in the superiority of Greek culture, he built huge libraries to house Greek books and culture instead of building jails and military outposts. In Egypt, for instance, he founded the greatest of the cities known by his name — Alexandria. Alexander did not merely want to conquer armies; he wanted to win the hearts of men and women to Greek culture and ideas.

Darius III was the last king of the Empire of Persia. It was under his rule that the Persian Empire was conquered during the wars of Alexander the Great.

The Battle of Gaugamela between Alexander the Great and Darius III of Persia resulted in a massive victory for the ancient Macedonians and led to the fall of the Persian Empire.

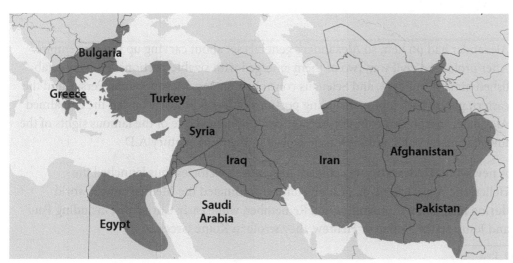

The extent of the empire of Alexander the Great.

Like most Greeks at that time, to Alexander one god was as good as another. Therefore he worshiped and sacrificed to the local gods. For instance, in Egypt he sacrificed to Apis, a sacred bull at Memphis, where the priests crowned him pharaoh. He also made a long pilgrimage to a famous oracle of the sun god Amon, or Amen-Re, at Siwa. The priest there duly recognized Alexander as the son of the god. Undoubtedly, Alexander, the son of Philip II, enjoyed his new notoriety!

Detail depicting the moment when Alexander the Great's forces crossed into Asia in 334 B.C. and engaged the Persian army on the banks of the river Granicus (Kocabas) near the site of ancient Troy, engraving by Gérard Audran, 1672 (PD-Art).

Finally, in the spring of 331, Alexander moved northeast into Mesopotamia, the heart of Persia proper. He defeated the Persian emperor Darius in the decisive battle of **Gaugamela**. His way was now open to the great Persian capital city of **Persepolis**.

In a symbolic gesture, conclusively ending the long wars between Greeks and Persians, he burned the palace of Xerxes — the same emperor who scourged the Greek homeland 700 years before — in 330. To make plain who now ruled the Persian Empire, Alexander adopted the ceremonial dress and court rituals of the Persian emperor.

For two years, Alexander subdued any pockets of opposition and established Greek settlements. Then he continued, in 327, through the mountain passes into India. In the following year, 323, after a banquet at Babylon, he died. The greatest conqueror in history, he was only 32 when he died.[2]

Discussion Question

How did Alexander administrate his empire?

Lesson 3

Alexander's Legacy

Alexander had no heir, so Alexander's generals set about carving up the new empire. After prolonged civil war, two of them emerged with sizable portions. Ptolemy established himself in Egypt, and Seleucus controlled Turkey, Mesopotamia, Persia, and the eastern part of the empire, including portions of India. Ptolemy buried the embalmed Alexander in a golden coffin in Alexandria. It remained one of the famous sights of the town for many years, until it was destroyed in the third century A.D.

A new word, **Hellenistic**, was coined. Alexander's victories thus launched the Hellenistic Age. Hellenism, or high culture, dominated the Mediterranean world during most of the Roman Empire. Remember, while early Christians, including Paul and Jesus, spoke Arabic or Hebrew, they wrote in Koine Greek.

---

2 Ibid.

Macedonia itself, Alexander's homeland, experienced many violent upheavals. In one of them his mother, Olympias, arrived with an army in 317 B.C. and killed his half-witted half-brother, Philip III, together with Philip's wife and 100 of his supporters. She lost her own life in the next coup the following year. In 276, descendants of Antigonus, another of Alexander's generals, established a stable dynasty. But it was relatively short-lived. As the most westerly part of Alexander's empire, Macedonia was the first region to be devoured by its imperial successor, Rome.

Whether or not Alexander had plans for a world empire cannot be determined. He had accomplished greater conquests than any before him, but he did not have time to mold the governments of the lands he had taken. Incontestably, he was one of the greatest military geniuses of all time and one of the most powerful history makers of antiquity. He influenced the spread of Hellenism throughout the Middle East and into Asia, establishing city-states modeled on Greek institutions that flourished long after his death.

Discussion Question

What was Alexander's most important legacy?

Nineteenth century depiction of Alexander's funeral procession based on the description of Diodorus ca.80–20 B.C. (PD-Art).

How "Great" Was Alexander?

by Ian Worthington, Ph.D.[3]

Why was Alexander III of Macedon called "Great"? The answer seems relatively straightforward: from an early age he was an achiever, he conquered territories on a superhuman scale, he established an empire that was, until his times, unrivalled, and he died young, at the height of his power. Thus, at the youthful age of 20, in 336, he

---

3 http://www.iranchamber.com/history/articles/how_great_was_alexander1.php.

inherited the powerful empire of Macedon, which by then controlled Greece and had already started to make inroads into Asia. In 334 he invaded Persia, and within a decade he had defeated the Persians, subdued Egypt, and pushed on to Iran, Afghanistan, and even India. Along with his vast conquests Alexander is credited with the spread of Greek culture and education in his empire, not to mention being responsible for the physical and cultural formation of the Hellenistic kingdoms — some would argue that the Hellenistic world was Alexander's legacy. He has also been viewed as a philosophical idealist, striving to create a unity of mankind by his so-called fusion of the races policy, in which he attempted to integrate Persians and Asians into his administration and army. Thus, within a dozen years Alexander's empire stretched from Greece in the west to India in the Far East, and he was even worshiped as a god by many of his subjects while still alive. On the basis of his military conquests, contemporary historians, and especially those writing in Roman times who measured success by the number of body bags used, deemed him great.

However, does a man deserve to be called "The Great" who was responsible for the deaths of tens of thousands of his own men and for the unnecessary wholesale slaughter of native peoples? How "great" is a king who prefers constant warfare over consolidating conquered territories and long-term administration? Or who, through his own recklessness, often endangered his own life and the lives of his men? Or whose violent temper on occasion led him to murder his friends and who towards the end of his life was an alcoholic, paranoid, megalomaniac who believed in his own divinity? These are questions posed by our standards of today of course, but nevertheless they are legitimate questions given the influence which Alexander has exerted throughout history — an influence which will no doubt continue.

Alexander sarcophagus showing Alexander in the battle of Issus (333 BC).

The aims of this paper are to trace some reasons for questioning the greatness of Alexander as is reflected in his epithet, and to add potential evidence dealing with the attitude of the Macedonians, Alexander's own people, in their king's absence. It is important to stress that when evaluating Alexander it is essential to view the "package" of king as a whole; i.e., as king, commander, and statesman. All too often this is not the case. There is no question that Alexander was spectacularly successful in the military field, and had Alexander only been a general his epithet may well have been deserved. But he was not just a general; he was a king too, hence military exploits form only a percentage of what Alexander did, or did not do. In other words, we must look at the "package" of him as king as a whole. By its nature this paper is impressionistic, and it can only deal rapidly with selected examples from Alexander's reign and discuss points briefly. However, given the unequalled influence Alexander has played in cultures and history from the time of his death to today, it is important to stress that there is a chasm of a difference between the mythical Alexander, which for the most part we have today, and the historical.

Alexander died in 323, and over the course of time the mythical king and his exploits sprang into being. Alexander himself was not above embellishing his own life and achievements. He very likely told the court historian Callisthenes of Olynthus what to say about his victory over Darius III at the battle of Issus in 333, for example. Contemporary Attic oratory also exaggerated his achievements, and so within a generation of his death erroneous stories were already being told.

As time continued we move into the genre of pulp fiction. In the third or second century B.C., Alexander's exploits formed the plot of the story known as the Alexander Romance, which added significantly to the Alexander legend and had such a massive influence on many cultures into the Middle Ages. Given its lifespan, deeds were attributed to Alexander that are unhistorical, such as his encounters with the tribe of headless men, his flying exploits in a basket borne by eagles, and the search for the Water of Life, which ended with his transformation into a mermaid. These stories became illustrative fodder for the various manuscripts of the Alexander Romance. One of the most popular episodes is Alexander's ascent to Heaven, inspired by the myth of Bellerophon's flight to Mount Olympus on Pegasus, which is found in many Byzantine and later art works, sculptures, and paintings. As a result of the Romance, Alexander astonishingly appears in the literature of other cultures: in Hebrew literature, for example, he is seen as a preacher and prophet, who even becomes converted to Christianity. In Persian literature, he is the hero Sikandar, sent to punish the impure peoples. In the West he appears as a Frank, a Goth, a Russian, and a Saxon.

Then there is Plutarch, writing in the late first and second century A.D., who has probably done the most damage to our knowing the historical Alexander. In his treatise, "On the Fortune or the Virtue of Alexander," Plutarch was swayed (understandably) by the social background against which he was writing and especially by his own philosophical beliefs, and he portrayed Alexander as both an action man and a philosopher-king whose mission was to impose Greek civilisation on the "barbarian" Persians. Plutarch's work is essentially a rhetorical exercise.

The Alexander legend was a ready feeding ground for artists throughout the centuries as well. When Alexander invaded Persia in 334 he detoured to Troy to sacrifice at the tomb of his hero Achilles. This was a stirring story, which became a model for heroic piety in the Renaissance and later periods; thus, for example, we have Fontebasso's painting of Alexander's sacrifice at Achilles' tomb in the 18th century. In modern Greece Alexander became both an art-work and a symbol, as seen in the painting by Engonopoulos in 1977 of the face-less Alexander standing with his arm around the face-less Pavlos Melas, a modern hero of the struggle for Macedonian independence.

Thus, we can see how the historical Alexander has faded into the invincible general, the great leader, explorer and king, as time continued, especially in the Middle Ages with its world of chivalry, warriors, and great battles: a superb context into which to fit Alexander, even if this meant distortion of the truth, and history subsumed to legend. Indeed, during the Middle Ages, Alexander was regarded as one of the four great kings of the ancient world.[4]

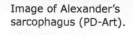

Image of Alexander's sarcophagus (PD-Art).

Discussion Question

Summarize Professor Worthington's argument. Do you agree or disagree with him? Why?

---

4 http://www.iranchamber.com/history/articles/how_great_was_alexander1.php.

Alexandria

Alexandria was the capital of Egypt and the cultural center of the Western world until supplanted by Rome; its founder was Alexander the Great, who planted the city in about 332 B.C. When **Ptolemy**, Alexander's main general, inherited Alexander's Egyptian empire, he made Alexandria its capital. Some historians claim that Alexander was later buried here.

Alexandria was the principal port of Egypt located on the western edge of the Nile delta. Built on a peninsula, a causeway connected the peninsula with **Pharos Island** and divided the harbor. The Pharos lighthouse, one of the Seven Wonders of the World, was visible for miles.

Like all ancient cities, Alexandria was divided into sections with different ethnic groups living in separate sections. The city had the finest library in the ancient world with more than 500,000 volumes that attracted many scholars. Judaism, in particular, found Alexandria to be a hospitable abode. It became the most important center of Judaism outside of Jerusalem. Jewish rabbis in Alexandria produced the **Septuagint** (LXX), the Greek translation of the Old Testament. **Octavian** incorporated Alexandria into the Roman Empire around 30 B.C., and it quickly became second in importance to Rome.

The educated Jews of Alexandria contended with Stephen (Acts 6:9). Apollos, the great Christian orator, came from Alexandria (Acts 18:24), and Paul rode the ships of that port (Acts 27:6, 28:11). Although the Christians suffered persecution there, they produced a school with such notables as **Clement** and **Origen** in leadership. The Alexandrian manuscripts were some of the most valuable biblical sources for the New Testament.[5]

Discussion Question

If you could fill a library with the most important books ever written, what would be your top ten choices?

Lighthouse of Alexandria, 17th century (PD-Art).

5   Gary C. Huckabay, *Holman Bible Dictionary* (Nashville, TN: Holman Bible Publishers, 1991).

Chapter 12

Roman Empire: The Bridge to Modern Times

Concepts

Indigenous

Latins

Plains of Latium

Rome

Contiguous

Tiber River

Etruscans

Phoenicians

Geopolitical World

Etruria

Republic

Romulus

Senate

Consuls

Empire

Autocrats

Emperors

Julius Caesar

Utilitarian

Eclectic

Temple of Vesta

Enculturation

Two Crop Rotation

First Thoughts

The Romans created the greatest empire ever — bar none. Napoleon's empire would barely fit into a province, and Hitler's empire was barely one-half the Roman Empire. Moreover, they had done it largely with relatively democratic forms of government. Amazing! While Rome was first ruled by kings, in the fifth century B.C. the kings were replaced by a republic. In the first century B.C., the republic was reluctantly transformed, but many of the democratic forms and practices (e.g., rule by the Senate) continued for another three centuries. Around A.D. 300, before Christianity was recognized as an official religion, the Roman government was reorganized as an absolute monarchy. This system used two emperors, one in the west, based in Italy, and the other in the east, based in Greece and Turkey. Both emperors cooperated with each other in matters that concerned the Empire as a whole, but each was supreme in his half of the Empire. By the late fifth century, the Empire in the west was overrun by numerous German barbaric tribes and collapsed. The eastern part of the Empire, with its capital in Constantinople (formerly called the city of Byzantium), survived until 1453.

Chapter Learning Objectives

We begin by examining the emerging Latin (Roman) civilization. We examine, in particular, the influence of the existing Greek and Etruscan influences on this thriving but still small people group. Next, we look at the three different governments that govern Rome in its history and observe how they all are undergirded by a powerful sense of democratic rule. Rome was perhaps the first truly secular state, and we examine how religion and secularism competed in this greatest of all empires. We observe how religious tolerance may have been the first casualty in this great anachronism. Next, we examine Roman family life. Finally, we examine more closely the Roman economy, and the fact that in spite of its sophistication, the Roman farmer remained the bedrock of the blossoming Empire.

As a result of this chapter you should be able to:

1. Predict the future of Roman relations between the Greeks and the Etruscans.

2. State why Republic Rome allowed despotic rule by emperors.

3. Analyze if such a thing is possible in the United States of America.

4. Evaluate how tolerant "tolerant, open" societies really are.

5. Describe what it was like to be a Roman young person.

6. Discuss why the Roman farmer was the most important part of the Roman economy.

Lesson 1

History: the Beginning

Rome lay central to the Italian peninsula, which in turn lay central to the entire Mediterranean Sea. Italy is guarded by the Alps to the north and by the sea all around.

The Romans were **indigenous** to the Italian Peninsula. The early people of Rome were from a tribe called **Latins**. They were from the **Plains of Latium**, contiguous to the **Tiber River**. The Latins were never nomadic food gatherers. They were an exception to the normal rule, where civilizations developed from nomadic beginnings to agrarian endings. For the beginning, living in the rich Tiber Valley, the Plains of Latium, the Latins were successful farmers and then merchants. They founded a small settlement/ city called **Rome** in about 1000 B.C.

From its early days, Rome was a rich city. Its wealth was to create jealousy and to bring the city of Rome into conflict with areas surrounding the city. In particular, the Romans fought against the **Etruscans**.

Rome had many advantages right from the start. Like many Greek city-states — for example, Athens — Rome lies only a few miles from the sea. It was close enough to trade with Mediterranean markets but far enough to be safe from **Phoenicians** and other seafaring raiders. But it was different from Athens in other important ways. For one thing, Rome lay in a vast and rich plain that promised agricultural support for the bustling city that grew at a phenomenal rate.

Speaking of the Greeks, they did help the early Romans a lot. The Greeks, who had no desire to control the **geopolitical world** in Italy, brought commerce, technology, and stability to southern Italy. From the Greeks, the Romans learned fundamental skills such as reading and writing, and even their religion was almost entirely derived from Greek mythology.

If the Greeks, who were no threat, settled to the south of them, then the Romans had the Etruscans to the north, which *was* a great threat. **Etruria**, too, was predominantly an urban society, drawing its considerable wealth from seaborne trade. The wealthy Etruscans were generally seen by ancient Romans to be decadent and weak.

At around 650 to 600 B.C., the Etruscans crossed the Tiber and threatened Rome. It was at this time that the Romans chose a king to lead them.

Abraham Ortel's 1595 map of ancient Latium (PD).

Discussion Question

From the information provided above, predict what the future would be between the Etruscans and the Greeks.

Government

Kingdom, Republic, Empire

Rome was governed by kings. However, ancient Rome, like Athens, preferred self-government. Kings seemed to be necessary in the beginning. But as soon as possible, Rome became a **republic** (meaning supreme authority lies with the people and their elected officials).

But for a season, Rome was ruled by kings. The first king of Rome was **Romulus**. He founded the **senate**, an elected body that advised the king in political matters. There were other, less noteworthy kings, but it is interesting and encouraging that a society that used its invincible army to conquer other nations and reduce people to slavery was democratic when its own citizens were concerned.

By 509 B.C. Rome was a republic. Citizens of Rome would gather to elect their own officials. The chief officials of Rome were called **consuls**. The consuls governed for a year. If they did not live up to expectations, they could be voted out of office at the next election.

If elections were reasonably democratic, the role of the Senate was not. Some Senates were sympathetic to the people; some became as autocratic as a despot. But it was during the time of the republic that Rome began its inexorable expansion into an **empire**. Rome went on to become the greatest power in the Mediterranean and in Europe.

From 509 to 27 B.C., Rome was governed as a republic, but this changed.

When the Roman Empire started to grow and Rome became a more powerful city, powerful rule by an executive monarch became more desirable. These early rulers believed fervently in republican government and saw their role as temporary. However, these rulers eventually become **autocrats** and called themselves **emperors**.

The first emperor was **Julius Caesar**. The republic was dead. Emperors would rule the Roman Empire until it collapsed in the middle of the fifth century A.D.

Augustus of Prima Porta, first century, Vatican Museum.

Discussion Question

Why would a perfectly good, successful republic reject democracy for autocratic rule?

Religion:
A Little of This and a Little of That

As previously stated, Rome borrowed Greek religion and modified it to suit its purposes. If anything, the Romans had a **utilitarian** attitude to all things, especially religion. To the Romans, religion was less a spiritual experience than a contractual relationship between mankind and the forces, which were believed to control people's existence. Rome basically embraced an **eclectic** faith that suggested that there were multiple paths to heaven and therefore was open to many different religions. Romans, then, if they were intolerant, were intolerant of faiths that claimed exclusive felicity to one God, namely Judaism and Christianity.

Temple of Vesta.

This sort of informal religious fervor led, to say the least, to an extraordinarily relaxed religious ambience. The practice of Roman religion was a confusing thing. In essence, Roman religion was an oxymoron. In some cases, a deity was worshiped for reasons no one really could remember. An example for such a deity is Furrina. A festival was held every year in her honor on the 25th of July. But by the middle of the first century B.C., there was no one left who remembered what she was actually goddess of.

On the other hand, the Romans had a dramatic flair. There were six vestal virgins. All were traditionally chosen from old noble families at a very young age. They would serve ten years as novices, then ten performing the actual duties, followed by a final ten of teaching the novices. They lived in a huge building next to the small **temple of Vesta** in the center of town. Their foremost duty was to guard the sacred fire in the temple. Other duties included performing rituals and baking the sacred salt cake to be used at numerous ceremonies in the year. Needless to say, the vestal virgins represented a type of public relations stunt that satisfied the most religious saint. To put it mildly, there was a certain cynicism about the casual way Romans handled their religion. In fact, Rome was perhaps the only empire that emerged in ancient times with a relatively insignificant appetite for religion.

Again, since Roman religion was not founded on some core belief that ruled out other religions, foreign religions found it relatively easy to establish themselves in the imperial capital itself. For that reason, among others, Christianity, when it came, spread like wildfire across the Roman Empire.

In summary, Rome was the first secular state that presaged the modern states that would follow. While it gave lip service to religion and its **enculturation** advantages, Rome's worldview was clearly motivated by secular, concrete, earthly concerns more than by metaphysical reality. When a religion like Christianity, with its claim that Jesus was the only way, the only truth, and the only life, came knocking at the Roman religious door, it found itself unwelcome.

Discussion Question

Some contemporary scholars warn that civilizations that accept all religions can easily become intolerant of one religion that claims authenticity. Explain.

Temple of Bacchus (CCA-SA2.5).

Sociology: Roman Family

In the Roman world, the father ruled the family. He owned all property and made all the important decisions — in theory! However, in many cases, the mothers had significant influence.

It was indeed the oldest living father who ruled over his family, regardless of how many generations had followed his own. And so it could be that a great-grandfather held sway over a family. And it could therefore well be that they all lived under the same roof. Roman homes were quite literally rambling palaces or shacks that might include three generations of families.

We might imagine that these large families would live all under one roof only due to economics, but that perception would be wrong. It was simply an essential part of the Roman way of life to live surrounded by one's family.

It might surprise modern readers that Romans would usually only work a six-hour day. This of course was only the case for working men. Women stayed at home.

Oldest sons usually followed in the footsteps of their fathers, inheriting their profession and their business. Siblings might pursue other professions, including the military.

Roman society was perhaps the only ancient civilization that allowed men to pursue politics as a profession. Romans would actually train and participate in politics as

Roman girls playing (PD).

a vocation. This created a professional **civil service** that was unmatched in the ancient world and greatly facilitated Roman expansion.

The highlight of every day was the bath. No one had an individual bath; everyone bathed in the public baths. The women, as well as the men, would head for the public bathhouses. Bathing was a social affair. Even the rich, who might have their own bathhouses, would hardly do so alone, but would invite friends to join them. It was considered unsociable to bathe alone. Taking a bath was the way the Roman working day came to a close, before one would finally retire for dinner.

Females enjoyed an education similar if not the same as boys' education in early childhood. However, beyond primary education it was generally only daughters of aristocratic families who continued their education; still, such training was not one of rhetoric or law such as the young men of noble families would learn. Women learned Greek and Latin literature as well as how to play a lyre, dance, and sing. They did not go to "finishing schools" like some civilizations insisted women do. They were taught the particulars of being a wife and mother by their own mothers.

In Roman society, nobody "fell in love" or chose his/her own spouse. It was the Roman custom to arrange marriages for boys and girls when they were still very young. They would then need to wait until the girl became an adult (15 or 16) before the marriage could take place. Being betrothed for such a lengthy time generally meant girls led a very sheltered life. To flirt, or even simply be in contact with other boys could be seen as an abrogation of the marriage arrangements.[1]

Discussion Question

Describe what it was like to be a Roman young person.

Relief found in Neumagen near Trier of a teacher with three disciples, 180–185 AD (Shakko/Wikipedia).

---

1 http://www.roman-empire.net/society/society.html.

Economics: Agrarian Base

For all of the largesse of ancient Rome, the Roman economy never developed into anything terribly complex. Ancient Rome was an agrarian, urban merchant and slave-based economy whose main concern was feeding the vast number of citizens populating the Mediterranean region. This was no small task. Rome conquered most of the known world, and it was difficult to keep grain flowing to Gaul, North Africa, and Persia. The Roman farmer managed it because, with advanced irrigation and the most advanced fertilizers and farming techniques in the ancient world, he was able to grow the most productive crops in history to that time. The Roman farmer raised two to three times the crop per acre compared to that which a Mesopotamian farmer raised. The Roman farmer, for instance, was the first farmer to use a two crop rotation in an organized, widespread fashion.

Olive oil and wine, outside of direct foodstuffs, were among the most important products in the ancient civilized world and led Italy's exports. Farmers could donate surplus crops to the government in lieu of a monetary tax. And this they did. This system allowed both republican and imperial rulers to gain popularity with the masses through free grain distribution and also helped to feed the legions at no direct monetary cost. Thus, in a real sense, successful farming and the resulting farm surpluses were the backbone of the Empire.

While the production and transportation of foods dominated the trading industry, there was also a vast exchange of other goods from all parts of Europe, Asia, and Africa. The prosperity of the empire and many of its citizens generated a need for luxurious imports. Silks from China, cotton from Egypt, spices from India, ivory and wild animals from Africa, iron ore from Spain and Britain, valuable gems from Germany, and slaves from all over enriched the Roman economy.

> The staple crops of Roman farmers in Italy were various grains, olives, and grapes.

Common coins of the Roman Empire, 280 B.C.–650 AD.

However, industry and manufacturing were always in the shadow of agriculture. Agriculture was the big mega-industry of Rome. At the same time, there was a large mining industry that provided the stones for the enormous building projects and metals for tools, as well as the weapons for the Roman army. Greece and northern Italy provided marble for the impressive buildings.

Extensive trade routes were established on land and sea. The so-called **Pax Romana** (the peace of Rome) greatly increased this trade. The Roman roads are one lasting legacy of Roman domination and many are still in use today.

The trading of goods for goods, or **barter system**, was popular in the ancient world. It was a way to avoid taxation. Merchants would exchange goods in a barter system and the emperor was cut out of revenue.

The Romans had the world's most developed **coinage systems**. Coins of brass, bronze, copper, silver, and gold were minted and circulated under strict rules for weights, sizes, value, and metal composition. Roman currency became the basis for all currency, much as the American dollar is the standard measure today.

Discussion Question

In spite of the fact that Rome was the most sophisticated and advanced civilization until modern times, the farmer remained the most important citizen in Rome. Why?

Chapter 13

Christianity: The People of the Way

First Thoughts

Phil Johnson, curator of The Hall of Church History, says, "Why would anyone want to study theology by reading A Bunch of Dead Guys? Shouldn't you focus mostly on current works, or risk becoming an irrelevant theological fossil?"[1] My answer: the truth about God is timeless. The last infallible book of theology was written nearly two thousand years ago. In theology, if it's new, it probably isn't true. The history of Christianity is the history of world civilization. Christianity has always been at the heart of world progress and morality. The three distinctives of the early Church were: separation from the world, unconditional love, and complete obedience to the teachings of Jesus Christ. This chapter will look at these distinctives and more.

Chapter Learning Objectives

This chapter explores the genesis of Christianity in the first century A.D. We will look at life in the first century, at a typical church service, and evaluate persecutions that devastated the Christian community.

As a result of this chapter you should be able to:

1. List what distinctives Christianity brought to the religious world in A.D. 50.

2. Describe what it was like to be a 13- or 14-year-old young person in the Middle East during the first century A.D.

3. Describe a typical early church service.

4. Contrast the life of a contemporary Christian with the life of a first-century Christian.

5. Evaluate what is the biblical way for Christians to respond to persecution.

Concepts

Emperor Nero

Messiah

Metaphysical

Inclusive

Urban

Galilee

Sepphoris

Nazareth

Rabbi

Papyrus Rolls

Home Meetings

Deacons

Presbytery

Elders

Christian Worship Assembly

Epistles

Gospels

Didache

Privatism

Montanist

Milan

Emperor Constantine

---

1 http://www.spurgeon.org/~phil//hall.htm.

Christianity: Overview

Christianity was founded in the first century by the followers of Jesus of Nazareth, a practicing Jew. The early Christians had no notion of founding a separate religion — none at all. They saw themselves as Jews first, Christians second. Peter and Paul had words about certain rituals that should be followed; however, no one seriously entertained the notion that Christianity was a separate religion. Not until the great persecution of **Emperor Nero**, when it was Judaism that rejected Christianity, not vice versa, did Christianity launch off into its own religious realm.

Peter, Paul and Jesus on glass windows in the apse of the parish church of Wiesloch, Germany (CC-by-SA3.0).

Christians made a bold assertion: Jesus Christ was the promised **Messiah**, the Son of the Living God. This was something completely new in the **metaphysical** world that existed in the first century. Christians loved one another; they met in homes and welcomed everyone into the fellowship — male, female, slave, and free. In Antioch they quite literally crossed over walls created to keep races and ethnic groups separated. Africans, former Jews, and converted Gentiles all worshiped and had fellowship together in this most **inclusive** of early religions. There was absolutely no religion quite like it, and it literally conquered the known world in one generation.

The founders of Christianity included those who had been disciples of Jesus, such as Peter, Matthew, James, and John, as well as others who never met Him in person but were influenced by accounts of His teachings from the Gospel writers Mark, Luke, and Paul of Tarsus, who actively encouraged the establishment of Christian communities or "churches" after his conversion.

Christianity spread initially from Jerusalem throughout the Near East. In the fourth century, it was successively adopted as the state religion by Armenia in 301, Ethiopia in 325, Georgia in 337, and then the Roman Empire in 380. It became common to all of Europe in the Middle Ages and expanded throughout the world during Europe's Age of Exploration from the Renaissance onward, to become the world's most populated religion.

Discussion Question

Which distinctive traits did Christianity bring to the religious world in A.D. 50?

Christianity: Demographics

Palestine's population in Jesus' day was approximately 500,000 to 600,000 (the population of Vermont). About 18,000 of these residents were priests. Jerusalem was a city of some 55,000 (about the size of Lancaster, Pennsylvania), but during Passover, would increase to 180,000.[2]

Children were perceived, as in all ancient cultures, as "small adults." Parents and other adults had no notion of treating children any differently from adults. They had to work and do their share. Children were dressed the same as adults and expected, as soon as maturation kicked in, to act the same as adults.

Jewish concerns about graven images meant that very few, if any, Jewish families had caricatures or portraits of family members. Everyone had two meals a day — no one, except the Romans, would eat lunch. The main staple was unleaved, or flat, bread, much like Mexican chaparejos. Breakfast consisted of bread, olives, dates, and dry cheese. Dinner was about the same, but with some fish or lamb thrown in.

Locals believed in the supernatural. Jesus wasn't the only miracle worker of His day. Everyone could list dozens of divinely inspired miracle workers. Nonetheless, Jesus seemed to have been different in that He offered no magical incantations, and more importantly, refused compensation.

> Like modern sports teams, craftsmen and mechanics would be recognizable by the symbols they wore. Barrel coopers wore barrel emblems on their tunics and robes.

A beautiful depiction of the Vale of Nazareth.

2 *Christianity Today*, "The Life and Times of Jesus of Nazareth: Did You Know?" http://www.christianitytoday.com/ch/1998/issue59/59h002.html.

Jesus grew up in an **urban** world. The vast majority of Palestinians lived in cities. Jesus lived close to three major ancient cities — the ancient capital of **Galilee**, **Sepphoris**, and **Nazareth**. Cities were no more than 500 to perhaps a thousand people. They were dark and unsavory places to many. Sewage was flowing in the streets, and there was no effort to control wood fires and smoke.

Jesus would have seen his **rabbi** read from **papyrus rolls**, which were often more than 30 feet long! This was about as long as any book could be. This as much as anything else determined the length of literary works. It is no accident that, for example, Luke's Gospel is the maximum length for an ancient document, and thus another papyrus roll had to be used to inscribe the Book of Acts.[3]

Papyrus rolls.

Discussion Question

Describe what it was like to be a 13- or 14-year-old young person in the Middle East during the first century A.D.

Lesson 3

Early Church Services

For the first 300 years or so of church history, there were no church buildings. It was mostly against the law. Church occurred in homes. Church services, quite literarily, were **home meetings**. The "pastors" were usually a couple, man and woman, who had been called forth from the **deacons** (vs. the **presbytery** or **elders**). Fairly early on, the church meetings occurred on Sunday — all day Sunday, usually.

The first part of an early **Christian worship assembly** was open to all, including strangers, who might be converted by the fellowship and preaching. Every church service had a meal during this time, and at the end, in a very informal way, communion, the Lord's Supper, was served. This part of the service involved the **Lord's Supper**, which only the baptized were allowed to partake of, so the **seekers** departed then. While there was no official altar call, nor was there a calling forth of the "gifts," it was during this time that miracles — healings, in particular — occurred. These were very natural phenomenon without any deliberate, emotional conjuring by the leadership. Prophecy and other gifts were encouraged and common.

Guest chamber of Ramallah, Palestine (LOC).

---

3 Ibid.

There was no Bible, of course. Paul's **epistles** were available by the middle of the first century, and then, slowly, Matthew, Mark, Luke, and then John wrote their **Gospels**. Again, though, copies were few and far between, so teaching was based on these early works, and a non-canonical work, the **Didache**. The Bible would come later.

Repentance was an involved process in the early Church. **Privatism** (the notion that the individual alone is important in society) is a modern phenomenon. Sin was not a personal matter but was viewed as something that destroyed the unity of the church. Penitents fasted and prayed for the forgiveness of their sins, appeared before the church to make public confession, and were barred from the Lord's Supper until they gave evidence of a change of heart and were absolved.

Discussion Question

Describe a typical early church service.

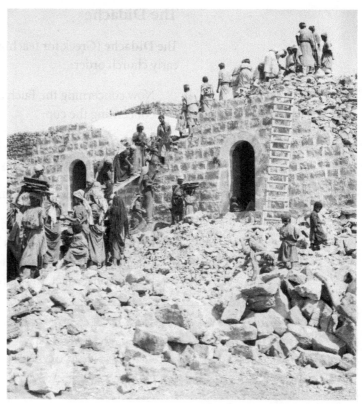

Building a native stone home in Palestine, 1896 (LOC).

Primary Source Material

A Roman Official's Report

Around A.D. 112, Pliny, the Roman governor of Bithynia (a province in northwest Turkey), wrote to the emperor Trajan in Rome:

> [The Christians] maintained that the amount of their fault or error had been this, that it was their habit on a fixed day to assemble before daylight and recite by turns a form of words to Christ as a god; and that they bound themselves with an oath, not for any crime, but not to commit theft or robbery or adultery, not to break their word, and not to deny a deposit when demanded. After this was done, their custom was to depart, and to meet again to take food, but ordinary and harmless food. — Letter X: 96:7[4]

Bust of Trajan who reigned from 98–117 AD.

---

4 http://www.christianitytoday.com/ch/1993/issue37/3721.html.

The Didache

The **Didache** (Greek for teaching) was a non-canonical manuscript written to describe early church order:

> Now concerning the Eucharist [or thanksgiving], give thanks this way. First, concerning the cup:
>
> We thank thee, our Father, for the holy vine David Thy servant, which You madest known to us through Jesus Thy Servant; to thee be the glory forever.
>
> And concerning the broken bread:
>
> We thank Thee, our Father, for the life and knowledge which You madest known to us through Jesus Thy servant; to Thee be the glory for ever. Even as this broken bread was scattered over the hills, and was gathered together and became one, so let Thy Church be gathered together from the ends of the earth into Thy kingdom; for Thine is the glory and the power through Jesus Christ for ever.
>
> But let no one eat or drink of your Eucharist, unless they have been baptized into the name of the Lord; for concerning this also the Lord has said, "Give not that which is holy to the dogs."
>
> But after you are filled, give thanks this way:
>
> We thank Thee, holy Father, for Thy holy name which You didst cause to tabernacle in our hearts, and for the knowledge and faith and immortality, which You madest known to us through Jesus Thy servant; to Thee be the glory for ever. Thou, Master almighty, didst create all things for Thy name's sake; You gavest food and drink to men for enjoyment, that they might give thanks to Thee; but to us You didst freely give spiritual food and drink and life eternal through Thy Servant. Before all things we thank Thee that You are mighty; to Thee be the glory for ever. Remember, Lord, Thy Church, to deliver it from all evil and to make it perfect in Thy love, and gather it from the four winds, sanctified for Thy kingdom which Thou have prepared for it; for Thine is the power and the glory for ever. Let grace come, and let this world pass away. Hosanna to the God of David! If any one is holy, let him come; if any one is not so, let him repent. Maranatha [Our Lord, come!]. Amen.
>
> But permit the prophets to make Thanksgiving as much as they desire.
>
> — Didache 9–10[5]

The title of the Didache in a manuscript discovered in 1873 (PD-Art).

---

5 http://www.earlychristianwritings.com/text/didache-roberts.html.

Charismatic Movement

Tertullian, a Christian leader, embraced the **Montanist** movement, a prophetic movement that made special claims about the Holy Spirit. In this selection, from *A Treatise on the Soul*, Tertullian gives a rare glimpse of charismatic experience in worship.

Quintus Florens Tertullian, 160–220 AD, church father and theologian.

> Seeing that we acknowledge spiritual charismata, or gifts, we too have merited the attainment of the prophetic gift, although coming after John [the Baptist]. We have now among us a sister whose lot it has been to be favored with sundry gifts of revelation, which she experiences in the Spirit by ecstatic vision during the sacred rites of the Lord's day in the church: she converses with angels, and sometimes even with the Lord; she both sees and hears mysterious communications; some men's hearts she understands; and to them who are in need she distributes remedies.
>
> Whether it be in the reading of Scriptures, or in the chanting of psalms, or in the preaching of sermons, or in the offering up of prayers, in all these religious services matter and opportunity are afforded her of seeing visions. . . . After the people are dismissed at the conclusion of the sacred services, she is in the regular habit of reporting to us whatever things she may have seen in vision (for all her communications are examined with the most scrupulous care, in order that their truth may be probed).
>
> "Among other things," says she, "there has been shown to me a soul in bodily shape, and a spirit has been in the habit of appearing to me; not, however, a void and empty illusion, but such as would offer itself to be even grasped by the hand, soft and transparent and of an ethereal color, and in form resembling that of a human being in every respect." This was her vision, and for her witness there was God; and the apostle most assuredly foretold that there were to be "spiritual gifts" in the church.[6]

Discussion Question

Contrast the life of a contemporary Christian with the life of a first-century Christian.

---

6 http://www.ccel.org/ccel/schaff/anf03.iv.xi.ix.html.

Sociology: Persecution

Christian persecution was a defining experience for the early Church. Jewish officials instigated the first persecutions, followed by the Romans. Persecution, however, was by no means constant.

In a secular state, a religion that claimed exclusivity naturally was a target for persecution. At the same time, whenever there was a crisis, the Christians were a convenient scapegoat. They invited exaggerated rumors. For instance, based on the early Christians' observance of the Lord's Supper, Christians were accused of cannibalism and incest.

Many Christians gave up their faith under the threat of persecution. In fact, the numbers of those who fell away produced a crisis for the Church in the 250s. Eventually, the question of whether or not to readmit the lapsed produced several splits.

One of the leading charges against Christians in the Empire was that they were "atheists"; that is, they did not worship the pagan deities, and so did not participate in the social and civic activities that involved homage to them.

Perhaps the most severe persecution, the "Great Persecution," was also the last, beginning in 303 and continuing off and on in places until 324.

Persecution ended officially with the "Edict of Milan" in 313 with a law issued at **Milan** by the **Emperor Constantine** that established Christianity as the state religion.

Discussion Question

What is the biblical way for Christians to respond to persecution?

Depiction of The Christian Martyrs' Last Prayer, painted between 1863 and 1883.

Chapter 14

Christianity:
The World Turned Upside-Down

First Thoughts

Antony of Egypt, the first Desert Father, wrote, "Wherever you find yourself, do not go forth from that place too quickly. Try to be patient and learn to stay in one place."[1] The contemporary Church would do well to revisit Antony and other Church fathers. The first- and second-century Church created patterns that are still functioning today. Struggling in a hostile place, the Church still managed, against overwhelming odds, to conquer the intellectual and religious world of its time!

Chapter Learning Objectives

Chapter 14 explores the emerging and expanding early Church. We look at the women in the early Church and marvel at both their effectiveness and their inspiring spirituality! We reflect upon evangelism and how it assured Christianity a permanent and important place in the first and second century. Next, we explore why aberrant heresies emerged and, in the next lesson, observe that this opposition stimulated the creation of the first canon, and subsequent Bible.

As a result of this chapter you should be able to:

1. Explain why Christian women were so valuable to early Church growth.

2. Evaluate why Christian evangelism was so effective in the early Church.

3. Discuss three early heresies.

4. Analyze why the Bible developed relatively late in early Church history.

5. Understand the allure of monasticism.

6. Evaluate what problems, if any, you might have with monasticism.

Concepts

Spiritual Gifts

Celsus

Agape Meal

Crossed the Jordan

Apologists

Historical Jesus

Church Fathers

Canon

Apostles

Apocryphal

Ascetics

Desert Fathers

Heretical Doctrines

Systematic Church Dogma

Desert Monasticism

Mennonite

Anabaptists

Quakers

Methodist Revival

---

1 www.ctlibrary.com/ch/131Christians

Women in the Early Church

Never in the history of the world has a religion so honored and empowered women as completely as Christianity. Women were the last disciples at the Cross and the first at the empty tomb. They remained a central part of the Christian Church. Women shared the pastoral role with their husbands and manifested many early **spiritual gifts**. Women were esteemed and honored by all in the Christian Church. Christianity was the first religion to do so.

Women were not merely "honored and esteemed." They were an important reason that the Church grew so quickly. They were valued Church members. In fact, the Church was the only community entity that really valued women.

Celsus, a pagan critic of Christianity, once taunted that the Church attracted only "the silly and the mean and the stupid, with women and children." Early Church leaders acknowledged that there were more women than in other faiths but that this was a distinct advantage. It wasn't that Christian leaders were in favor of "women's liberation." The fact was that women were a critical part of the infrastructure that emerged in the first century. They cooked and served the meals during home church meetings. They freely manifested supernatural gifts in church services. They were prayer warriors. They were tireless workers on behalf of our Lord!

Women were hard workers and ironically, as a labor force, were readily available. As society enjoyed the enforced peace and security of Roman occupation, women had more and more spare time. They used it to advance the cause of Christ.

Why were women attracted to the early Church? For one thing, the common practice of killing unwanted female children among Hellenistic society was forbidden. Quite literally, Christian families had more female children than pagan families. Christian husbands were forced to be monogamous, an unprecedented practice among ancient people groups.

Women founded the first Christian hospital in Europe. Church widows were especially generous and supported many early Christian benevolent causes. And there were many such causes! With no need to maintain a building or support a paid clergy, the Church devoted most of its resources to ministry to the poor.

In a letter to his wife, Tertullian gives us a glimpse into some of the ministries of Church women in his time. He charges her, in case of his own death, to not marry a pagan. "Who would be willing to let his wife go through one street after another to other men's houses, and

From the Royal Gold Cup, showing scenes from Saint Agnes' life and death, British Museum, 14th century.

indeed to the poorer cottages, in order to visit the brethren? Who would like to see her being taken from his side by some duty of attending a nocturnal gathering? At Easter time who will quietly tolerate her absence all the night? Who will inauspiciously let her go to the Lord's Supper, that feast upon which they heap such calumnies? Who will let her creep into jail to kiss the martyr's chains? Or bring water for the saints' feet?"[2]

Discussion Question

Why were Christian women so valuable to early Church growth?

Evangelism in the Early Church

For more than 150 years after the Resurrection, some argue it was longer — up to 300 years, Christians had no official church buildings. During this time, evangelism was conducted mainly in homes, in the context of worship and care-giving. There were virtually no evangelists or revival services.

Friends were invited to the potluck dinners that were the heart of early Church liturgies. Toward the end of the service, unsaved visitors were invited to commit their hearts to Christ, and, if they agreed, they were invited to the last, most important ritual, the **agape meal** (the Lord's Supper). Then, in the next few weeks the new converts "**crossed the Jordan**" or were baptized in the Jordan River. It is unlikely that the first converts were immersed. Nor were they "sprinkled." It *is* likely that early converts had water poured over their heads as they stood in the shallow Jordan River. They were now members of the Body of Christ, the Church!

It was generally expected that everyone would participate in a religion of some sort, but few people thought it necessary to take religion seriously. When a people group — like the Christians — really took their religion seriously, it made a great impact on society.

At first, Christianity and Judaism were the only monotheistic religions. By the end of the first century, virtually every popular religion — especially Mithraism — aligned itself in some way with solar monotheism (worship of the sun). Thus, Christians often talked of the similarities and differences

Saints Peter and John Baptizing the Samarians by Willem Vrelant, The J. Paul Getty Museum, c 1460 (PD-US, PD-Art).

---

2 Catherine Kroeger, "The Neglected History of Women in the Early Church," https://www.christianhistoryinstitute.org/magazine/article/women-in-the-early-church/.

between the sun god and the Light of the World. Jesus said, "I am the light of the world." This had great appeal to first-century Middle Eastern people.

During the early years, Christians were mostly defending themselves against competing faiths. Evangelism, informally, or otherwise, was not intentional. Eventually, **apologists** defended the truths of Christianity, and that became the first form of formal evangelism. In other words, Christians were not trying to recruit new converts. They were merely trying to hold their own in a very hostile culture!

Growth was phenomenal. In 250, after more than 200 years of evangelistic effort, Christians still made up only 1.9 percent of the Empire. By the middle of the next century, though, about 56 percent of the population claimed to be Christians.

Discussion Question

Why was Christian evangelism so effective in the early Church?

Lesson 3

Heresy in the Early Church

Emperor Constantine and the Council of Nicaea; the burning of Arian books is illustrated below, ca. 825 (PD-Art).

112

Fairly early in Church history **heretical doctrines** emerged. Usually these doctrines contained some truth but overemphasized a good thing. For instance, a movement called Montanism correctly emphasized the gifts of the Holy Spirit but carried things too far when it tied the gifts to salvation. Likewise, a nasty heresy, gnosticism, drew many converts away from the Gospel. Gnosticism argued that Jesus was not really a man.

Though the debate about Christ's deity extended over centuries, the debate about the Holy Spirit's divine nature lasted only about 20 years. Some of the greatest early theologians were confused about Christ's nature. Clement of Alexandria, for example, masterfully refuted the gnostic heresy that said Christ did not have a real human body and therefore did not eat and drink. Clement held that Jesus did indeed eat and drink but not because He needed food and drink to stay alive — Jesus, Clement argued, only wished to keep His disciples from heretical beliefs about Him. Of course, Jesus Christ was wholly man, wholly God. As a man He did need to eat.

Not all defenders of orthodoxy stayed orthodox themselves. Tertullian and Novatian, for example, two major anti-Gnostic theologians of the 200s, each fell out of favor with the Church: Tertullian because of his conversion to the Montanist heresy, and Novatian because of his unforgiving stance against those who had denied Christ under persecution.[3]

---

3 Tony Lane, *Exploring Christian Thought: Nelson's Christian Cornerstone Series* (Nashville, TN: Thomas Nelson, 1996).

Heretics often provided a great service to the Church. For example, Marcion rejected the Old Testament and the Gospels of Matthew, Mark, and John, thus forcing the Church to define the New Testament canon. It is fair to say we would not have had a Bible without Marcion. Arius, in denying the deity of Christ, made the Church articulate the Nicene Creed that became critical to early Christian orthodoxy.

The burning of the Amalrician heretics, circa 1210 (PD-Art).

Discussion Question

Discuss three early heresies. In your discussion, explain what kernel of truth was in each heresy.

The Canon

Until the middle of the second century, there was no Bible. In fact, most people did not see much of a need. For one thing, the early Church had Paul's letters that were circulating through the churches. At the same time, there were no church buildings and therefore no church property or church infrastructure to maintain. Besides, there was no need for a **systematic church dogma** because there was no serious aberrant, alternative church dogma. That was to change.

The reason Christians have 27 books in their New Testament, some scholars say, is because a Christian leader named Marcion created a New Testament with 12. Marcion, among others, claimed authority through questionable sacred works. This was a problem, especially concerning the **historical Jesus**.

Different theories arose. Was Jesus really a man? Was He equal to God? Should people be baptized in the name of the Father? The Son? All three? And so forth. A Bible emerged because the Christian community needed it. Ultimately, the whole world benefited!

The oldest surviving manuscript of any part of the New Testament is a papyrus fragment containing verses from John 18; it was written in about 125.

But what writings would go into the Bible? Which would be left out? The **Church fathers** were forced to pick and choose, and finally decided upon what they called the **canon**.

> The word *Bible* comes from the Greek word for "papyrus plant" (*biblos*), since the leaves of that plant were used for paper.

The Book of Esther from the 13th or 14th century (CCA-SA3.0).

In classical Greek, the world "canon" signifies "a straight rod" or "a carpenter's rule." The Canon of Truth — referring to the restriction of the number of books that compose the Bible — was first used in the year A.D. 367.

Why was the canon necessary?

So long as the **apostles** were alive, there was no pressing need for a canon of Scripture. Under the inspiration of God they knew what was inspired, but when they died, it became necessary that their writings be gathered together for others to know their messages to the churches, and to preserve those writings from corruption.

Likewise, there was a need to limit other aberrant **apocryphal** works that purportedly were "inspired."

Still another powerful reason for the formation of the canon lay in the fact that the Emperor Diocletian issued an edict in A.D. 302 that all the sacred books should be destroyed by fire. Secular authorities, demanded, then, to know what writings were sacred.

By the end of the fourth century A.D., the Bible as we know it emerged. Of course, it was not in a bound book, but existed in papyrus manuscript form all over the Western world.

Discussion Question

Why did the Bible develop relatively late in early Church history?

The Abisha Scroll; the oldest scroll among the Samaritans in Nablus and possibly the oldest surviving Pentateuch scroll on Earth; photo taken 1900–1920 (LOC).

Desert Fathers: Christian Radicals

Saint Poimen The Great (CC by-SA3.0).

As the Church matured, a group of radical Christians emerged. These people were called the **Desert Fathers**. The Desert Fathers were hermits and **ascetics** who lived mainly in the Egyptian desert beginning around the third century A.D. The most famous was Anthony the Great, who moved into the desert in 270–271. He founded **desert monasticism**. Monasticism was a relatively new idea in Christianity. A monastic, or monk, purposed to live a sheltered life so as to concentrate on God alone. Some monks lived solitary lives, taking a vow of silence. Others lived openly in community.

The desert monastic communities that grew out of the informal gathering of hermit monks became the model for Christian monasticism. All of the monastic revivals of the Middle Ages — and there were several — looked to the desert for inspiration and guidance. Even religious renewals such as the **Mennonite Anabaptists**, the **Quakers**, and the **Methodist Revival** were influenced by the Desert Fathers.

The following are several quotes from the Desert Fathers.

On Fasting

Abba John the Short said, "If a king wants to take a city whose citizens are hostile, he first captures the food and water of the inhabitants of the city, and when they are starving subdues them. So it is with gluttony. If a man is earnest in fasting and hunger, the enemies which trouble his soul will grow weak."

On Purity of Heart

Abba Poemen said, "Teach your heart to keep what your tongue teaches others."

On Judging

A brother asked Abba Poemen, "I am troubled in spirit, and want to leave this place."

And the old man said, "Why?"

And he said, "I have heard unedifying stories about one of the brothers."

And the old man said, "Are the stories true?" And he said, "Yes, Father. The brother who told me is a man of trust."

And the old man answered, "The brother who told you is not a man of trust. For if he was so, he would not have told you these stories. When God heard the cry of the men of Sodom, he did not believe it until he had gone down and seen with his own eyes."

And the brother said, "I too have seen it with my own eyes."

When the old man heard this, he looked down and picked off the ground a wisp of straw, and he said, "What is this?"

And he answered, "Straw."

Then the old man reached up and touched the roof of the cell, and said, "What is this?"

And he answered, "It is the beam that holds up the roof."

And the old man said, "Take it into your heart that your sins are like this beam, and that brother's sins are like this wisp of straw."[4]

Discussion Question

What was the allure of Monasticism? Why, suddenly, in the third century, did so many Christians flee to the desert to walk with God?

Desert landscape from southern Jordan.

---

4 "Antony and the Desert Fathers: Did You Know?" http://www.christianitytoday.com/ch/1999/issue64/64h002.html.

Saint Augustine by Antonio Rodríguez (1636–1691), Museo Nacional de Arte (PD-US, PD-Art).

Chapter 15

Age of Augustine: The Church Prospers in a Hostile Culture

First Thoughts

Arguably, after Jesus and Paul, Augustine of Hippo was the most influential figure in the history of Christianity. He lived at a time when the waves of barbarians surging into the Roman Empire must have created public anxiety similar to that experienced today because of the threat of Al-Qaida. The barbaric Goths sacked Rome in A.D. 410, and the Vandals were besieging the city of Hippo even as Augustine, the city's bishop, lay on his deathbed. Smoke from Vandal-set fires was wafting through the windows of his room as he breathed his last. But he had much for which to give thanks. His Church was ready. The Barbarians conquered Rome but the Church of Jesus Christ, so well-loved and well-represented by Augustine, conquered the Barbarians.

Chapter Learning Objectives

We will discuss the life of Augustine and his impact on history. We will revisit the Donatist and Pelagian heresies and speculate as to whether or not Augustine and the Church handled it properly. Finally, we will examine Augustine's handling of barbarian incursions and determine how we can apply this knowledge to our present situation.

As a result of this chapter you should be able to:

1. Outline Augustine's conversion.
2. Discuss the impact that Church growth and expansion had on the Church's witness in society.
3. Judge whether or not Augustine was too harsh with the Donatists.
4. Gauge the impact of the post-Christian world upon the Church of the future.
5. Review Augustine's conversion and discuss one's own conversion.

CONCEPTS

Barbarians

Manichaeanism

Cicero

Atonement

Dualistic

Exegesis

Donatism

Pelagianism

Visigoth Alaric

Hegemony

Young Augustine

Augustine was born in North Africa in A.D. 354 and died almost 76 years later in Hippo (present-day Algeria) only 60 miles away. In his lifetime, Augustine bridged the gap between the defeated Roman Empire and the nascent Christian Middle Ages. No doubt, Augustine had no **concept** of his historical importance, because from the moment of his conversion, his life was centered on God and "the city of God," not on his participation in it.

Augustine's African homeland was an older part of the Roman Empire. It had been part of Roman hegemony since the destruction of Carthage 500 years before his birth. Carthage had been completely destroyed and then rebuilt by Rome as a modern metropolis of Roman Africa. It was, in short, one of the most cosmopolitan parts of the sprawling Roman Empire.

But at the same time, Roman Africa was a military backwater. Africa had no **barbarians** on its borders threatening peace. The only emperors who ever spent much time in Africa were the ones who had been born there, and by Augustine's time, decades had passed without any notable visit from a high Roman official.

By the time of Augustine's tenure, the dominant religion of Africa was Christianity — a religion that violently opposed the traditions of old Rome but that could not have spread as it did without the prosperity and peace that Roman power brought.

Therefore, as one historian explained, "A young man like Augustine could belong irretrievably to the world Rome had made, but still feel that he was living on the periphery of that world. Augustine set out to make himself more Roman than the Romans and to penetrate to the center of the culture from which he found himself alienated by his provincial birth."[1]

Augustine's parents, Patricius and Monica, belonged to the declining middle class. They were well off enough to have educational ambitions for their son, but too poor to finance those ambitions themselves. Whereas Monica was a pious Christian, Patricius was not. Moreover, like most Roman husbands, he was unfaithful to Monica and had several mistresses. Monica continued to pray, however, and Patricius accepted the Lord and was baptized on his deathbed.

Augustine by Simone Martini, c. 1320–1325 (PD-Art).

Historians suggest that Augustine was an ordinary child, "good at his lessons but not fond of school, eager to win the approval of his elders but prone to trivial acts of rebellion, quick to form close friendships but not always able to foresee their consequences. He studied Latin with some enthusiasm but never loved Greek."[2] Like most middle-class

---

1 James J. O'Donnell, "Augustine the African," http://www9.georgetown.edu/faculty/jod/twayne/aug1.html.
2 Ibid.

parents of promising students, his parents worried about paying for his education. Finally, with the help of an affluent family friend, Augustine was able to go to college.

Although raised in a Christian home, Augustine rebelled in his teenage years. He abandoned his childhood faith and joined an intellectual sect, some called it a religion, called **Manichaeanism**. During Augustine's college years, his live-in girlfriend became pregnant and they had a son. Later, Augustine regretfully left his first love to marry a society scion. Their son died prematurely and Augustine always felt badly about this event, as if God might be punishing him.

The School of Tagaste detail, 1464 (PD-Art).

Discussion Question

Why was the Manichaean faith so appealing to the intellectual Augustine? What contemporary worldview temptations exist?

Augustine's Conversion

Augustine was a powerful intellectual, particularly fond of the works of the Roman statesman **Cicero**.

Always the intellectual darling, and wishing to advance himself politically, the ambitious Augustine thrived in the politically correct Manichaean sect. Augustine, who could not escape the prayers and silent moral turpitude of his faithful mother, found the Manichaeans a most desirable escape from what Augustine saw as the demanding Christian faith. Manichaean faith claimed that security could be attained without sacrifice and guilt removed without **atonement**.

The world the Manichaeans imagined was **dualistic**, competing between two contrary powers: the perfectly good creator and the perfectly evil destroyer. The convert could obtain salvation by intellectually overcoming the devil, who, after all, was not that clever. If the devil did cause one to sin, then he need not feel guilt, because the Manichaean was saved through knowledge, not through any religious act. What a metaphysical deal! If it were only true!

But it was not true, and Augustine was too clever to settle for vague theology for long. Besides, his faithful mother continued to pray for him! It was only a matter of time before God brought other believers into his midst.

St Augustine reading the epistle of St Paul, 1464 (PD-Art).

First, his mother entered the picture again. She continued to pray for him and connected him with other Christians, notably Ambrose, Bishop of Milan. Ambrose was Augustine's intellectual equal. One historian explains, "Here Christianity began to appear to him in a new, intellectually respectable light. As before, his most pressing personal problem was his sense of evil and his responsibility for the wickedness of his life; with the help of technical vocabulary borrowed from Platonic philosophy Ambrose proposed a convincing solution for Augustine's oldest dilemma. Augustine had besides a specific objection to Christianity that only a professor of rhetoric could have: he could not love the Scriptures because their style was inelegant and barbaric. Here again Ambrose, elegant and far from barbaric, showed Augustine how Christian exegesis could give life and meaning to the sacred texts."[3] Finally, Augustine responded to the Holy Spirit and gave his life to Christ.

Ambrose was a bishop of Milan, Italy, who became one of the most influential ecclesiastical figures of the fourth century.

Discussion Question

Trace Augustine's spiritual journey to Christ.

Lesson 3

Pastor Augustine

Baptism of St Augustine, 1464 (PD-Art).

In the spring of A.D. 387, on the night of the Saturday before Easter, Augustine was baptized by Ambrose. At a time when Christianity was the fashionable road to success in the Christian Roman Empire, many may have viewed such a move as a career maker. But not Augustine. From the get-go, Augustine was sold out to Christ.

During the first few months, some think a year, after his conversion, Augustine withdrew for a season of retreat and meditation. It was during this time that his mother died. He was devastated, but, under the discipleship of Ambrose, he grew strong in the Lord!

Now Augustine felt called to the priesthood. Fifth-century pastors were not trained in seminaries; normally they were assigned to an older pastor who taught the young man Bible **exegesis** and Church history.

Two years later, by default really, the young Augustine, preparing to be a pastor, became the interim pastor of a church in Hippo, North Africa. He stayed in leadership there the rest of his life.

By this time, the Roman Catholic Church was fully established. The fourth-century Church was centered upon the worship of the community. On a Sunday, every Christian in Hippo could be found jammed into Augustine's church, standing through a service that must have lasted at least two hours.

---

3 Ibid.

We know from the hundreds of sermons that survive how much creativity Augustine put into preaching, tailoring his remarks to suit the needs and capacity of his audience. Augustine was the R. C. Sproul of his time — he preached well, but his sermons were full of theological sophistication and import.

Historian James J. Donnell writes:

> But even the homiletics of Augustine did not efface the dignity of the central act of worship. God was present on the altar for these people and this event was the center of Christian community life. Lukewarm believers in the throng attended out of respect for social pressure and a fear of divine wrath and were not much moved, but for Augustine, this was his central task. The controversies were only sideshow, important only when they threatened to disrupt the unity of the community's worship.
>
> But we know Augustine for his writings, and many of them were controversial. Three great battles had to be fought: the first was an ecclesiastical struggle for the very life of his community, the second a philosophical battle to affect the Christianization of Roman culture, and the last a theological quarrel of great subtlety over the essentials of faith and salvation.[4]

Augustine teaching in Rome detail, 1464 (PD-Art).

Discussion Question

By the fourth century, the Church no longer met in homes but met in church buildings and was increasingly controlled by a tertiary ecclesiological government (i.e., the Roman Catholic Church). What advantages and disadvantages did this offer the early Church?

Lesson 4

New Heresies

Donatism was the movement Augustine opposed, named after a bishop at Carthage some 80 years before Augustine. The Church had just recovered from the last bitter wave of persecution begun in A.D. 303 by the Emperor **Diocletian**. When the persecution ended, Christians brought charges against other Christians who had succumbed to temptation and denied the faith.

The official position of the Church was that those Christians who had compromised their religion in time of persecution could, with due repentance and atonement, be readmitted to full membership. But this was easier said than done. Christians who had watched their loved ones tortured and murdered were not ready to forgive those who

---

4 Ibid.

had betrayed the faith. Some Christians insisted that cooperation with the authorities in time of persecution was tantamount to total apostasy and that if any traitors wanted to re-enter the church they had to start all over again, undergoing rebaptism. Evaluation of the credentials of those who sought re-entry would be in the hands of those who had not betrayed the church.

This position was called the "Donatist" position.

Augustine opposed the Donatists. His first letters to Donatist leaders were friendly and emphasized their good will. He assumed that they could settle this controversy peaceably. But Augustine quickly discovered that this was not the case. The Donatists were injured and angry and in no mood to compromise. They meant to purify the Church.

Saint Augustine Disputing with the Heretics by Vergós Group, Museu Nacional d'Art de Catalunya c.1470 (PD-US, PD-Art).

In the late 390s, then, Augustine resigned himself to a more radical course. Augustine was dismayed at coercion in matters of religion, but in this case he felt that the Donatists must be handled roughly. For one thing, unforgiveness would undermine the effectiveness of the Gospel and ruin the Church's witness to the world. The Donatists were driven from the Church.

The final heresy that Augustine confronted was **Pelagianism**. Pelagianism was theologically rather similar to Donatism in that it argued that people could, by their own virtue, set themselves apart as the ones whom God particularly blessed. To Augustine, such a view violated the very sovereignty of God.

Augustine and the Orthodox Roman Catholic Church won both conflicts, but the results were mixed. The net result, though, was that the Church in general declined in North Africa, and even today the Church is mostly absent from North Africa. Apparently, Augustine won the battle only to lose the war (so far at least).

Discussion Question

Were the Donatists correct in arguing that recalcitrant, unfaithful believers should not be readmitted into the Church even with extensive penance and repentance?

Waiting for the Barbarian

In A.D. 410, the city of Rome, with all its glories, was taken by barbarians under the leadership of the **Visigoth Alaric**. It is customary to say that shock waves ran throughout the Roman world at this event, but it is more correct to say that shock waves ran through those citizens of the Roman world prosperous enough to care about expensive symbols of Roman **hegemony**. A fair number of wealthy Romans fled the city to country estates in Campania, Sicily, and North Africa. Enough of them showed up in Hippo for Augustine to warn his flock that they should receive the refugees with open arms and charity. Ultimately, the Visigoths, and other barbarians, conquered Rome. But Augustine and his community conquered the barbarians. How? The following essay gives the author's take on how Christians can prosper in a post-Christian, hostile world that was much like the world in which Augustine lived. He is addressing his own community, the evangelical Christian community.

Alaric entering Athens, c. 1920s (PD-US).

The Time of Obadiah Is Ending[5]

In 49 B.C., the crossing of a small stream in northern Italy by ambitious Roman general Julius Caesar became one of the pivotal events in world history. From it sprang the Roman Empire and the genesis of modern Europe. An ancient Roman law forbade any general from crossing the Rubicon River and entering Italy proper with a standing army. To do so was treason. Caesar was well aware of this. Coming up with his troops on the banks of the Rubicon, he halted, and reminded his fellow officers of the importance of the next step.

"Still we can retreat!" he said. "But once let us pass this little bridge, and nothing is left but to fight it out with arms!" (Suetonius). He crossed the river and we all know the rest.

America is very different from the America in which my family began home schooling in 1985. Really different. Moral boundaries are violated; sacred fences are down.

America in the beginning of the 21st century is spinning out of control. We are stretching our wings adventurously, but drifting farther away from our God. We are in trouble. In 1 Kings 18–19, Elijah and his peers lived in a similar world. Choleric Elijah was coming home — and no one wanted him home. He is crossing his Rubicon. After a long time, in the third year, the word of the Lord came to Elijah: "Go and present yourself to Ahab, and I will send rain on the land." King Ahab and Queen Jezebel, of course, hate him. But even Obadiah, a faithful follower of God and trusted advisor to the king and queen, who had learned so

5 James P. Stobaugh, *World History — Teacher: Observations and Assessments from Creation to Today* (Green Forest, AR: Master Books, 2012), p. 48.

well to survive in this hostile land, who has done so much good for God's people — Obadiah was not too thrilled to see him either. In fact, no one welcomed Elijah — not the hostile king and queen nor the pious evangelical Obadiah.

Even though Elijah brings good news — it is finally going to rain — no one welcomes him. Elijah's fish-or-cut-bait prophetic messages were irritating the life out of the status quo. That was bad enough. But what really scares the dickens out of everyone is the fact that Elijah has come home to Zion, to the City of God, to challenge the gods of the age to a duel.[6]

Fellow believers, I don't know when we crossed the Rubicon. Was it when we turned off the television or refused to buy the latest entertainment center? Was it when we drove our old cars another year so we could buy the best curricula for our kids? Or was it when we decided to read classics together in our homes? Somewhere, sometime, we crossed the Rubicon and there is no going back.

Jezabel and Ahab meeting Elijah in Naboth's Vineyard by Sir Frank Dicksee (PD-US).

To push my metaphor further, we were first "Obadiahs," perhaps from 1985 to today. There is nothing wrong with being Obadiah. Faithful, godly Obadiah, like Daniel, was very influential in a very evil regime. Obadiah served evil Ahab and Jezebel well, and he also served God's people well. For instance, he was able to protect hundreds of prophets who otherwise would have been killed by Ahab.

King Ahab and Jezebel are very capable, and, in many ways, successful monarchs. From their perspective, they are the true leaders. Elijah and the prophets were radical, unreasonable, uncompromising troublers of Israel. They are not team players. No doubt, Ahab and Jezebel could not understand why Elijah could not carry on a civil discussion about what they saw as tangential, civil issues. Likewise, recently our president was genuinely concerned that "conservatives cannot be civil and polite in their discussions about abortion." To many of us pro-lifers, and to Elijah, murder and apostasy do not engender etiquette.

This present generation is the Elijah generation. To Elijah, the behavior of Ahab and Jezebel is absolutely appalling. While claiming to worship the Hebrew God they also fill the land with syncretism, with apostate worship of the Baals. The crowning blow, to Elijah, is when these scoundrels placed the Asherah poles on the hill next to the temple. Enough was enough, and Elijah was ordered home to confront these evil powers on Mt. Carmel. And Elijah was not accommodating nor was he running away — don't you just wish, Ahab and Jezebel! — he is coming home to challenge the gods of this age.

Ahab and Jezebel are postmodernists. They celebrate the subjective. They are committed to compromise. Live and let live! What is the big deal? Well, you see, Elijah cannot compromise with the stuff they are doing. There is no wriggle

---

6 James P. Stobaugh, *World History — Teacher: Observations and Assessments from Creation to Today* (Green Forest, AR: Master Books, 2012), p. 48.

room in Judah and there is getting to be precious little wriggle room in the USA too.

There is some good news here. The world of the Baals, folks, is falling apart. And quickly. As my old friend Professor Harvey Cox at Harvard coyly observed, "Once Americans had dreams and no technology to fulfill those dreams. Now Americans have tons of technology, but they have no dreams left."

In short order the Ahabs and Jezebels are going to find out that Elijah is not in a compromising mood either. Folks, there are some things one cannot compromise. Elijah and Jezebel are going to meet a man of God who speaks with concrete clarity, who carries the weight of truth. Elijah is coming, Christian brothers and sisters. The days of Obadiah are over. Elijah is coming to town.

Christian parents, you are not only discipling your children to be faithful believers and good students. You are preparing them to fight a war, a culture war.

Are you ready? Can you give up your anonymity? Will you risk everything this year to prepare this generation to be salt and light in a world that is losing its light and flavor? Will you go the extra mile in your home schooling to make sure that this generation will stand on Mt. Carmel and proclaim the sovereignty and goodness of our God so they can bring the Kingdom on this earth as it is in Heaven?

The stakes are high; the potential rewards astounding. We have a chance, perhaps in our lifetime, to experience an unprecedented cultural revolution. In your homes are the new revolutionaries, who will go to the high places of this nation and proclaim the radical goodness of our God.

This is the generation of Elijah, the generation that will have to walk the long, arduous walk up Mt. Carmel, and they will challenge the gods of this age. Bring it on! We are ready! Every knee shall bow, every tongue shall profess, that Jesus Christ is Lord. Bring on the fire of Elijah, again, on this nation! God is calling forth our children — Elijahs who will go to the high places of our nation to challenge the prophets of Baal — in the courts, in the university, in the shop, in the home, in the churches.

The southwest face of Mount Carmel, taken from the entrance of Kibbutz Ma'agan Michael by Chadner 2008 (PD-US).

Elijah window, St. Matthew's German Evangelical Lutheran Church, Charleston, South Carolina (CC by SA3.0).

Elijahs brought Good News but not welcome news. Good News that we gave them in our modest homes. Year after year, one music lesson after another . . . we raised this generation. And today, they are on the threshold of changing their world. They are housewives; they have small businesses. They are writing scripts in Hollywood. Writing speeches for presidents. Lobbying for godly causes in Congress.

Do we have a vision of what lies ahead? Will we seek the Lord's face to cooperate in His equipping, enabling, and empowering process? Will we trust God? Elijahs are wild and crazy! They will move beyond our traditions and our comfort zones. Elijahs always do.

Challenge the gods of this age![7]

After coming so far, after working so hard, have we forgotten why we came? Are we at the place where we can get the solution to our problems, but we have forgotten why we came? The challenge for us in the future is to sit down together and talk, to look around at all that God has done and give thanks. And then go forth, Elijahs, and challenge the gods of this age — at Harvard, at the Supreme Court, in Hollywood. Give no quarter and ask for none. We must give God everything we are and will ever be. The God we serve deserves nothing less, accepts nothing less!

Discussion Question

How can Christians prosper in this post-Christian era?

---

7 Ibid., p. 48–49.

Chapter 16

African Kingdoms: Benign Neglect

First Thoughts

While European knights were defending castles and maidens in distress from blood-thirsty Vikings, central Africa was enjoying unprecedented prosperity and peace. While the Mongols conquered most of Asia, Africa was quietly being ruled by an ingenious group of people who used entrepreneurship to conquer a whole continent. In particular, Ghana and Mali were fabulously wealthy and enlightened. How did this happen? Why is it that we know so little about this exotic part of the world?

Chapter Learning Objectives

Chapter 16 first explores the emergence of the kingdoms of Ghana and Mali in the African Sub-Sahara. We will observe how a small but ingenious people can conquer and then maintain a vast empire without a huge army. These kingdoms were created by economic élan, not military might. Finally, we will visit the exotic, romantic Timbuktu and will be inspired by a gentle, thriving people who changed the course of history along the Niger River.

As a result of this chapter you should be able to:

1. Discuss how African kingdoms were different from other ancient civilizations.

2. Delineate some unique features of the Ghanaian kingdom.

3. Summarize the Ghanaian economy and why it had such a profound impact on African history.

4. Analyze how Mali was able to conquer Ghana without a military conquest.

5. Evaluate what lessons Americans can learn from African kingdoms.

6. Analyze why most Western history books hardly mention Timbuktu.

Concepts

Ghana

Mali

Sahel

Sahara Desert

Commodities

Mauritania

Industrial State

The Gold Coast

Enculturation Agent

Benevolent Autocracy

Senegal River

Zaghawa

Niger

Sundjata

Timbuktu

Songhay

Overview

In many ways, the African kingdom, isolated on a continent, developed in unique and significant ways. Besides Egypt, there were two distinct kingdoms: **Ghana** and **Mali**. The **Sahel**, which is the region of West Africa just south of the **Sahara Desert**, a vast and inhospitable place, became established as an important area of trade around A.D. 700. Advancements in transportation, such as camels instead of horses, allowed for long-distance travel across the Sahara. This one event, more than any other, had a profound impact on the economy of Sub-Saharan Africa. **Commodities** could be transported long distances across inhospitable areas with relative ease. These were mostly nomadic kingdoms with agricultural products imported from southern Africa. In fact, these were the most advanced and richest nomadic kingdoms in the entire ancient world.

Trade with various parts of Africa, Europe, and Asia connected this region and the kingdoms which arose in it. In the course of less than a millennium, it flourished at varying times as an economic, political, cultural, and religious center.

Ghana was the oldest kingdom in Africa. This kingdom lasted from A.D. 750 to 1200. The Mali kingdom emerged in A.D. 1200 and lasted until A.D. 1500. It encompassed most of West Africa.

It is extraordinary that such significant civilizations emerged in the most inhospitable land possible. These were not rich river civilizations. They emerged primarily because of their trading savvy. Unlike the Mongols, who conquered through military hegemony, these African kingdoms emerged through commercial hegemony. These kingdoms became vulnerable when Islamic and Western invasions occurred in the early 17th century.

Discussion Question

How were African kingdoms different from other ancient civilizations?

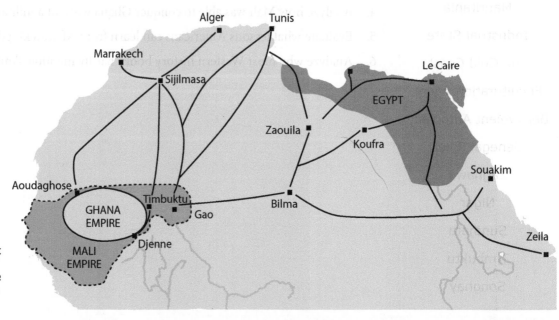

Map showing the extent of Egypt, the Ghana Empire, the Mali Empire and desert trade routes around 1400.

Ghana

Ghana was once the largest empire in West Africa. Long after Egypt had disappeared from the world stage, Ghana was a thriving power in west central Africa.

Geographically, the country included what is today referred to as western Mali and southeastern **Mauritania**. During the fifth century A.D., Ghana began to emerge as a thriving nation, becoming an established center of the iron industry. Skilled ironworkers produced weapons which made Ghana the leading military **industrial state** of the continent. No other nation or people group could produce the quality weapons that Ghana did. Thus, with its technological weapons, Ghana maintained a mobile, aggressive and highly effective military force that ruled one-half of the African continent.

Metalwork was not limited to iron, for the country was rich in gold, found along mountain ranges in its coastal region, called the Gold Coast by the Portuguese. In fact, Ghana cornered the gold market on the African continent and experienced obscene prosperity. The riches of Ghana would have rivaled the most extravagant Chinese emperor or Egyptian pharaoh. From approximately A.D. 300 through the mid-1000s, Ghana rivaled Rome as the most thriving trading center in the world. Arab caravans traveled on camels from North Africa across the Sahara to exchange salt, dried fruits, and copper for Ghanaian gold, ivory, leather goods, and jewelry. Artisans crafted gold and exotic wooden products. At the same time, Ghana developed a vital agrarian industry. Much like the present American economy, Ghanaian agriculture was a minor part of the larger economy. But its farmers harvested cocoa, plantains, yams, corn, and peanuts in abundant levels. Ghana, then, while remaining primarily a nomadic nation, was able to maintain a flourishing agrarian economy that fed the entire empire and even provided products as far away as Egypt. Fishing and forestry were also thriving industries.

Desert scene characteristic of the Mauritanian landscape (CCA-SA2.5).

While Ghanaian marriages were polygamous, the Ghanaian family was strong and sustaining. The family was the key **enculturation agent**: cultural values, religious structure, and pride that were all maintained by the family. While the Ghanaian government was an autocracy, it was a **benevolent autocracy**, and the family remained the strongest component of Ghanaian society.

During this period, most Ghanaians embraced traditional animism religions. Animism argues that there is no separation between the spiritual and physical (or material) worlds, and souls exist in humans and all other animals, plants, rocks, natural phenomena such as thunder, geographic features such as mountains or rivers, or other entities of the natural environment. Islam had begun to emerge as a result of interaction with Arab traders and indigenous inhabitants from the North African region.

Discussion Question

What are some unique features of the Ghanaian kingdom?

African Camel.

Economics: Controlling the Gold Trade

Slavery was once the second most profitable business in Africa. This would have a tragic impact in the years ahead.

Ghana, and subsequent African kingdoms, prospered because of their economic success, not because of military victories. Admittedly, much warfare goes on among nations, enabling the ruler of the most powerful state to demand the submission of the others. But this is only the background to the main business of controlling the caravans of merchants and camels.

These routes run north and south through the Sahara, specifically through Ghana. And the most precious of the commodities moving north is African gold.

Ghana was well placed to control the traffic in gold from the valley of the **Senegal River**. This is the first of the great fields from which the Africans derived their alluvial gold (meaning gold carried downstream in a river and deposited in silt, from which grains and nuggets can be extracted). This was not gold that had to be mined from hillsides or caves. It could easily be extracted from rivers and creeks.

While gold was the most valuable African commodity, slavery was unfortunately a close second. Slaves came mainly from the region around Lake Chad, where the Zaghawa tribes made a habit of raiding their neighbors and sending them up the caravan routes to Arab customers in the north.

Ghana also exported other exotic and very valuable products. These included elephant tusks, ostrich feathers, and the cola nut popular in precursors of the carbonated soft drink.

Natives with ivory tusks in Dar Es Salaam, Tanganyika between 1880 and 1923 (LOC).

After the gold and slavery trade, the most important commodity coming south with the caravans was salt, essential in the diet of African agricultural communities. The salt mines of the Sahara were extremely valuable. Salt was a valuable seasoning and preserving agent, and there was great demand for it. There is evidence that even European and Asian traders bought Ghanaian salt.

In summary, the fact that Ghana was able to sustain a successful and highly profitable culture in the midst of such an inhospitable environment is a remarkable testimony to this ingenious people group who, in their time, was one of the most advanced, civilized people groups in the world.

Discussion Question

Summarize the Ghanaian economy and why it had such a profound impact on African history.

Mali

Around A.D. 1200, for reasons unknown, the Mali people from the south conquered Ghana. Mali developed around the upper Niger valley near the Gold Coast. Unlike the people of the older kingdom of Ghana, who had only camels, horses, and donkeys for transport, the people of Mali also used the Niger River. By river, they could transport bulk goods and larger loads much more easily than by land. In a sense, then, Ghana was conquered by an even more skillful commercial nation! Mali did not defeat Ghana on a military battlefield; it put Ghana out of business!

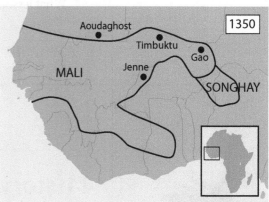

Map of the Mali Empire.

For one thing, living on the fertile lands near the **Niger**, people suffered less from severe droughts that occurred in the 12th century than those living in the drier regions farther north in Ghana. Food crops were grown on the level areas by the river, not only for local people but also for those living in cities farther north on the Niger River and in oasis towns along the trade routes across the desert. The Mali farmers put the Ghanaian farmers out of business. Thus, the Niger River enabled the kingdom of Mali to develop a far more stable economy than Ghana had enjoyed and contributed to the rise of the Mali Empire.

The Mali King **Sundjata** built up a vast empire that stretched eventually from the Atlantic coast south of the Senegal River to Gao on the east of the middle Niger bend. It extended from the forest in the southwest through the savannah (grassland) country of the Malinke to the Sahel and southern Saharan "ports" of Walata and Tadmekka. It included the gold fields of Bumbuk and Bure and the great cities of Timbuktu, Djenne, and Gao on the Niger River, and extended to the salt mines of Taghaza. Many different peoples were thus brought in to what became a federation of states, dominated by Sundjata and the Malinke people.

In its day, the Mali Empire was huge. Its mercantile approach was not unlike the earlier Athenian Empire and colonials. The Mali Empire was based on outlying areas — even small kingdoms — pledging allegiance to Mali and giving annual tribute in the form of rice, millet, lances, and arrows. Slaves were used to clear new farmlands where beans, rice, sorghum, millet, papaya, gourds, cotton, and peanuts were planted. Cattle, sheep, goats, and poultry were also bred. Agriculture, quite literarily, became "gold" to Mali. As the population in Africa increased astronomically, the Mali officials were ready to provide food and sustenance, and they had a trading industry to make it possible.

Like Ghana, Mali prospered from the taxes it collected on trade in the empire. All goods passing in, out of, and through the empire were heavily taxed. Mali was so rich that it did not barter a great deal. Gold was used as currency.

The empire of Mali reached in zenith in the 14th century, but its power and fame depended greatly on the personal power of the ruler. The capital Timbuktu was eventually raided and burned, several states revolted and seized their independence, and eventually Mali rule ended.[1]

Image of a Saracen king of West Africa, believed to be Mansa Musa, Emperor of Mali 1375 (PD).

---

1 http://mali.pwnet.org/history/history_mali_empire.htm.

Discussion Questions

A. Some historians argue that Mali conquered Ghana by doing what Ghana did "better." Explain.

B. America relies on its juggernaut economy and its small but effective military. What lessons can we learn from Mali and Ghana?

Lesson 5

Like this father and son, who haunt the area of Timbuktu, most of the nomads of the Sudan are relatively light-skinned and descendents of ancient Arabs. ca. 1948 – ca. 1955 (National Archives and Records Adminstration).

History of Timbuktu

The popular statement, "From here to **Timbuktu**," conjures up images of remote, isolated, and exotic parts of this earth. Timbuktu was located in the western African nation at the edge of the Sahara and was a major commercial center in the Mali Empire. Originally, it was part of a minor ancillary civilization called **Songhay** but was conquered by Mali early in the 13th century.

The historic town of Timbuktu is located at the precise point where the Niger flows northward into the southern edge of the desert. It was a natural starting and ending point of the profitable trading routes. Thus, Timbuktu became the New York City — the financial capital — of Africa, and, some historians claim, the world. In its time, Timbuktu was a very wealthy and powerful city indeed.

Gold came from the south and salt from the north. Financial centers and banks prospered in Timbuktu. Merchants had goods to buy and to sell, and bankers financed both.

Discussion Question

While Rome, London, and Paris, were insignificant, inhospitable cities in the 12th century, Timbuktu was a thriving, modern, wealthy city full of gold, libraries, and opportunities. However, most Western history books hardly mention it. Why?

When Christopher Columbus sailed in 1492, Timbuktu was one of the richest cities in the world.

Timbuktu seen from a distance by Heinrich Barth's party, September 7, 1853 (PD).

132

Chapter 17

Ancient North America: Hunter-Gatherers

First Thoughts

Throughout their history, Native Americans have been dynamic agents of change. Food discovered by Native Americans would transform the diet of Europe and Asia. In fact, maize, in particular, would save thousands of lives. Native Americans also made many crucial contributions to modern medicine, art, and architecture. They cultivated new plants for dyes, medicines, and textiles; domesticated animals; built cities; produced monumental architecture; and constructed a wide variety of systems of social and political organization ranging from kin-based bands and tribes to city-states. Native Americans not only adapted to diverse and demanding environments, they also reshaped the natural environments to meet their needs.[1]

Chapter Learning Objectives

Chapter 17 analyzes North American Native Americans. Arriving from Asia after the Great Flood, Native Americans built cities, domesticated the horse, and transformed North America. Indigenous to Native Americans were vigorous, critical kinship ties. Finally, the Native American culture was robust, sustaining, and laudable in scope and style.

As a result of this chapter you should be able to:

1. Explain why early North American natives were "semi-nomads."
2. Analyze why Native American villages were created and why they disappeared.
3. Speculate if you were a Native American, which native group would you prefer.
4. Describe what effect kinship had on Native American societies.
5. Evaluate how the horse transformed Native American culture.

CONCEPTS

Native Americans

Maize

Mound Building

Cahokia Mounds

Monk's Mound

Deforestation

Shamans

Matrilineal

Sedentary Hunter-Gatherers

Kinship

Domicile

Patrilineal

---

1 http://www.digitalhistory.uh.edu/era.cfm?eraid=1&smtid=1.

The First Americans

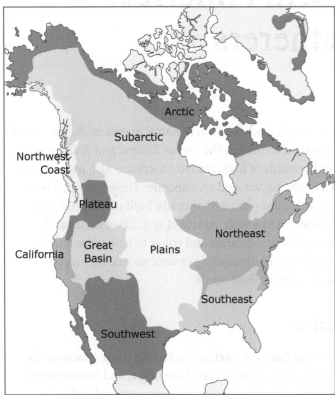

Map showing general locations of Native American groups in North America.

After the Great Flood and the subsequent Ice Age, native peoples from Siberia walked across a land bridge between Asia and North America and began the inexorable movement down the continent to the tip of present-day Argentina. No one knows how long this took, but undoubtedly it took many hundreds of years.

This first people group was called **Native Americans**.

How did these people manage to move so quickly down the coast to the end of South America? Most historians agree that Native Americans moved in roving bands down and through North America, but they also argue that some Natives, now called Native Americans (the Clovis culture) moved in boats, hop-scotching down the Pacific Ocean coast.

Ancient North Americans lived in a wide range of environments. On the east side of the continent there were vast dense woodlands, where Native Americans killed elk and deer. On the grass plains of the Midwest they hunted to extinction several American species, including the camel, mammoth, and horse. In the desert regions of the southwest, human subsistence depended on smaller animals such as rabbits. In the Arctic north, where there is much more hunting than gathering, fish and seals were plentiful.

Whatever they ate, wherever they lived, Native Americans were mostly nomads. They would build cities — large cities — but these cities were abandoned as the seasons of the year changed. During and after this period, two regions of North America developed quite advanced agrarian societies — the Mississippi Valley and the southwest pueblo villages. Farming, accompanied by village life, spread up the east coast, where fields were cleared from the woodlands for the planting of **maize**. But in most parts of the continent the tribes continued to live a semi-nomadic existence in the traditional manner of hunter-gatherers, although they lacked the one animal that makes movement on the plains easy. That animal would return (for it once was in North American) with Spanish conquistadors: the horse.

A peculiar Native American habit was **mound building**. Great burial mounds were constructed around tomb chambers of log or wood. The earliest burial mounds in North America were those of the Adena culture of the Ohio valley, closely followed by nearby Hopewell tribes. The period of greatest activity is from the first century B.C. to the fifth century A.D., by which time a vast number of mounds were built throughout North America.

Discussion Question

Explain why early North American natives were "semi-nomads."

Ancient Burial Mounds

Burial mounds can be found in many countries around the world. One of the best examples of a burial mound complex is found in the United States. Located near Collinsville, Illinois, the **Cahokia Mounds** archaeological site was the largest earthen construction in the Americas. We have no notion of when the Cahokia Mounds were built — Native Americans were prehistoric, in that they did not have a written language. The only examples of their writing consisted of symbols that were found on stone and pottery. Usually burial sites were separated from human habitation. However, in Cahokia, there is evidence Native Americans lived on or near burial mounds. Why? Some historians argue that Native Americans used these burial mounds as refuge from floodwaters that plagued the Mississippi valley.

In fact, the mounds were located in a city. The city of Cahokia was settled around A.D. 600 and evolved into a sophisticated city with plazas, stockades, and watchtowers. This was not surprising considering that the city was a center for trade and, at one time, was the largest urban center north of Mexico. There may have been as many as 40,000 people living at Cahokia at the city's peak. This is extraordinary.

The main feature that dominates the area is **Monk's Mound**. This mound is ten stories or 92 feet high. It is a massive 951 feet in length and 836 feet long. The mound took several centuries to complete.

One of the most interesting features is actually the Grand Plaza that stretches out from Monk's Mound. The Grand Plaza seems to be where ceremonies were held by the residents who were living at the mound. Studies have shown that while the landscape was originally undulating, the residents were able to level and fill it in order to make a flat area where they could worship.

Another example of the site's sophistication includes the Woodhenge. This was a circle of posts that was used in astronomy. It was made up of a series of posts that were placed so that they marked equinoxes and solstices. The wooden posts served much the same purpose as the stones that make up Stonehenge. Archaeologists were able to prove that not only was Woodhenge rebuilt several times during the past, remnants of another Woodhenge were also found near another of the area's burial mounds.

Cahokia mound in Illinois,
taken October 16, 1907 (LOC).

Grave Creek mound, Moundsville, West Virginia (CCA-SA2.5).

Although Cahokia was home to a sophisticated civilization, it eventually began to decline. This began in A.D. 1300, and the site was completely abandoned by the time Europeans arrived. There have been many theories as to why the site was abandoned, ranging from disease to over hunting, **deforestation,** and environmental issues that may have caused the area to become uninhabitable.[2]

Discussion Question

While Central and South American Native American cities prospered into the 16th century, North American Native American cities disappeared before the end of the 13th century. Why?

Monks mound, Cahokia, as seen from the site's central plaza (CCA-SA3.0).

2 http://ancientstandard.com/category/ancient-north-america/.

Native American Culture

There is little commonality among Native Americans. All Native Americans came from Asia and all Native Americans had a profound understanding and close relationship with nature.

However, beyond these few similarities, Native Americans varied from region to region. For instance, Native Americans in the Southeast were largely agrarian people groups that included the Cherokee, Choctaw, Chickasaw, and Muskhogee tribes. The members of the southeastern culture practiced many of the same ceremonies. They were a very warlike people. They all lived in close communities and practiced polygamy. All tended to live in cabin structures in villages of about 100 which included a chief, one or more **shamans** and a dozen or so extended families. Their ties to other villages within their nations were close, and ceremonies would often bring numerous villages together.

Southwest Pueblo culture also included agrarian people groups, but they lived in more secluded people groups. Each family occupied a single apartment style rock. The Pueblos included the Hopi, Zuni, and Pecos. The Pueblos were peaceful avoided war at all costs. They were advanced artisans, were **matrilineal**, and were monogamous. The Pueblos all descended from the Anasazi. This ancient Native American group disappeared before the first millennium, and no one knows why. The Pueblos farmed a greater number of crops than did any other culture in the present United States. Arid conditions forced them to diversify. They domesticated and raised animals for meat and feathers, a unique ancient practice.

Arapaho or Kiowa village, by William S. Soule, 1870s (PD).

Northwest culture was comprised of **sedentary hunter-gatherers** that relied heavily on fishing. Acorns were an important food source as well. They were active. Each nation was one or more villages which were totally capitalistic, had no government, and were usually monogamous.

The Plains culture was comprised of **nomadic hunter-gatherer** tribes. All were driven westward from the Northeastern woodlands by wars except for the Comanche and Kiowa, who were driven out onto the plains from the Rockies by other plains tribes. The other Plains tribes included the Sioux (Dakota and Lakota), Assiniboin, Crow, Blackfeet (Piegan, Blood, Siksika), Arapaho, and Cheyenne. The Plains culture was dependent upon the buffalo. The Plains culture did not exist until about 1650 when the Blackfeet and Arapaho were forced onto the plains. Once horses proliferated onto the plains, more eastern woodland tribes joined the culture. As they did when they were eastern woodlands tribes, all of the tribes were communal, practiced polygamy, and were matrilineal.[3]

Discussion Question

If you were a Native American, which native group would you prefer?

---

3 http://www.fourdir.com.

Sociology: Kinship

Many Native American societies were organized around principles of **kinship**. Kinship ties — based on bloodlines and marriage — were very important to Native Americans. Kinship formed the basis of the political, economic, and religious system. In other words, in Native American culture, kinship was the primary sociological function. Native American kinship systems were pervasive and intricate. They included regulations governing marriages, relations with in-laws, and even **domicile** after marriage. In **patrilineal** societies, like the Cheyenne and Lakota Sioux, kinship lineage, through the father, was seminal. Native American land ownership and participation in the political process were related to family ties.

Most Native American groups placed less emphasis on the nuclear family and more upon the extended family or the tribe. One sign of the relative unimportance of the nuclear family as opposed to larger kinship ties is that many Native American societies provided for relatively easy access to divorce.

Apart from a common emphasis on kinship, Native American societies also practiced certain religious beliefs and practices. Native Americans were animistic, but included a rich ceremonial life and an elaborate creation.

The horse created a cultural revolution. It radically reshaped the lives of the Plains Native Americans, transforming hunting, transportation, and warfare. The introduction of the horse encouraged groups like the Cheyenne, who had been farmers, to become

Photo of Apaches at home by Gentry, c.1909 (LOC).

hunters. This is one of the few examples in world history where farmers abandoned their agrarian practices to become nomadic food gatherers. The horse and the abundant buffalo herds made nomadic life quite appealing.

Discussion Question

What effect did kinship have on Native American societies?

Arapaho camp with buffalo meat drying near Fort Dodge, Kansas, 1870 (National Archives and Records Administration).

Anthropology: The Impact of the Horse

The Plains Native Americans lived on the plains and rolling hills of the Great Plains of North America. They were fierce warriors and, by the 16th century, totally dependent upon the horse.

Plains Native Americans were usually divided into two broad groups. The first group was completely nomadic, following the vast herds of buffalo. This group included the Blackfoot, Arapaho, Cheyenne, Crow, Kiowa, and Lakota Sioux.

The second group of Plains Native Americans consisted of the semi-sedentary tribes who, in addition to hunting buffalo, lived in villages and raised crops. These tribes included the Iowa, Mandan, Missouria, Omaha, Osage, Otoe, Pawnee, and Quapaw, Santee, and Wichita.

> The **horse** created a cultural revolution among Native Americans. The only comparable event in world history was the introduction of the railroad in the early 19th century.

The nomadic tribes followed the seasonal grazing and migration of bison. The Plains Native Americans lived in tepees because they were easily disassembled and assembled. Plains Native Americans were the first people group to be impacted by Europeans. Once they could obtain Spanish horses, the Plains tribes rapidly integrated them into their daily lives.

The horse enabled the Plains Native Americans to gain their subsistence with relative ease from the seemingly limitless buffalo herds. The horse enabled villages to spend more time in culture-building activities like artisan crafts and religious rituals. The horse enabled the Plains Native Americans to travel faster and farther in search of bison herds and to transport more goods, thus enjoying a richer material environment than their pedestrian ancestors. The horse impacted Native American culture more than the railroad changed early western culture.

Painting entitled Doomed by Charles Schreyvogel c 1901 (LOC).

It was the Comanche, coming to the attention of the Spanish in New Mexico in 1706, who first realized the potential of the horse. As pure nomads, hunters, and pastoralists, well supplied with horses, they swept the mixed-economy Apaches from the plains and by the 1730s were dominant in the Great Plains south of the Arkansas River. The success of the Comanche encouraged other Native American tribes to adopt a similar lifestyle. The southern Plains Native Americans acquired vast numbers of horses. By the 19th century, Comanche and Kiowa men owned an average of 35 horses and mules each — and only six or seven were necessary.

Before horses were introduced, hunting was a more complicated process. The Native Americans would surround the bison, and then try to herd them off cliffs or into places where they could be more easily killed. Native Americans would build a corral and have people herd the bison into it to confine them in a space where they could be killed.

Discussion Question

In what ways did the horse transform Native American culture?

Chapter 18

Ancient South and Central America: The End of All Things

First Thoughts

The early people of the Americas traveled from Asia across the Bering Straight and eventually populated North and South America. The South American Natives adapted to radically different topography: the Amazon rainforests and the Andes desert plateaus. The two most notable South American Native groups were the Mayans and the Incans. These people groups developed and administered complex societies and large urban centers that would rival the cities of Europe, Asia, and Africa.

Chapter Learning Objectives

Chapter 18 explores the emergence of human communities in the South American continent. First, we examine the impact of geography and typography on these people groups. Next, we observe that these groups emerged in isolation and we evaluate what impact isolation had on these cultures. We explore why the Mayans disappeared and finally we examine a mountain people, the Incas.

As a result of this chapter you should be able to:

1. Describe the typography of South America.

2. Discuss the effect of isolationism on South American culture.

3. Analyze animism and discuss how it conflicted with Western Christianity.

4. Speculate upon what happened to the Mayas.

5. Evaluate in what ways the mountainous topography of the Andes affected the Incan civilization.

CONCEPTS

Andes Mountains

Glaciers

Talismans

Cosmology

Gypsum

Functionality

Aesthetics

Machu Pachacutec

Conquistadors

Bureaucracy

Geography of South America

The geography of South America manifests many different regions and diverse climates. Geographically, South America is a continent forming the southern portion of the American landmass.

South America became attached to North America only after the Great Flood. The **Andes Mountains** run down the western edge of the continent; the land to the east of the Andes is largely tropical rainforest, the vast Amazon River basin. The continent also contains drier regions such as eastern Patagonia.

The South American continent also includes islands. However, the Caribbean islands are grouped with North America.

The continent's topography is often likened to a huge football stadium, owing to its flat interior almost ringed by high mountains. There are three main topographic features: the Andes, central rainforests, and the extensive Brazilian high country.

In their northern parts, the Andes exhibit expansive plateaus and valleys. These contain three of the world's highest capitals: Bogotá, Quito, and highest of all, La Paz, Bolivia. The Andes also exhibit several **glaciers**.

The climate of South America is a study of extremes. The arid Andes meet the torrid, humid Amazon jungles in east Peru.

The very fertile soils from the erosion of the Andes attracted the early Native American people groups. Nearly all settled and expanded from these areas. Only in Greece did geography have as profound an impact on people groups as did the geography of South America.

Discussion Question

Describe the topography of South America.

Centers of Civilization in the Americas: Isolationism

Far from the rest of the world, far from Western culture, religion, and commercial practices, Central and South American, and for that matter, North American people groups experienced relatively uninterrupted prosperity for more than one thousand years.

For example, the earliest people groups were the Olmecs, who, in relative isolation developed an elaborate autocratic government and rich religion. They built huge monuments that would rival the Egyptian pyramids. They practiced advanced agricultural techniques, including fertilization and irrigation.

The centers of civilization of the Americas had no contact with the international network forming in Europe, Asia, and Africa. Within America itself, though, there was much contact.

Native Americans traveled widely, embarked on far-flung commercial ventures, and engaged in extensive cross-cultural exchange. Through well-established trading networks, the civilizations of ancient Mexico came to share basic customs and beliefs. In time, products and ideas spread to the cultures of North America.

Merchants traded ritual objects like macaw feathers and copper bells for precious turquoise mined by the Anasazi of the American Southwest. Turquoise mosaic mirrors adorned with the Feathered Serpent served as a royal emblem for the Mayan kings of Chichen Itza, in the Yucatan Peninsula.

Along with commerce, the Native Americans enjoyed a game that was like soccer. Ancient soccer fields can still be found all over North and South America!

By A.D. 900, South American culture had spread to the woodland tribes of North America. North American tribes adopted corn agriculture that made agricultural life far more successful.

Nonetheless, no contact occurred with other people groups any-where else in the world until Europeans arrived in the 15th century. For this reason, as well as the paucity of domesticated animals, American Natives were far behind contemporaries in other parts of the world technologically. For instance, Native Americans did not use plows and they did not use a wheel. This is interesting, since children's toys with wheels have been found in archeological digs. Why wouldn't farmers build carts and wagons? None did. There is not a single instance of a cart or wagon being built by Native Americans, either in North or South America. Native American culture remained, essentially, in the Stone Age until European encroachment.

Nevertheless, without the wheel, without iron implements and without the plow, the capital of the Aztec Kingdom was significantly larger than any European, Asian, or

> **Isolationism** had a profound impact on the western hemisphere. Far from the rest of the world, far from western culture, religion, and commercial practices, North and South American people groups experienced relatively uninterrupted prosperity for more than a thousand years.

San Lorenzo Monument 3 in the Museo de Antropología de Xalapa, Veracruz, Mexico (CCA-SA2.0).

143

African ancient city. Furthermore, the farmers surrounding these cities were able to sustain huge populations without any trouble whatsoever.

These anachronisms created problems when later European, more technologically advanced, civilizations came. The American civilizations were unable to adjust to new technology, to a new religion and to a new work ethic that would ultimately doom these amazing civilizations.[1]

Discussion Question

What effect did isolationism have on South American Native American culture?

Cliff Palace of the Anasazi, Mesa Verde National Park.

1   Peter N. Stearns, *World History in Brief* (New York: Longman, 2010), p. 246–248.

Overview of People Groups

South American Native Americans appeared in the Argentina area, in southern South America, thousands of years ago. Fifty-one tribes and more than 30 different languages emerged.

South American Native Americans were, in their own way, very pious people with a good knowledge of astrology, mathematics, and other sciences. Yet they were a prehistoric people with no written language.

The animistic religious views of these people included a world of spirits, ghosts, and witches. Thus omens, dreams, and **talismans** were important to them. They performed several rituals, each carrying their own significance. Most also practiced human sacrifices. These sacrifices were presented to the polytheistic gods of the sun, moon, serpent, and jaguar.

Mayan plate of Mythological Bird, A.D. 550–700 Northern Campeche, Mexico (PD).

Native American tribes in South America included the Mayas who lived in Guatemala and Mexico, the Aztecs who lived in Mexico, and the Incas who lived in Peru. All practiced some form of human sacrifices.

The animist **concept** of "Mother Land" was widespread in the Americas. The **cosmology** of many Native American people started with the concept that they were children of the land. They believed they could sustain the lands with rituals, and sometimes the offering of human sacrifices. The rationale behind that was to preserve the cosmic balance.

In the West, the idea was the opposite. Human beings were the most important creatures on the planet, and all the animals and plants were created to serve mankind. Nature, to South American Native Americans, existed to be preserved and nurtured. Nature, to Christian Europeans, was primarily an obstacle to overcome, something to be conquered. It was only after man started to consider the possibility of becoming extinct in the 20th century because of ecological problems that the paradigm shifted.

Discussion Questions

How did animism conflict with western Christianity?

Aztec Teotihuacan Pyramid of the Moon.

Lesson 4

What Happened to the Maya?

The Maya were perhaps the most famous classical civilization of the Americas. They are thought to have first originated around in the Yucatan and their society flourished from A.D. 300 to 900. They inhabited the land presently known as Southern Mexico, Guatemala, Northern Belize, and Honduras. The Maya were adept in architecture, as is seen by their numerous pyramids. They were also skilled farmers that managed to clear dense tropical forest in order to build underground reservations for water. They did this with Stone Age technology!

The ancient Maya created the most advanced civilization in the New World. The Maya forged strong political and commercial alliances with the civilizations of central Mexico. Through long-distance trade, luxury goods as well as religious beliefs eventually reached the Anasazi people of the American Southwest, and Native American tribes living east of the Mississippi River.

Around A.D. 900, for unknown reasons, the Maya suddenly declined. The most popular theory for the decline of the Maya was climate change. There was precedence. For example, a drought in the northern area of the Mesopotamian Valley wiped out the Akkadian Empire, which stretched for almost 800 miles into the Persian Gulf. Between A.D. 800 and 900, when the Mayan Native Americans were reaching their apex period, they disappeared. Like the Akkadians, the decline was pronounced and precipitous.

Uxmal Maya ruins in Yucatan, Mexico.

Around the year 800, the Yucatan suffered a 200-year drought, and it left the region drier than it had ever been. Evidence taken from the Yucatan Lakes shows that the sediments were especially rich in **gypsum**. This mineral is present in many places and it dissolves in water; therefore, researchers gather that there must have been no water in the lakes to dissolve the sediments. The notion of such a large body of water going completely dry is hard to imagine, so there must have been an incredible drought as historians predicted.

This makes sense. The Maya's survival relied on the cultivation of their crops, such as maize, which requires rainfall. With this 200-year-long drought, the soil would have gone almost completely dry, and there would have been crop failure resulting in widespread famine and probably susceptibility to disease as well.

In any event, by A.D. 1200, the Mayan civilization had disappeared completely.

Discussion Question

What happened to the Maya?

Stucco head of K'inich Janaab Pakal I (603–683 AD), king of Palenque in the National Museum of Anthropology, Mexico City (CCA-SA2.0).

The Incas: A Mountain People

The Inca civilization lasted from the 13th to the 16th century and existed in Peru and Chile. The Incas had no written language and passed their history down orally from one generation to the next.

The Incas were a polytheistic people. Most of these gods were attached to natural objects such as the sun, the moon, and the earth. They believed that their emperors were descended from the sun god Inti. This gave Inca emperors the same kind of demigod status that oriental monarchs enjoyed.

Inca art was plain. They valued **functionality** over **aesthetics,** and most of their sculpture had ceremonial purposes. Their architecture was plain and utilitarian but magnificent! The artistic discipline so carefully maintained in pottery was abandoned in the exuberance of large public buildings. The Inca buildings rivaled anything the Greeks or Egyptians built.

Portrait of Pachacutec in the Beguine Convent of Our Lady of Copacabana, Lima, Peru from the 17th century (PD).

The greatest achievement of Inca civilization was the architecture. The Inca created their buildings by placing stones together in such a tight fashion that not even a thin knife blade could fit between them. This method of building required no mortar and was extremely resistant to seismic activity. As a result, sites like **Machu Picchu** remained largely intact.

For the first two hundred years, the Inca were a small group of people; however, around 1438 **Emperor Pachacutec** turned the Inca civilization into the most powerful nation in South America. After the death of Pachacutec, the Inca Empire was split into two factions, each led by one of the emperor's sons. The division eventually led to a civil war that wouldn't be resolved until 1532, the same year the Spanish conquistadors arrived.

In their quest for gold and silver, the **conquistadors** would melt down countless examples of Inca metalwork. While some aspects of Inca civilization would remain after the Spanish conquest, most of it would disappear.

The Inca Empire was governed perhaps better than any ancient civilization. It was divided into four provinces, each with its own governor. The Incas developed a fairly effective **bureaucracy** that provided civil stability for hundreds of years.[2]

Discussion Question

In what ways did the mountainous topography of the Andes affect the Inca Civilization?

Macchu Picchu near Cusco in Peru (CCA3.0).

---

2   http://www.about-peru-history.com/inca-civilization.html.

Chapter 19

Byzantium:
Saints Standing in God's Holy Light

First Thoughts

English poet William Butler Yeats wrote a poem about Byzantium:

> O sages standing in God's holy fire
> As in the gold mosaic of a wall,
> Come from the holy fire, perne in a gyre,
> And be the singing-masters of my soul."

Byzantium is full of contradictions, full of anachronisms.

By A.D. 364, the Roman Empire had been definitively split into two separate states: the Eastern Roman Empire and the Western Roman Empire. The Western Empire soon collapsed under the weight of attacks by barbarians, and Europe entered the so-called Dark Ages or Medieval era. While the Western Roman Empire collapsed, imperial rule in the east survived for almost one thousand years. The Byzantines were especially important to eastern Europe for its influences in art and religion. However, as western Europe grew more prominent, foreign pressure brought the Eastern Roman empire to a decline. The empire collapsed to the Ottoman Turks in 1453, one of the events that also precipitated the end of the Medieval period.

Chapter Learning Objectives

Chapter 19 explores the maintenance and eventual collapse of the Eastern Roman Empire called Byzantium. We will meet Justinian, a controversial but capable ruler who administered a vast empire at the end of the sixth century. Next, we will look at the Bosporus Strait and observe how important it has been in world history. We will see that the Eastern Orthodox Church — not conquering armies — left a lasting Byzantium legacy on eastern Europe. Finally, we will examine the Black Death which made its first appearance in Europe during the Byzantium period.

As a result of this chapter you should be able to:

1. Analyze historian Edward Gibbon's analysis of Byzantium.

2. Evaluate why Justinian was such an effective leader.

3. Discuss why the Bosporus Strait is so strategically important.

4. Describe eastern and western churches separation in A.D. 1054.

5. Assess the impact that the Black Death had on world history.

CONCEPTS

Ottomans

Holy Roman Empire

Constantinople

Balkan

Turkish

Justinian I

Legal Precedence

Civil Law

Excommunication

Pandemics

Anti-Semite

Bubonic Plague

Bosporus Strait

Sea of Marmara

Black Sea

Ionian Sea

Constantine the Great

Eastern Orthodox Church

Icons

Patriarchs of Constantinople

Byzantium

The Byzantine Empire preserved Christianity and blocked Islamic invasions for a century.

Byzantium is the name given to both the state and the culture of the Eastern Roman Empire in the middle ages. Both the state and the inhabitants always called themselves Roman, as did most of their neighbors, until the Empire succumbed to **Ottoman invaders** in the 15th century. Western Europeans, who had their own **Holy Roman Empire**, called them Orientals or Greeks, and later Byzantines after the former name of the empire's capital city, Constantinople. Again, however, if we stopped a resident of 12th-century Byzantium and asked him who he was, he would not know what Byzantium meant — he saw himself as a Roman citizen.

Such is the diverse history of Byzantium. Whatever it became, it was the continuation of the Roman state, and until the seventh century, preserved the basic structures of late Roman Empire culture — a large multi-ethnic urban Christian state defended by a mobile, highly specialized and effective army.

View of Constantinople (Istanbul) around 1490, from the Nuremberg Chronicle (PD).

After the Arab/Islamic conquest of Egypt and Syria, Byzantium became much more of a Hellenistic state, all the cities except **Constantinople** faded away to small fortified outposts. The Byzantines governed and administrated their declining empire the same way earlier Romans handled Roman Britain.

There is then a persistent contradiction about the beginning of Byzantine history, between the building of Constantinople by Constantine I and the mid-seventh-century collapse of late antique urban culture. And who were the Byzantiums? Greeks? Romans?

The seventh to ninth centuries were tough times in Byzantine history. This was a time when Roman Christian Byzantium changed to Eastern Orthodox Byzantium.

The main struggle in the Church, and in the Empire, was the struggle over icons. Until the Eastern Orthodox Church prevailed, there was some unease in the Byzantium Empire.

From A.D. 900 to 1100, Byzantium's political power reached its apogee as former colonies were annexed into the empire, and the military carved out a small but secure empire between emerging Russia and nascent medieval Europe.

This period is also significant as the time in which Byzantine culture was spread among the **Balkan** peoples. Following massive **Turkish** attacks in the late 11th century, the empire quickly declined until it was conquered by the Turkish Ottoman Empire in the 15th century.[1]

Discussion Question

The English historian Edward Gibbon stated that the Byzantium Empire experienced one thousand years of constant decline. Disagree with Gibbon and explain what really happened.

---

1 http://www.fordham.edu/halsall/byzantium/.

The Emperor Justinian (A.D. 527–565)

Justinian I, commonly known as Justinian the Great, was Byzantine emperor from 527 to 565. During his reign, Justinian sought to revive the Roman Empire and recover the lost western half of the Empire. Although his achievements were short term, he accomplished a lot. Justinian and his generals briefly succeeded in re-establishing Roman hegemony in western Europe and even in North Africa.

Justinian was more than a great general; he also established a law code that was based on **legal precedence** — a major breakthrough in the rule of law. In other words, legal arguments, in Justinian's Byzantium, had greater weight if they were based on legal precedence. This so-called "Corpus Juris Civilis" or **Civil Law**, is still the basis of law practices in many modern states. His reign also marked a revival of Byzantine culture, particularly in church buildings, which made Constantinople the center of Eastern Orthodox Christianity for many centuries. Justinian was able to weaken the power of the two most important institutions in Byzantium: the army and the Church.

A devastating outbreak of **bubonic plague** in the early 540s marked the end of an age of splendor. The Empire entered a period of territorial decline not to be reversed until the ninth century.

Mosaic image of Justinian in Ravenna before 547 (PD).

Discussion Question

Why was Justinian such an effective leader?

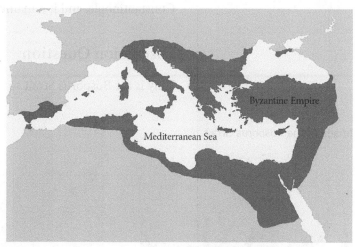

The Byzantine Empire at its greatest extent in 555 AD under Justinian the Great.

Geography: Bosporus Strait

Antique map of Turkey and the Black Sea with the Bosporus Strait circled.

The **Bosporus Strait** is the most salient geographical feature of the Byzantium Empire. It is a natural strait (as opposed to a built waterway) connecting the **Black Sea** to the **Sea of Marmara**, thus being a very strategic waterway. It is, in effect, the only warm water route for Russia to reach the Mediterranean Sea.

It is a treacherous waterway. The surface current flows always from north to south; however, a strong countercurrent under the surface creates swirls and eddies.

Bosporus comes from a Greek word which means "passage of the cow," deriving from the name of Lo, one of the many consorts of Zeus. When Hera, Zeus' wife, suspected her husband of being involved with Lo, Zeus transformed Lo into a small cow and tried to send her away from Hera's rage. Lo (the cow) swam across the strait but Hera discovered her and sent big flies after the cow to bite and disturb her all the time there in the Aegean Sea (in ancient times called the **Lonian sea**).

The Bosporus Strait is approximately 19 miles (30 km) long, with a maximum width of 2.3 miles (3,700 m) at the northern entrance, and a minimum width of .43 miles (700 m). The depth varies from 118 to 407 feet (36 to 124 m) in midstream.

The Bosporus Strait is considered the boundary between Europe and Asia. It has always been strategically important, and control over it has been an objective of a number of hostilities in modern history. Certainly this was the case during the Byzantium period.

Its shores are heavily populated by the large city of Constantinople, now called Istanbul. Constantinople, at first called Byzantium, was the only city in the world to bridge two continents. Byzantium had first been reconstructed in the fourth century as a model of Rome itself. Later, **Constantine the Great** chose it as his new capital, renaming it Constantinople, and it remained the capital of the eastern part of the Roman Empire.

Discussion Question

Why is the Bosporus Strait so strategically important?

Image of the Bosporus Strait.

The Hagia Sophia in Contantinople which was begun 325 and rebuilt under Justinian I after a devastating fire.

Eastern Orthodox Church

More important than the Byzantine expansion into the Balkans was the influence of the **Eastern Orthodox Church**. A major missionary effort was mounted for several centuries in eastern Europe and, while the political entity called Byzantium disappeared in the 1500s, the Eastern Orthodox Church remains today.

Until A.D. 1054, Eastern Orthodoxy and Roman Catholicism were branches of the same body — the Roman Catholic Church. This date designates the very first major division in Christianity and the beginning of "denominations." Disagreement between these two branches of Christendom had already long existed, but the widening gap between the Roman and Eastern churches increased after A.D. 1000 until there were two different Christian churches.

On religious matters, the two branches disagreed over issues pertaining to the nature of the Holy Spirit, the use of **icons** in worship, and the correct date for celebrating Easter. Cultural differences played a major role, too, with the eastern mindset more inclined toward philosophy, mysticism, and ideology, and the western outlook guided more by a practical and legal mentality.

Profound separation was encouraged in A.D. 330 when Emperor Constantine decided to move the capital of the Roman Empire to the city of Byzantium (Byzantine Empire, modern-day Turkey) and called it Constantinople. When he died, his two sons divided their rule, one taking the eastern portion of the empire and ruling from Constantinople, and the other taking the western portion, ruling from Rome. The political separation of the Roman into a western and eastern branch put a great strain on the Church, especially when Rome fell and the ecclesiological authorities lost touch with the east.

In A.D. 1054 a formal split occurred when Pope Leo IX (leader of the Roman branch) excommunicated the **Patriarch of Constantinople**, Michael Cerularius (leader of the eastern branch), who in turn condemned the pope in mutual **excommunication**.

Michael Cerularius was the patriarch of Constantinople from A.D. 1043 to 1058, during Eastern Orthodoxy's formal separation from the Roman Catholic Church. He played a prominent role in the circumstances surrounding the great east-west schism.

During the time of the Crusades (1095), Rome joined with the east to defend the Holy Land against the Turks, providing a ray of hope for potential reconciliation between the two churches. But by the end of the Fourth Crusade (1204), and the sacking of Constantinople by the Romans, all hope ended as the degree of hostility between the two churches continued to worsen. To date, the eastern and western churches remain divided and separate.[2]

Discussion Question

Why did the eastern and western churches separate in A.D. 1054?

Lesson 5

The Black Death

A larger percentage of Europeans died in the Black Plague than any other catastrophic event in history.

The Black Death, or the Bubonic Plague, the most severe epidemic in human history, ravaged Europe in the sixth century. Twenty-five million people (one-third of Europe's population at the time) were killed during this short period. Thousands of people died each week. Perhaps no event in human history affected the social life of the world as much as this single terrible disease.

This plague killed entire families at a time and destroyed whole villages. Families were wiped out. Parents abandoned their children, and parentless children roamed the streets in search of food. Life was in total chaos.

The plague was a disaster without parallel, causing dramatic changes in Europe and Asia. The Black Death (or Bubonic Plague) had many effects beyond its immediate symptoms. Not only did the Black Death take a devastating toll on human life, it also played a major role in shaping European life in the years that followed.

---

2 http://christianity.about.com/od/easternorthodoxy/a/orthodoxhistory.htm.

There is no modern facsimile of the Black Death. It is believed to consist mainly of bubonic plague, but pneumonic and septicaemic plagues were also thought to be present in the epidemic. The Bubonic Plague is caused by a bacterium transmitted primarily by fleas and rats.

The symptoms were described as convulsions; followed by a rise of temperature; with vomiting, headache, giddiness, and intolerance to light; pain in the lower abdomen, back, and limbs; sleeplessness; apathy; and delirium. The body temperature varied greatly from 101 to 107°F, but fell two or three degrees on the second or third day. Terrible headaches ensued. The eyes became red, the tongue swelled and became covered with a white fur everywhere except on the tip. Constipation was the rule but there might be diarrhea — an even worse sign. The patient might die within 24 hours, but more commonly death occurred on the second or third day. Recovery was very rare. Historically, 60 percent of all those infected died.

Historiated initial 'C' containing a scene showing monks, disfigured by the plague, being blessed by a priest. James le Palmer, 1360–1375 (PD-Art).

The disease probably came from China. In A.D. 46, an epidemic in Mongolia killed two-thirds of the population. In 312, northern and central China became a wasteland and in the province of Shensi. In 468, 140,000 people died in the Chinese cities. During the next 900 years this pestilence traveled slowly throughout China and the Middle East, though major outbreaks were not common. It was inevitable that it appeared in the crossroad between Asia and Europe: Byzantium.

Three **pandemics** (an epidemic that strikes literally everywhere within a short time) that spread across Europe have been recorded. The Bubonic Plague reached Byzantium in 540. This pandemic stuck Europe and was thought to have been brought to the West by Justinian's armies in 547.

The most common belief was that the plague had been sent by God, and that it was His punishment for the sins humankind had committed. Even innocent people, such as infants, had to suffer for the horrible crimes of others. Thus, the Bubonic Plague (Black Death) encouraged asceticism in the Church. Furthermore, the Church was quick to condemn gambling, excessive drinking, the immodesty of women, and the laziness of peasants. The first measures taken against the plague were not medicinal but spiritual. Patients were encouraged to confess all sins and to beg for forgiveness. The Black Death also encouraged **anti-Semitism**. Jewish people were accused of spreading the pestilence.

Miniature out of the Toggenburg Bible (Switzerland) of 1411. The disease is widely believed to be the plague (PD-Art).

The Black Death did not disappear from world history until the 20th century.

Discussion Question

What impact did the Black Death have on world history?

Mosaics from the Hagia Sophia

Southwestern entrance mosaic. The Virgin Mary is standing in the middle, holding the Child Christ on her lap. On her right side stands emperor Justinian I, offering a model of the Hagia Sophia. On her left, emperor Constantine I, presenting a model of the city.

Detail of Empress Zoe mosaic (11th-century).

The Virgin and Child (Theotokos) mosaic.

Imperial Gate mosaics. The emperor Leo VI the Wise is bowing down before Christ Pantocrator. In medallions: on the left of Christ, the Archangel Gabriel; on his right, Mary.

Sailing to Byzantium

By William Butler Yeats

I

That is no country for old men. The young
In one another's arms, birds in the trees
— Those dying generations — at their song,
The salmon-falls, the mackerel-crowded seas,
Fish, flesh, or fowl commend all summer long
Whatever is begotten, born, and dies.
Caught in that sensual music all neglect
Monuments of unaging intellect.

II

An aged man is but a paltry thing,
A tattered coat upon a stick, unless
Soul clap its hands and sing, and louder sing
For every tatter in its mortal dress,
Nor is there singing school but studying
Monuments of its own magnificence;
And therefore I have sailed the seas and come
To the holy city of Byzantium.

III

O sages standing in God's holy fire
As in the gold mosaic of a wall,
Come from the holy fire, perne in a gyre,
And be the singing-masters of my soul.
Consume my heart away; sick with desire
And fastened to a dying animal
It knows not what it is; and gather me
Into the artifice of eternity.

IV

Once out of nature I shall never take
My bodily form from any natural thing,
But such a form as Grecian goldsmiths make
Of hammered gold and gold enamelling
To keep a drowsy Emperor awake;
Or set upon a golden bough to sing
To lords and ladies of Byzantium
Of what is past, or passing, or to come.[3]

---

3 http://www.poemhunter.com/poem/sailing-to-byzantium/.

Chapter 20

Early Russia: A People Formed by Geography

First Thoughts

Russia was initially settled by Slavic people groups during the Roman Empire. Initially, the center of geo-political Russia was in the Ukraine, specifically Kiev. That was to change in the 12th century as Kiev fell to the Tatars and the capital was moved to Moscow. The Tatars, however, did the Russians a big favor: they unified a divergent people and Russia emerged as a nation. Several themes emerge in this early history: Is Russia part of Asia? Europe? How does Russia govern such a large, divergent area? How does Russia defend such a vast nation?

Chapter Learning Objectives

Chapter 20 examines Russian history from its genesis to the end of the Tatar era. We will examine the impact of the Tartars on Kievan Russia, which ultimately paved the way for the modern state that emerged in the Middle Ages. We will examine a fascinating primary source, and, finally, examine the emerging city of Moscow, that, as history moves forward, will be the pre eminent center of Russian society, government, and culture.

As a result of this chapter you should be able to:

1. Understand why the Kievan Russians prospered so quickly after A.D. 500.

2. Evaluate why the Tatar invasion was good for Russia.

3. Analyze what advantages and disadvantages the Russian vastness brought to its history.

4. Discuss why the author of the *Novgorod First Chronicle* explains events in the context of Christian theology.

5. Trace the history of Moscow's evolution as capital of Russia.

History: Kievan Russians

The Russians' ancestors were the **Slavic tribes**, whose original home is thought to have been the wooded areas along the Pripyat River. Relatively little is known about East Slavs prior to approximately A.D. 800. Moving into the lands populated by the migrating **Germanic tribes**, the Eastern Slavs — the ancestors of the Russians who occupied the lands between the Carpathians and the Don River — were subject to Eastern Orthodox Christian influences. The culture of the declining Byzantine Empire had a continuous influence upon the development of Russia in its formative centuries.

The **Khazars** were Turkish people who lived in the **Volga steppes** between the Caspian and Black Seas from the seventh to 13th centuries. The Khazars were the main commercial link between the Baltic and the Arabian Empire centered in Baghdad. In the eighth and ninth centuries, many East Slavic tribes paid tribute to the Khazars who became quite wealthy and powerful.

By the late ninth century, the city of **Kiev** supplanted the Khazars and established power over a large area that gradually came to be known as Russia. Kievan Russia, the first East Slavic state, emerged in the ninth century along the Dnieper River Valley. The Kievan Russians controlled the northern trade route for furs and slaves between Scandinavia and the Byzantine Empire along the Dnieper River.

Kievan Russians were very impressed with Byzantium, and ties were very strong. They introduced a Slavic variant of the Eastern Orthodox religion, making a synthesis of Byzantine and Slavic cultures that defined Russian culture for the next thousand years. Thus, the Church, more than any other institution, created the Russian character.

Principalities of Kievan Russia (1054–1132) (CCA-SA3.0).

By the 11th century, Kievan Russia, in sophistication and economics, could boast that it could match any European nation.

Kievan Russia ultimately disintegrated because of economic struggles and **Tatar** invasions.

Discussion Question

Why did the Kievan Russians prosper so quickly after A.D. 500?

Prypiać River, Belarus (CCA-SA3.0).

Tatars

The Tatars were a derivative tribe of the Mongols and dominated Asia and most of Russia beginning in the 12th century. The Russians coined the term for the Mongols. The term "Tatar" was derived from the place of punishment (i.e., Hades) in Greek mythology. Thus, to call someone a Tatar was to call him a person from hell!

The Tatars invaded Kievan Russia in 1236 and quickly conquered most of it — but not all of it.

The Russian leaders who survived learned from how to fight the Tatars. They created more centralized governments. They created cavalry regiments (e.g., the **Cossacks**) who could defeat the Tatars. Russian cities learned to defeat the Tatars at their own game. Russians also learned how to use the vastness of their land to defeat their enemies. Russian armies retreated and gave the Tatars vast stretches of Russian territory. Eventually, when the Tatars were spread out and disorganized, Russian Cossacks would attack and destroy their enemies. Besides, the same problems that occurred in Mongol China occurred in Tatar/Tatar Russia: the Mongols were better soldiers than administrators and eventually lost all that they won.

> The **Tartars** were a people group who dominated Russian history for a century. They preferred a nomadic life to a sedentary life.

Russian Cossacks fighting Tatars of Crimea (PD-Art).

But the Tatars were not finished. They turned to the Balkans. In initial military encounters with European forces in east Europe, the Tatars were successful. However, the Tatars eventually concluded that Balkan conquests were not worth the trouble and eventually retreated to their Asian base.

The truth is that Russia benefited from the Tatar invasions. Besides the revelation of having a strong central government, the Russians overcame significant ethnic differences to defeat the cruel, ruthless Tatars. After the Tatars departed, familial ties remained that ultimately led to the genesis of the Russian nation. At the same time, power shifted from the southern, more vulnerable capital of Kiev, to the more northern capital of **Moscow**. Founded in the 12th century, the Principality of Muscovy was able to emerge from more than two hundred years of Mongol domination (13th–15th centuries), and to gradually conquer and absorb surrounding principalities. In the early 17th century, a new **Romanov Dynasty** continued this policy of expansion across Siberia to the Pacific.

Discussion Question

Why was the Tatar invasion a good thing for Russia?

Cossacks of the Russian army during World War I, 1915 (PD).

159

Lesson 3

Geography: Vastness

Adjacent to the **North Pole**, in a huge arc, Russia spans almost half the globe from east to west and about 2,500 miles (4,000 km) from north to south. Divided into 11 time zones, Russia is by far the world's largest country. It occupies much of eastern Europe and northern Asia. The country's terrain is diverse, with extensive stands of forest, numerous mountain ranges, and vast plains. The land includes extensive reserves of natural resources that provide the nation with enormous potential wealth.

The **Ural Mountains**, which extend more than 1,300 miles (2,200 km) from north to south, form the boundary separating the unequal European and Asian sectors of Russia. The continental divide continues another 854 miles (1,375 km) from the southern end of the Ural Mountains through the **Caspian Sea** and along the **Caucasus Mountains**. Asian Russia is about as large as China and India combined, occupying roughly three-quarters of the nation's territory. But it is the European western quarter that is home to more than 75 percent of Russia's inhabitants. This acutely uneven distribution of human and natural resources is a striking feature of Russian geography and population.

Abundant natural resources, numerous rivers, and vast rich plains have deeply impacted Russian history. Russia's topography includes the world's deepest lake and Europe's highest mountain and longest river.

Discussion Question

What advantages and disadvantages did the Russian vastness bring to its history?

View of the North Ural Mountains.

The Caspian Sea.

The vast Siberian landscape.

Mount Elbrus, the highest point of the Caucasus Mountains.

Primary Source:
The Novgorod First Chronicle

The Republic of Novgorod was one of the earliest Russian states situated around the city of Novgorod and nearby territories. The main areas of the Republic were around Lake Ilmen. Later on, when the power of Novgorod grew, she joined areas that were far north, behind the lakes of Onega and Beloje. In the east, the power of Novgorod stretched to the northern Urals. The people in Novgorod dealt with agriculture, fishing, hunting, pottery, and salt production.

The city was situated on an important trade route from Russia to the Baltics and to western Europe. The *Novgorod First Chronicle* is the most ancient extant chronicle of the Novgorod Republic. It is a very reliable resource for a history of the Tatar invasion.

> In the same year (1224), for our sins, unknown tribes came. No one knows accurately who they are . . . what their language is, or race, or faith, but they called them Tatary (Tatars) . . . God alone knows . . . We know not whence they came, nor where they hid themselves again. God knows whence he fetched them against us, for our sins. But let us return to what lies before us . . . The godless Tatars entered the Church of the Holy Mother of God . . . people were already perishing, some by fire and others by the sword, took refuge in the Church of the Holy Mother of God and shut themselves in the Sacristy. The pagans breaking down the doors, piled up wood and set fire to the sacred church; and slew all, thus they perished, giving up their souls to God.[1]

"Novgorod Marketplace," a painting by Appolinary Vasnetsov, 1909 (PD-Art).

Discussion Question

The author of the *Chronicle* discusses historical events in the context of Christian theology. What dangers result from such an interpretation?

1 https://archive.org/stream/chronicleofnovgo00michrich/chronicleofnovgo00michrich_djvu.txt.

Lesson 5

Demographics: Moscow

Moscow in the 12th century was nothing like Paris or London in the 12th century. It was more or less a large village. Whatever was there, however, was to be destroyed in less than 50 years.

The **Vikings** came to Russia in 862 B.C. and founded the first Russian dynasty in **Novgorod**. Viking tribes from Scandinavia moved southward into European Russia, tracing a path along the main waterway connecting the Baltic and Black Seas. The various tribes were united by the spread of Christianity from Byzantium in the 10th and 11th centuries.

In 1240, Kiev was destroyed by the Mongols, and the Russian territory was split into numerous smaller states. The next two centuries saw the rise of Moscow as a provincial capital and center of the Christian Orthodox Church.

The city of Moscow gradually grew around the Moscow Kremlin, beginning in the 14th century. The first reference to Moscow dates from 1147. In 1156, Moscow was fortified with a timber fence and a moat. This did not matter when the Tatars came. The Tatars burned the city to the ground and killed its inhabitants. In 1328, Moscow became the capital city of all Russian lands.

Discussion Question

Trace the history of Moscow's evolution as capital of Russia.

The Kremlin in Moscow.

Chapter 21

Eastern Europeans: A People Conflicted

First Thoughts

Eastern Europe has been, and remains, a volatile area. It is a region of barbarians, demagogues, and ethnic fighting. The great Attila the Hun heralded from this area. To western Europe, the Huns and east Europe failed to achieve any effect other than a rearrangement of barbarian power, the relocation of the Goths westward, and the founding of Venice by those who fled the Huns in northern Italy. Thus, in Western history, the Huns are one of the bloodthirsty barbarian groups that contributed to the collapse of civilization. In eastern Europe, however, in countries such as Hungary, Attila is regarded as a hero. Whether Attila was a ruthless barbarian or a man of bravery and courage, the Huns will always be remembered for the ferocity of their warriors and the thoroughness of their victories.

Chapter Learning Objectives

Chapter 21 begins by summarizing eastern European history. Next, we examine a primary source description of the Gauls (Germans). Then, we examine the Huns and their most famous leader Attila. We finish by looking at the Cossacks.

As a result of this chapter you should be able to:

1. Explain why the ethnic rich Balkans have always been an area of Europe full of turmoil.

2. Examine Roman Tacitus' observations of the Germans.

3. Discuss why the Huns were so feared in eastern Europe.

4. Analyze why Attila showed much discipline by refusing to completely destroy his Roman enemies.

5. Describe who the Cossacks were and why they had such an impact on world history.

Lesson 1

Overview

During the first one thousand years after Christ lived, the **Huns**, the **Visigoths**, and the **Ostrogoths** had all passed through southeastern Europe, driving out the Romans, who had occupied all the lands south of the Danube River just around the beginning of the era. However, these nomadic tribes passed through burning and pillaging, but not establishing permanent settlements. They were never able to establish an agrarian culture.

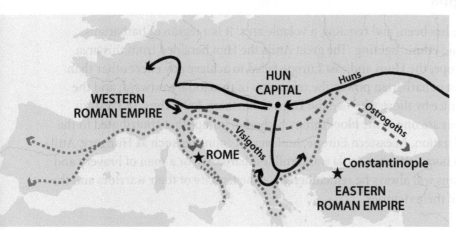

Map showing invasion of the Roman Empire by the Huns, Ostrogoths, and Viigoths, 100–500 A.D.

Then, some of the Slav tribes, who for at least a thousand years had lived in the plains between the Vistula and Dnieper Rivers, moved westward into areas vacated by the Visigoths, and southward into the abandoned areas as far as Greece, and settled in what today are the Czech and Slovak Republics and the Balkan states.

The original Illyrian peoples of the Danube Basin retreated into the mountains bordering the Adriatic Sea and became the modern-day Albanians. In the ninth century, a nomadic warrior people from east of the Ural mountains, the **Magyars**, moved across the Carpathian passes, and finally settled down in the rich plains of the Danube valley, displacing the Slavs who had arrived earlier, and founding the Hungarian nation.

In the area north of the Danube, in the Carpathian Mountains, lived the ancient **Dacians**. The Romans had previously invaded and colonized the area, but cut off from Rome by the advance of Slavs to the west, the remaining Romans departed or intermarried with the local population. As a result, modern Romania has a language strikingly similar to Italian. A Turkic tribe, the **Bulgars**, moved across the steppes north of the Black Sea into the mountainous region south of the Danube. There they settled down and became assimilated by the Slavic peoples.

At the end of the first millennium of the New Era, all of central and eastern Europe was beginning to stabilize. For the next thousand years, continued pressure existed. From the west, the Germans pushed relentlessly eastward. From the east, for several centuries, transient onslaughts of Mongols and Tatars caused devastation. Later, the growing Russian Empire pushed westward. From the south, the Turks pushed northward.

But the tribes that had settled the region coalesced first into principalities, then into kingdoms as they converted to Christianity.[1]

Discussion Question

The Balkans have always been a place of turmoil and warfare. From the above discussion, offer some explanations about why this is so.

---

1 http://biega.com/historylinks.html.

Primary Source:

Germania by Tacitus

The Germans, or Gauls, posed a constant threat to eastern Europeans, and for that matter, to all Europeans, and to the Romans. Tacitus (A.D. 56–117) was a senator and a historian of the Roman Empire. This essay, part of his *Histories*, offers great insights to these first cousins of the Huns and Visigoths.

Tacitus, from an antique bust (PD).

The Germans, I am apt to believe, derive their original from no other people, and are in nowise mixed with different nations arriving amongst them: since anciently those who went in search of new dwellngs, travelled not by land, but were carried in fleets, and into that mighty ocean so boundless, and, as I may call it, so repugnant and forbidding, ships from our world rarely enter. Moreover, besides the dangers from a sea tempestuous, horrid and unknown, who would relinquish Asia, or Africa, or Italy, to repair to Germany, a region hideous and rude, under a rigorous climate, dismal to behold . . . unless the same were his native country? . . .

They have a tradition that Hercules also had been in their country, and him above all other heroes they extol in their songs when they advance to battle. Amongst them too are found the kind of verses by the recital of which (by them called Barding) they inspire bravery; nay, by such chanting itself they divine the success of the approaching fight. For, according to the different din of the battle, they urge furiously, or shrink timorously. Nor does what they utter so much seem to be singing as the voice and exertion of valor. They chiefly study a tone fierce and harsh, with a broken and unequal murmur, and therefore apply their shields to their mouths, whence the voice may by rebounding swell with greater fullness and force. . . .

Their lands, however somewhat different in aspect, yet taken all together consist of gloomy forests or nasty marshes — lower and moister towards the confines of Gaul, more mountainous and windy towards Noricum and Pannonia, very apt to bear grain, but altogether unkindly to fruit trees; abounding in flocks and herds, but generally small of growth. Nor even in their oxen is found the usual stateliness, no more than the natural ornaments and grandeur of head. In the number of their herds they rejoice, and these are their only and their most desirable riches. Silver and gold the gods have denied them, whether in mercy or in wrath, I am unable to determine. Yet I would not venture to aver that in Germany no vein of gold or silver is produced; for who has ever searched? For the use

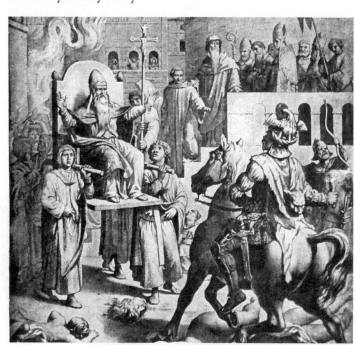

The Pope and Attila, the Hun, detail by Chenavard (PD).

and possession, it is certain they care not. Amongst them indeed are to be seen vessels of silver, such as have been presented to their Princes and Ambassadors, but holden in no other esteem than vessels made of earth. The Germans, however adjoining to our frontiers, value gold and silver for the purposes of commerce, and are wont to distinguish and prefer certain of our coins. They who live more remote are more primitive and simple in their dealings, and exchange one commodity for another. The money which they like is the old and long known, that indented, or that impressed with a chariot and two horses. Silver too is what they seek more than gold, from no fondness or preference, but because small pieces are more ready in purchasing things cheap and common.

Neither in truth do they abound in iron, as from the fashion of their weapons may be gathered. Swords they rarely use, or the larger spear. They carry javelins . . . pointed with a piece of iron short and narrow, but so sharp and manageable, that with the same weapon they can fight at a distance or hand to hand, just as need requires. Nay, the horsemen also are content with a shield and a javelin. . . .

Affairs of smaller moment the chiefs determine: about matters of higher consequence the whole nation deliberates; yet in such sort, that whatever depends upon the pleasure and decision of the people, is examined and discussed by the chiefs. Where no accident or emergency intervenes, they assemble upon stated days, either, when the moon changes, or is full: since they believe such seasons to be the most fortunate for beginning all transactions. Neither in reckoning of time do they count, like us, the number of days but that of nights. In this style their ordinances are framed, in this style their diets appointed; and with them the night seems to lead and govern the day. From their extensive liberty this evil and default flows, that they meet not at once, nor as men commanded and afraid to disobey; so that often the second day, nay often the third, is consumed through the slowness of the members in assembling. They sit down as they list,

A 19th century depiction of the Hun invasion (PD).

promiscuously, like a crowd, and all armed. It is by the Priests that silence is enjoined, and with the power of correction the Priests are then invested. Then the King or Chief is heard, as are others, each according to his precedence in age, or in nobility, or in warlike renown, or in eloquence; and the influence of every speaker proceeds rather from his ability to persuade than from any authority to command. If the proposition displease, they reject it by an inarticulate murmur: if it be pleasing, they brandish their javelins. The most honorable manner of signifying their assent, is to express their applause by the sound of their arms. . . .

Yet the laws of matrimony are severely observed there; nor in the whole of their manners is aught more praiseworthy than this: for they are almost the only Barbarians contented with one wife, excepting a very few amongst them; men of dignity who marry divers wives, from no wantonness or lubricity, but courted for the luster of their family into many alliances. . . .

In all their houses the children are all nourished with the milk of their own mothers, and never surrendered to handmaids and nurses.[2]

Discussion Questions

From Tacitus' observations, what can we conclude about Germanic families, government, and warfare?

Lesson 3

The Huns

In A.D. 376 the barbarian **Huns** north of the Danube turned to their civilized rival, the Romans, and begged for protection. For good reason. Perhaps no other people have struck greater fear in the west than the Huns. In the end of the fourth century the Huns appeared out of nowhere and they pushed into the Hungarian plains. From there they extended their domains south of the Danube River, into Gaul and then northern Italy, leaving a trail of destruction and terror wherever they went.

The Huns were nomads from the Central Asian Steppes, but the exact origins of the Huns remain a mystery. The Huns had already settled in the area northwest of the Caspian Sea as early as the third century. Around A.D. 370, the Huns moved west and destroyed every eastern European village in their path.

Print of a Don Cossack, c.1820 (PD).

2 Various authors, Thomas Gordon, translator, *Voyages and Travels: Ancient and Modern* (P.F. Collier, 1910), p. 95–107.

Although the nomadic food-gathering Huns soon became a prominent force in Europe, they did not have the political unity to stage a massive and serious campaign. More often than not, the Huns before **Attila** were a loose confederation of many kings rather than an empire. There existed the title of "high king," but few of such rank had the competence to control all of the Huns. For the most part the Huns attacked and operated in separately commanded groups without a unified objective.

Discussion Question

Why were the Huns so feared in eastern Europe?

The Zaporozhian Cossacks writing a letter to the Sultan of Turkey, 1880–1891 (PD-Art).

Attila

Attila was indisputably the greatest leader of the Huns. He was the first, and the only, barbarian king to force the Romans to sign a non-aggression treaty. The Huns agreed to desist from all violent activity toward the Romans as long as they paid a yearly tribute.

With the southern border secured, Attila campaigned eastward and subjugated many tribes. He returned home a victor, but when he realized that the Romans failed to pay tribute, he was furious. Furthermore, the Roman **bishop of Margus** had crossed the Danube and robbed royal Hun graves, stealing their burial treasures. Attila and his hordes poured into the eastern Roman Empire and devastated it.

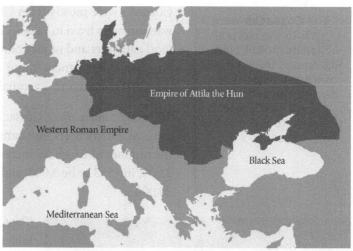

The empire of Attila the Hun.

The Huns reached Constantinople and defeated the Imperial army in the outskirts of the city. However, the defense at Constantinople was stronger than expected. Attila continued his path of destruction elsewhere.

The victory against the Romans was only a beginning of Attila's power. The year 447 saw yet another Hun campaign against the eastern Roman Empire. Attila led his men south and laid waste to the Balkans.

Discussion Questions

Attila showed much discipline by refusing to completely destroy his Roman enemies. Why?

Attila in the Nuremberg Chronicle (1493).

Lesson 5

Hungarian Cossacks

The **Cossacks** were vital to the cultural significance of both Russia and Ukraine, who were established as a democratic people with a fierce military-type presence to protect their people.

Cossacks were mostly from Ukraine and of Tatar descent. Cossacks were fierce warriors who lived in eastern Europe and southern Russia. Cossacks were nomadic food gatherers and never connected with other people groups to form a nation state. Poorly inhabited and without efficient administration, their territories attracted potential conquerors. Eventually the Cossacks united to oppose the Tatars.

The ethnic make up of Cossacks is interesting. The **Ukraine** element prevailed, but there were still many Poles, Russians, Tatars, Germans, and Hungarians. In the16th century the number of Cossacks increased rapidly. In 1534 their number was assessed to be 2,000, in 1553 to be 3,000, and in the beginning of the 17th century to be more than 20,000.

The Cossacks were a match for all invaders. Since Poland maintained small forces on the borderlands, the Cossacks were often the only defenders for Ukraine against Tatar raids.

Discussion Questions

Who were the Cossacks and why did they have such an impact on world history?

Cossack Mamay, circa 1890 (PD-Art).

Chapter 22

Fringe History

First Thoughts

History is not merely cold facts. It is human life with all its foibles and triumphs, defeats and victories. Questions and eyebrows have often been raised concerning the study of history, and, in particular, whether the merits of historical knowledge and research have anything to do with real life. Too often historical figures seem to be bigger than life. We are fatigued by wars and cataclysmic events and we forget that ordinary folks made history — people like you and me. Spike Milligan once posed the poignant and philosophical question, "Is it because with the future unknown, the present traumatic, that we find the past so secure?"[1] Whatever the reasons for searching out what has occurred before, it seems that our past has always had an influence on our present lives, regardless of whether we know it or not. Why can't that be fun, too? Let's have some fun this week.

Chapter Learning Objectives

Chapter 22 begins by examining the most mundane of subjects: the importance of bread in history. Next we will look at dogs and show how man's best friend has stood with him throughout history. Next we will examine legends that emerged from real, and not so real, historical figures. We will look at something ordinary but discover it was very important indeed: the discovery of paper. Finally, we will look at sly, and not so sly, kings and how they were helped and hindered by their illiteracy.

As a result of this chapter you should be able to:

1. Explain what bread symbolizes in history.

2. Tell how dogs were used in warfare.

3. Examine some legends that are circulating today that surely are false.

4. State how the battle among animal skins, papyrus, parchment, and paper turned out.

5. Analyze when in world history illiteracy perhaps would be a distinct advantage.

---

1 http://www.allempires.com/article/index.php?q=Education_From_History.

Bread

Is anything in history more important than bread? Yet how often do historians assess its importance?

Governments, kings, and armies come and go. But bread was, and is, part of all of history.

Bread and circuses was the basic Roman formula for the well-being of the population, and hence a political strategy unto itself. Bread and entertainment in the coliseum were frequently used to placate the masses.

Bread is the central symbol of many religions. Jesus said, "I am the bread of life" (John 6:35 and 48). In Judaism, the unleavened bread of the **Passover** is a central symbol. The sharing of bread and salt is a traditional basis of hospitality and creates a usually unbreakable mutual obligation of protection.

Bread and sickle in the museum at Boscoreale in Italy. Both items were buried under ash and pumice by the eruption of Mount Vesuvius in AD 79 (CCA-SA3.0).

Almost all cultures, no matter what else they eat, have some sort of bread. It is still one of the staples that all cultures partake of.

To most of us, flour means white wheat flour. Not so in the past. The first flours were nothing more than very coarse seeds ground from grass. Later, it was discovered that corn and some ancient varieties of wheat could be ground more uniformly to produce a better and more edible product. There have been ancient grains found in Egypt that have been grown today, as well as bread produced in the described ways. The product was amazingly good, but it still wasn't white bread. There was no white bread until the Middle Ages, when cooks began separating the bran from the mix. They even flirted with bleaching it. White, bleached flour was very expensive, due to the labor intensity of producing it, and became a status symbol. Ironically then, in bread-making history, it was the rich who ate the least nutritious product!

Discussion Question

What are some things that bread symbolizes in history?

Man's Best Friend

While horses were the **archetypal** animal of war, and by far the most common companion to man, animals have been used in battle for as long as horses.

The earliest records of the use of canines in war are from 2100 B.C., when Hammurabi employed dogs to fight alongside his most elite Sumerian warriors.

The Greeks had special canine units at the Battle of Marathon. Man's best friend was present at every fortress siege in the Peloponnesian Wars.

Image of the Battle of Agincourt from the early 15th century (PD).

Later, the Celts, a Briton native group, bred fearsome war dogs, an act that was promptly copied by the Romans who did one better and created huge, ferocious **Mastiffs** that could literally devour Roman enemies.

During the Middle Ages, Great Danes were used to jump onto the backs of horses, throwing the rider off, and allowing their master to kill the horseman. They were also used to scare horses and pursue fleeing enemies.

The U.S. Marines use bomb-sniffing dogs in Afghanistan and other places around the world.

In ancient battles, dogs were also sent out to search for and either stand over or drag back fallen soldiers to camp, while others would remain at the baggage camp to protect camp followers during the battle.

A legendary tale has arisen from the Battle of Agincourt, where Englishman Sir Peers Legh was severely wounded, but his Mastiff stood over him until the end of the battle.

In the New World, the 16th-century conquistadors employed tactics not dissimilar to those of the Celts and Romans over a millennium earlier. Dressing their huge Mastiffs in quilted overcoats, they were released into native villages, attacking the residents and wreaking havoc. They were also used to pursue and combat Aztec warriors at several battles.

Dogs, man's best friend, have been, since time immemorial, man's comrade in arms too!

Discussion Question

How were dogs used in warfare?

Mastiffs were sometimes used in warfare.

173

Legends

Howard Pyle illustration from the 1903 edition of *The Story of King Arthur and His Knights* (PD).

History becomes **legend** and legend becomes myth. **King Arthur**, **Robin Hood**, Jason and the Argonauts — these are all legends, some of which are based on some historical figure.

One notable legend was the legend of **Prester John**.

The legend of Prester John and his empire of wonders was established at the same time the first crusade was launched. Islam was considered a ferocious threat to Christian Europe and, probably in order to encourage the soldiers of Europe, legends were told of a Christian king situated in the Far East with a large army ready to defeat their Islamic opponents.

Prester John never existed, although there were Christian congregations in the Far East; regardless, the legend remained for centuries.

Legends such as Prester John, the Holy Grail, or the realms of Eldorado are mere fiction. Some of them have a historical foundation, but eventually they evolve into legends and the truth pales in comparison to the legend. Nonetheless, these myths and legends ignited exploration through centuries, and led to expeditions through the Americas, Africa, Asia, and, of course, the vast oceans. Knights searched for the Holy Grail for centuries.

Not all legends are harmless. The **Protocols of the Elders of Zion** were written by Russians in order to justify their **pogroms** — suppression of Jews. The Protocols purported to offer secret, harmful, conspiratorial information about the Jewish people. The pogroms started in the late 19th century, but they escalated even more after the Russian defeat in the Russo-Japanese War of 1904–05.

Recently, a medieval legend — the Da Vinci Code — surfaced. It has no basis in fact. Holy Blood and Holy Grail — and, thus, consequently, the Da Vinci Code — are in many ways a culmination of centuries of pseudo history. Some legends are based on truth, such as the realms of Eldorado and Saguenay, others are merely hoaxes, like the Protocols of the Elders of Zion, while others are based on deceptions like Holy Blood and Holy Grail. What it proves, however, is that regardless of age and era, humans are easily deceived and easily impressed.

Discussion Question

Which of the legends circulating today are surely false?

The Importance of Paper

By the time scribes were copying their first works onto parchment in Europe, animal skins had been used as a writing material for thousands of years. The ancient Egyptians, Assyrians, and Persians all wrote on hides, although at this stage the manufacturing process was most likely still so primitive it was only possible to write on one side of the animal skin. Also, frankly, it was an awkward, expensive, and stinky process! Often insects, and other animals, would eat the written work, too!

Proper parchment as we know it was not invented until about 200 B.C., in the city of **Pergamon** in Asia Minor, from which **parchment** derives its name. The bright minds of Pergamon achieved this by soaking raw animal hide in limed water, which dissolved fats and made remnants of hair and flesh loosen from the skin. The hide was then suspended on a rack to dry, while being scraped and cleaned further, before being rubbed with finely grained chalk and finally smoothed over with a pumice stone.

Papyrus plant.

A more popular paper was **papyrus**, made from the reeds of the plant by the same name, which was much cheaper but not as durable. Eventually, most Europeans favored parchment, whereas papyrus remained popular in the Middle East.

Parchment was without a doubt a more solid material to work with than papyrus; one could make corrections by erasing with less risk of destroying the sheet. If prepared properly it presented a smoother surface to write on as well. Taking into account the missionary activities of the early Christians, parchment had the ability to survive even if exposed to inclement weather conditions and was more immune to humid climates, whereas papyrus had a tendency to rot outside the hot and dry climate of Egypt. Perhaps most importantly, however, parchment entailed the first binding of written works into books rather than scrolls, the book form we still use to this day.

In any case, the Christians carried with them parchment as an integral part of their written culture, and when their faith rose to prominence in the fourth century, parchment also began superseding papyrus in many regions of the Roman Empire.

Fragments of Turin papyrus of an ancient Egyptian mining map (right half), for Ramesses IV's quarrying expedition, 12th century BC (New Kingdom).

Paper was in circulation but not preferred by anyone in the West. Invented in A.D. 105 in China, paper was at first kept secret, but the Arabs managed to learn the technique in the eighth century. With them it travelled to the areas of southern Europe under Arab dominion, most notably the southern half of Iberia, and by the 12th — no later than the 13th century — western Europeans knew how to make paper. France initiated its own paper production in the 14th century, Germany in the 15th with England, the Low Countries, and Scandinavia following subsequently. Paper was, in other words, readily available by the late Middle Ages, yet parchment still retained a high status, paper sometimes being regarded with outright disdain. Fortunately, many historical documents were recorded on parchment, and thanks to its durability, these documents are available hundreds of years later.

Discussion Questions

How did the battle among animal skins, papyrus, parchment, and paper as a medium for writing and sharing text turn out?

Lesson 5

Dumb Kings

Charlemagne acted like he could not read so he could gain advantages of his opponents.

Most kings who ruled in the ancient world were highly educated, intelligent leaders. A few, though, were completely illiterate. Some were even proud of it!

Ateas was the king of the Scythians who conquered most of Euro-Asia. Ateas lived to a very old age and it was he who united the Scythian tribes under a single leadership. During his life, the Scythians flourished, having good relations with the Macedonians and being successful in conquests around their own lands. He conquered Euro-Asia but could not read one word!

Likewise Attila the Hun. Attila was an inspiring leader and fierce warrior; he was also a mediocre administrator who could not read one single word!

Genghis Khan, the first main khan of the Mongols, was one of the most well-known lords of the steppe. He conquered most of his neighboring states and his son Kubla conquered most of the known world. Despite this, Genghis Khan never needed writing, though he didn't discard those who could — he often hired Chinese engineers for great effect, and they were very well educated. But he never learned to read or write a letter.

But perhaps the most famous illiterate monarch was **Charlemagne**, the most famous and powerful monarch in Europe before Napoleon. Creator of a large empire, Charlemagne never disliked education. As a young man, he just never learned reading or writing — usual for the Frankish kingdom. Some historians think Charlemagne had a severe learning disability. However, Charlemagne often feigned ignorance to cause his opponents to underestimate him. He was, in fact, a very shrewd, capable man.

After he became the king, he valued literacy and education in general. It is told that he wanted to learn writing and he managed to spell his own name but almost nothing else. Did not seem to hurt him much!

All of the above kings could probably have learned to read and write if they wished. They were pretty smart. But there are examples of ancient rulers who were just plain dumb! For example, Emperor Commodus was obviously of an extremely low intelligence and barely read at all. His low intelligence was a quiet joke shared throughout the Western world. He was the quintessential "dumb jock" who preferred gladiatorial sporting games above everything else. Like Jimmy Jones hung around the Dallas Cowboys, Commodus hung around his sporting teams. Nonetheless, Commodus had the last laugh: he was one of the most successful of the Roman emperors.

Discussion Question

When in world history would illiteracy perhaps be a distinct advantage?

Charlemagne at Cologne Cathedral.

Chapter 23

Early Britain: Island Topography

First Thoughts

The history of England concerns the study of the human past in one of Europe's oldest and most influential national territories. For thousands of years, Britons, Celts, Picts, and Scots populated this mystical, relatively small island. The end of Roman rule in Britain enabled the Anglo-Saxon settlement of Britain, which is often regarded as the origin of England and the English people.

Chapter Learning Objectives

Chapter 23 examines English history up to the Norman conquest. We will see that the Britons were conquered by the Romans and later by the Anglo-Saxons. We will examine in greater depth the Roman rule by reading a passage by G.K. Chesterton. Next we will examine the importance of the Magna Carta and finish by reading a portion of the Robin Hood legend.

As a result of this chapter you should be able to:

1. Give a summary of English history until the departure of the Romans.

2. Discuss G.K. Chesterton's history of Roman occupation.

3. Analyze why the Domesday Book was so important to English history.

4. Understand why the Magna Carta was so important in English history.

5. Evaluate what British values are cherished by examining the Robin Hood legend.

CONCEPTS

Celts

Picts

Scots

Britons

Anglo-Saxons

Alfred the Great

Battle of Hastings

Domesday Book

Magna Carta

King John

Charter of Liberties

King Henry I

Constitutional Law

A Short History

The United Kingdom was inhabited by English native people groups: **Celts**, **Picts**, **Scots**, and **Britons** before the Romans came in A.D. 43. In fact, the rural areas of England were more populated in 100 B.C. than they are today!

Anglo-Saxons, (A.D. 500–1000) *Costumes of All Nations*, Albert Kretschmer and Dr. Carl Rohrbach, 1882 (PD).

England is an island, and it reaped all the privileges of an island. Reasonably immune from invasion until the Romans came, England enjoyed a relatively quiet peaceful existence. That all changed in A.D. 43 with the arrival of the Romans.

Roman control lasted for 400 years when the Romans withdrew for tactical reasons. They simply could not sustain outposts in these remote parts of their kingdom. Nonetheless, the Roman influence was so pervasive and profound that Englishmen today point to the Roman occupation as their golden age. The Romans built the first roads and cities in England, many of which still exist today.

The **Anglo-Saxons** then conquered the Britons and other indigenous people groups. The History of Anglo-Saxon England spanned early medieval England from the end of Roman Britain and the establishment of Anglo-Saxon kingdoms in the fifth century until the conquest by the Normans in 1066. The King Arthur legends approximately recount Briton resistance to Anglo-Saxon conquests.

During the Anglo-Saxon era, the dominant themes of the seventh to tenth centuries were the spread of Christianity and the political unification of England. Christianity came from three directions — Rome from the south, and Scotland and Ireland to the north and west. Seven Anglo-Saxon kingdoms populated the Kingdom of England during the early tenth century. These included Northumbria, Mercia, East Anglia, Essex, Kent, Sussex, and Wessex. These kingdoms were ruled by warlords, not kings. Anglo-Saxon rule would end when the Normans conquered all of England in 1066.[1]

Discussion Question

Give a summary of English history until the departure of the Romans.

---

1 http://www.shvoong.com/humanities/1694503-history-england/#ixzz1jZdxhxE5

Secondary Source:

Excerpt from Chapter II, Introduction, A Short History of England by G.K. Chesterton (1917)

The land on which we live once had the highly poetic privilege of being the end of the world. Its extremity was ultima Thule, the other end of nowhere. When these islands, lost in a night of northern seas, were lit up at last by the long searchlights of Rome, it was felt that the remotest remnant of things had been touched, and more for pride than possession. . .

The great rationalist hero who first conquered Britain, whether or not he was the detached demigod of "Cæsar and Cleopatra," was certainly a Latin of the Latins, and described these islands, when he found them, with all the curt positivism of his pen of steel. But even Julius Cæsar's brief account of the Britons leaves on us something of this mystery, which is more than ignorance of fact. They were apparently ruled by that terrible thing, a pagan priesthood. Stones, now shapeless yet arranged in symbolic shapes, bear witness to the order and labor of those that lifted them. Their worship was probably Nature-worship, and while such a basis may count for something in the elemental quality that has always soaked the island arts, the collision between it and the tolerant Empire suggests the presence of something that generally grows out of Nature-worship—I mean the unnatural. But upon nearly all the matters of modern controversy Cæsar is silent. He is silent about whether or not the language was "Celtic"; and some of the place-names have even given rise to a suggestion that, in parts at least, it was already Teutonic. I am not capable of pronouncing upon the truth of such speculations, but I am of pronouncing upon their importance; at least, to my own very simple purpose. And indeed their importance has been very much exaggerated. Cæsar professed to give no more than the glimpse of a traveler; but when, some considerable time after, the Romans returned and turned Britain into a Roman province, they continued to display a singular indifference to questions that have excited so many professors. What they cared about was getting and giving in Britain what they had gotten and given in Gaul. We do not know whether the Britons then, or for that matter the Britons now, were Iberian or Cymric or Teutonic. We do know that in a short time they were Roman.

Every now and then there is discovered in modern England some fragment such as a Roman pavement. Such Roman antiquities rather diminish than increase the Roman reality. They make something seem distant which is still very near, and something seem dead that is still alive. It is like writing a man's epitaph on his front door. The epitaph would probably be a compliment, but hardly a personal introduction. The important thing about France and England is not that they have Roman remains. They are Roman remains. In truth they are not so much remains as relics; for they are still working miracles. A row of poplars is a more Roman relic than a row of pillars. Nearly all that we call the works of nature have but grown like fungoids upon this original work of man; and our woods are mosses on the bones of a giant. Under the seed of our harvests and the roots of our trees is a foundation of which the fragments of tile and brick are but emblems, and under the colors of our wildest flowers are the colors of a Roman pavement.

Britain was directly Roman for fully four hundred years, longer than she has been Protestant, and very much longer than she has been industrial. What was meant by being Roman it is necessary in a few lines to say, or no sense can be made of what happened after, especially of what happened immediately after. Being Roman did not mean being subject, in the sense that one savage tribe will enslave another, or in the sense that the cynical politicians of recent times watched with a horrible hopefulness for the evanescence of the Irish. Both conquerors and conquered were heathen, and both had the institutions which seem to us to give an inhumanity to heathenism: the triumph, the slave-market, the lack of all the sensitive nationalism of modern history. But the Roman Empire did not destroy nations; if anything, it created them. Britons were not originally proud of being Britons; but they were proud of being Romans. The Roman steel was at least as much a magnet as a sword. In truth it was rather a round mirror of steel, in which every people came to see itself. For Rome as Rome the very smallness of the civic origin was a warrant for the largeness of the civic experiment. Rome itself obviously could not rule the world, any more than Rutland. I mean it could not rule the other races as the Spartans ruled the Helots or the Americans ruled the blacks. A machine so huge had to be human; it had to have a handle that fitted any man's hand. The Roman Empire necessarily became less Roman as it became more of an empire; until not very long after Rome gave conquerors to Britain, Britain was giving emperors to Rome. Out of Britain, as the Britons boasted, came at length the great Empress Helena, who was the mother of Constantine. And it was Constantine, as all men know, who first nailed up that proclamation which all after generations have in truth been struggling either to protect or to tear down. . .

<aside>**Rome** controlled Britain for some 400 years — almost twice as long as the United States has been a nation.</aside>

But while a million little priests and monks like mice were already nibbling at the bonds of the ancient servitude, another process was going on, which has here been called the weakening of the Empire. It is a process which is to this day very difficult to explain. But it affected all the institutions of all the provinces, especially the institution of Slavery. But of all the provinces its effect was heaviest in Britain, which lay on or beyond the borders. The case of Britain, however, cannot possibly be considered alone. The first half of English history has been made quite unmeaning in the schools by the attempt to tell it without reference to that corporate Christendom in which it took part and pride. I fully accept the truth in Mr. Kipling's question of "What can they know of England who only England know?" and merely differ from the view that they will best broaden their minds by the study of Wagga-Wagga and Timbuktu. It is therefore necessary, though very difficult, to frame in few words some idea of what happened to the whole European race.

Rome itself, which had made all that strong world, was the weakest thing in it. The centre had been growing fainter and fainter, and now the centre disappeared. Rome had as much freed the world as ruled it, and now she could rule no more. Save for the presence of the Pope and his constantly increasing supernatural prestige, the eternal city became like one of her own provincial towns. A loose localism was the result rather than any conscious intellectual mutiny. There was anarchy, but there was no rebellion. For rebellion must have a principle, and therefore (for those who can think) an authority. Gibbon called his great pageant of prose "The Decline and Fall of the Roman Empire." The Empire did decline, but it did not fall. It remains to this hour.[2]

---

2   G. K. Chesterton, *The Collected Works of G. K. Chesterton, Volume XX*, p. 427–435.

Discussion Question

What does Chesterton mean when he says, "Rome itself, which had made all that strong world, was the weakest thing in it. The centre had been growing fainter and fainter, and now the centre disappeared. Rome had as much freed the world as ruled it, and now she could rule no more"?

Normal Invasion

The Kingdom of England was not founded until the seven separate petty kingdoms were unified under **Alfred the Great King** of Wessex, who later proclaimed himself king of the English after liberating London from the Danes in 886. For the next few hundred years, the Kingdom of England would fall in and out of power between several West-Saxon and Danish kings.

However, the political ties and direction of England were changed forever by the Norman conquest in 1066. The Norman conquest of England was the conquest of the Kingdom of England by William the Conqueror (Duke of Normandy), in 1066 at the **Battle of Hastings** and the subsequent Norman control of England. It is an important watershed in English history for a number of reasons. The conquest linked England more closely with continental Europe and lessened Danish influence. The success of the conquest established one of the most powerful monarchies in Europe, created the most sophisticated governmental system in Europe, changed the English language and culture, and set the stage for English-French conflict that would last into the 19th century. The events of the conquest also paved the way for a pivotal historical document to be produced — the *Domesday Book*. The *Domesday Book* was the record of the great survey of England completed in 1086, executed for William the Conqueror. The survey was similar to a census by a government of today and is England's earliest surviving public records document.[3]

Discussion Question

Why was the *Domesday Book* so important to English history?

Bayeux Tapestry of The Battle of Hastings with Norman knights and archers, 1070s (PD).

---

3 http://www.shvoong.com/humanities/1694503-history-england/#ixzz1jZfjmswW.

Government and Law: The Magna Carta

> The **Magna Carta** sets an important precedence in English history: the rule of law, not the monarchy, had the final say in political and legal matters.

Magna Carta is an English charter, or agreement, originally issued in the year 1215 and reissued later in the 13th century in modified versions. The Great Charter of the Liberties of England, and of the Liberties of the Forest, still remains on the statute books of England and Wales.

The 1215 charter required **King John** to protect certain liberties given by God and the state and not to be removed by the king. The main law stated that no "freeman" could be punished except through the law of the land, a right which is still in existence today.

Magna Carta was the first document forced onto an English king by a group of his subjects, the feudal barons, in an attempt to limit his powers by law and protect their privileges. It was preceded and directly influenced by the **Charter of Liberties** in 1100, in which **King Henry I** had specified particular areas wherein his powers would be limited.

The charter was an important part of the extensive historical process that led to the rule of **constitutional law** in the English-speaking world. Wherever Englishmen went, they carried their sense of law and justice with them. Perhaps no document has had more impact on English-speaking people than the Magna Carta![4]

Discussion Questions

Why was the Magna Carta so important in English history?

"King John Signing Magna Carta" by Ernest Normand published in 1906 (PD-Art).

---

4 http://www.archives.gov/exhibits/featured_documents/magna_carta/.

How Robin Hood Came To Be an Outlaw

The Merry Adventures of Robin Hood, **by Ernie Pyle**

In Merry England in the time of old, when good King Henry the Second ruled the land, there lived within the green glades of Sherwood Forest, near Nottingham Town, a famous outlaw whose name was Robin Hood. No archer ever lived that could speed a gray goose shaft with such skill and cunning as his, nor were there ever such yeomen as the seven-score merry men that roamed with him through the greenwood shades. Right merrily they dwelled within the depths of Sherwood Forest, suffering neither care nor want, but passing the time in merry games of archery or bouts of cudgel play, living upon the King's venison, washed down with draughts of ale of October brewing.

Not only Robin himself but all the band were outlaws and dwelled apart from other men, yet they were beloved by the country people round about, for no one ever came to jolly Robin for help in time of need and went away again with an empty fist.

And now I will tell how it came about that Robin Hood fell afoul of the law.

When Robin was a youth of eighteen, stout of sinew and bold of heart, the Sheriff of Nottingham proclaimed a shooting match and offered a prize of a butt of ale to whosoever should shoot the best shaft in Nottinghamshire. "Now," quote Robin, "will I go too, for fain would I draw a string for the bright eyes of my lass and a butt of good October brewing." So up he got and took his good stout yew bow and a score or more of broad clothyard arrows, and started off from Locksley Town through Sherwood Forest to Nottingham.

It was at the dawn of day in the merry Maytime, when hedgerows are green and flowers bedeck the meadows; daisies pied and yellow cuckoo buds and fair primroses all along the briery hedges; when apple buds blossom and sweet birds sing, the lark at dawn of day, the throstle cock and cuckoo; when lads and lasses look upon each other with sweet thoughts; when busy housewives spread their linen to bleach upon the bright green grass. Sweet was the greenwood as he walked along its paths, and bright the green and rustling leaves, amid which the little birds sang with might and main: and blithely Robin whistled as he trudged along, thinking of Maid Marian and her bright eyes, for at such times a youth's thoughts are wont to turn pleasantly upon the lass that he loves the best.

As thus he walked along with a brisk step and a merry whistle, he came suddenly upon some foresters seated beneath a great oak tree. Fifteen there were in all, making themselves merry with feasting and drinking as they sat around a huge pasty, to which each man helped himself, thrusting his hands into the pie, and washing down that which they ate with great horns of ale which they drew all foaming from a barrel that stood nigh. Each man was clad in Lincoln green, and a fine show they made, seated upon the sward beneath that fair, spreading tree. Then one of them, with his mouth full, called out to Robin, "Hulloa, where goest thou, little lad, with thy one-penny bow and thy farthing shafts?"

Ernie Pyle was an American writer and illustrator who compiled the text for *The Merry Adventures of Robin Hood*, which was published in 1883.

The frontispiece of Howard Pyle's *The Merry Adventures of Robin Hood,* 1883 (PD).

Then Robin grew angry, for no stripling likes to be taunted with his green years.

"Now," quote he, "my bow and eke mine arrows are as good as shine; and moreover, I go to the shooting match at Nottingham Town, which same has been proclaimed by our good Sheriff of Nottinghamshire; there I will shoot with other stout yeomen, for a prize has been offered of a fine butt of ale."

Then one who held a horn of ale in his hand said, "Ho! listen to the lad! Why, boy, thy mother's milk is yet scarce dry upon thy lips, and yet thou pratest of standing up with good stout men at Nottingham butts, thou who art scarce able to draw one string of a two-stone bow."

The first meeting between Robin Hood and Little John, from Howard Pyle's *The Merry Adventures of Robin Hood*, 1883 (PD).

"I'll hold the best of you twenty marks," quote bold Robin, "that I hit the clout at threescore rods, by the good help of Our Lady fair."

At this all laughed aloud, and one said, "Well boasted, thou fair infant, well boasted! And well thou knowest that no target is nigh to make good thy wager."

And another cried, "He will be taking ale with his milk next."

At this Robin grew right mad. "Hark ye," said he, "yonder, at the glade's end, I see a herd of deer, even more than threescore rods distant. I'll hold you twenty marks that, by leave of Our Lady, I cause the best hart among them to die."

"Now done!" cried he who had spoken first. "And here are twenty marks. I wager that thou causest no beast to die, with or without the aid of Our Lady."

Then Robin took his good yew bow in his hand, and placing the tip at his instep, he strung it right deftly; then he nocked a broad clothyard arrow and, raising the bow, drew the gray goose feather to his ear; the next moment the bowstring rang and the arrow sped down the glade as a sparrowhawk skims in a northern wind. High leaped the noblest hart of all the herd, only to fall dead, reddening the green path with his heart's blood.

From Howard Pyle's *The Merry Adventures of Robin Hood*, 1883 (PD).

"Ha!" cried Robin, "how likest thou that shot, good fellow? I wot the wager were mine, an it were three hundred pounds."

Then all the foresters were filled with rage, and he who had spoken the first and had lost the wager was more angry than all.

"Nay," cried he, "the wager is none of thine, and get thee gone, straightway, or, by all the saints of Heaven, I'll baste thy sides until thou wilt ne'er be able to walk again." "Knowest thou not," said another, "that thou hast killed the King's deer, and, by the laws of our gracious lord and sovereign King Harry, thine ears should be shaven close to thy head?"

"Catch him!" cried a third.

"Nay," said a fourth, "let him e'en go because of his tender years."

Never a word said Robin Hood, but he looked at the foresters with a grim face; then, turning on his heel, strode away from them down the forest glade. But his heart was bitterly angry, for his blood was hot and youthful and prone to boil.

Now, well would it have been for him who had first spoken had he left Robin Hood alone; but his anger was hot, both because the youth had gotten the better of him and because of the deep draughts of ale that he had been quaffing. So, of a sudden, without any warning, he sprang to his feet, and seized upon his bow and fitted it to a shaft. "Ay," cried he, "and I'll hurry thee anon." And he sent the arrow whistling after Robin.

It was well for Robin Hood that that same forester's head was spinning with ale, or else he would never have taken another step. As it was, the arrow whistled within three inches of his head. Then he turned around and quickly drew his own bow, and sent an arrow back in return.

"Ye said I was no archer," cried he aloud, "but say so now again!"

The shaft flew straight; the archer fell forward with a cry, and lay on his face upon the ground, his arrows rattling about him from out of his quiver, the gray goose shaft wet with his; heart's blood. Then, before the others could gather their wits about them, Robin Hood was gone into the depths of the greenwood. Some started after him, but not with much heart, for each feared to suffer the death of his fellow; so presently they all came and lifted the dead man up and bore him away to Nottingham Town.

From Howard Pyle's *The Merry Adventures of Robin Hood*, 1883 (PD).

Meanwhile Robin Hood ran through the greenwood. Gone was all the joy and brightness from everything, for his heart was sick within him, and it was borne in upon his soul that he had slain a man.

"Alas!" cried he, "thou hast found me an archer that will make thy wife to wring! I would that thou hadst ne'er said one word to me, or that I had never passed thy way, or e'en that my right forefinger had been stricken off ere that this had happened! In haste I smote, but grieve I sore at leisure!" And then, even in his trouble, he remembered the old saw that "What is done is done; and the egg cracked cannot be cured."

And so he came to dwell in the greenwood that was to be his home for many a year to come, never again to see the happy days with the lads and lasses of sweet Locksley Town; for he was outlawed, not only because he had killed a man, but also because he had poached upon the King's deer, and two hundred pounds were set upon his head, as a reward for whoever would bring him to the court of the King.

From Howard Pyle's *The Merry Adventures of Robin Hood*, 1883 (PD).

Now the Sheriff of Nottingham swore that he himself would bring this knave Robin Hood to justice, and for two reasons: first, because he wanted the two hundred pounds, and next, because the forester that Robin Hood had killed was of kin to him.

But Robin Hood lay hidden in Sherwood Forest for one year, and in that time there gathered around him many others like himself, cast out from other folk for this cause and for that. Some had shot deer in hungry wintertime, when they could get no other food, and had been seen in the act by the foresters, but had escaped, thus saving their ears; some had been turned out of their inheritance, that their farms might be added to the King's lands in Sherwood Forest; some had been despoiled by a great baron or a rich abbot or a powerful esquire—all, for one cause or another, had come to Sherwood to escape wrong and oppression.

So, in all that year, five-score or more good stout yeomen gathered about Robin Hood, and chose him to be their leader and chief. Then they vowed that even as they themselves had been despoiled they would despoil their oppressors, whether baron, abbot, knight, or squire, and that from each they would take that which had been wrung from the poor by unjust taxes, or land rents, or in wrongful fines. But to the poor folk they would give a helping hand in need and trouble, and would return to them that which had been unjustly taken from them. Besides this, they swore never to harm a child nor to wrong a woman, be she maid, wife, or widow; so that, after a while, when the people began to find that no harm was meant to them, but that money or food came in time of want to many a poor family, they came to praise Robin and his merry men, and to tell many tales of him and of his doings in Sherwood Forest, for they felt him to be one of themselves. [5]

Discussion Questions

The Robin Hood legend, while fictional, is based on fact. There was a historical character somewhat like the legendary figure Robin Hood. Regardless, what does this legend tell us about the values that medieval England cherished?

Statue of Robin Hood near Nottingham Castle (CCA-SA2.0).

_____
5 http://www.gutenberg.org/files/964/964-h/964-h.htm#2H40002.

Chapter 24

Islam:
For Allah and Caliph

First Thoughts

Islam has captured most of the headlines for the first decade of the 21st century. But what is Islam? What is militant Islam? Is it an aberration of the norm? Who is Muhammad, the founder of Islam? How should Americans, then, perceive and react to Islam?

Chapter Learning Objectives

We explore the life of Muhammad, the purported author of the Koran. We will compare Islam to Christianity. Next, we will read an editorial by Marvin Olasky, editor of *World Magazine*, as he gives his views on militant Islam. Finally, we will read and react to another contemporary response to Islam.

As a result of this chapter you should be able to:

1. Understand who Muhammad was and what impact he had on history.

2. Compare and contrast Christianity and Islam.

3. Evaluate one view on militant Islam.

4. Form your own views on Islam.

5. Respond to an article calling for peace among all faiths.

CONCEPTS

Bedouin

Koran

Muhammad

Abyssinia

Wailing Wall

9/11

Islamic
Fundamentalism

Modernity

Lesson 1

Muhammad, a Student Essay

Ironically, Muhammad and his followers found refuge in a Christian nation, a nation that practiced freedom of religion and protected Muhammad and his followers from persecution.

In A.D. 571, a child was born to an important **Bedouin**, nomadic food gatherer from an Arabian tribe living near Mecca, and was given by his mother a name which may remain forever uncertain. His tribe called him **al-Amin** (the faithful), apparently an honorific title but fairly common name. The form which his name takes in the **Koran** is **Muhammad**, and once Ahmad. The name, which means "highly praised," is borne by more male children than any other in the world. The baby's father died before his birth, the mother when he was about six years old. So Muhammad was an orphan by age six.

Very little is known about Muhammad's early life, but it must have been hard. We know however, that at age 25 he was married to the wealthy and intelligent 40-year-old widow, Khadijah. His new wife was a well-to-do merchant. Many argue that Khadijah was his one and only true love.

Muhammad spent much time meditating on a hill outside of Mecca. It was in the course of one of these periods of reflection that Muhammad heard a voice commanding: "Recite thou in the name of thy Lord who created" (Koran 96:1). He claimed that this was the Angel Gabriel speaking. Muhammad felt inspired to write a sacred book. Interestingly, he shared that the Jews and Christians had a sacred book and appeared to be quite prosperous. Why couldn't the Arabians have their own sacred book?

So Muhammad wrote one.

It was apparently, though, like the one that inspired him, the Hebrew Old Testament. There are striking parallels.

In any event, the message of the Arabian Muhammad was a parallel of the message of the Hebrew prophets of the Old Testament. God is one. He is all-powerful. He is the Creator of the universe. There is a judgment day with splendid rewards in paradise awaiting those who carry out God's commands, and terrible punishment in hell for those who disregard them. Such was the gist of his early message.

Muhammad then announced that he was a prophet, the anointed one. He went among his own people teaching, preaching, and delivering the new message. Most thought he was crazy. Even his family only acknowledged him as a prophet. They never said he was the "anointed one" or "Messiah."

Initially, Muhammad and his followers were persecuted in Arabia. They had to move to **Abyssinia**. Ironically, Muhammad and his followers found refuge in a Christian nation, a nation that practiced freedom of religion and protected Muhammad and his followers from persecution. It was in this Christian nation that Muhammad wrote most of the Koran.

Now things became more bizarre. Muhammad had a vision where he traveled to heaven. Unfortunately, one place he visited was the **Wailing Wall** in Jerusalem. So in his mind, this place — the Temple — belonged to Islamic people.

Portrait of Mohammed from Michel Baudier's *Histoire générale de la religion des turcs* (Paris, 1625) (PD).

The religion grew in numbers. In 628, Muhammad led a body of fourteen hundred believers to Mecca. Even at the height of his glory, Muhammad lived an unpretentious life in a very modest house. He was often seen mending his own clothes and was at all times open to visits from friends.[1]

Discussion Question

What do you know of Muhammad from things you have read, the media or what others have said?

Lesson 2

Islam	Christianity
Islam considers Jesus a prophet just like Moses, Abraham, and Noah. Muhammad and the Arabs are descendants of Ishmael, which Islam claims Jesus said by their interpretation of Matthew 21:42–44 would supersede the Israelite nation. Islam rejects the divinity of Jesus Christ: "The Messiah, Jesus the son of Mary, was no more than Allah's apostle and His Word which He cast to Mary; a spirit from Him. So believe in Allah and His apostles and do not say: 'Three.' . . . Allah is but one God . . ." (Koran 4:171). "Then Allah will say: 'Jesus, the son of Mary, did you ever say to mankind: 'Worship me and my mother as gods beside Allah?' " (Koran 5:114).	Jesus was more than a prophet. He is God (Matthew 17:5; Mark 1:1; Luke 1:35; Philippians 2:6; Hebrews 1:8; 1 John 4:15). He claimed to be God: John 4:26, 8:23, 10:30, 13:13, 14:7–10. He accepted worship: Matthew 8:2, 9:18, 14:33, 15:25, 18:26, 28:9, 17; Mark 5:6; Luke 24:52; John 5:22–23; John 9:38. He forgave sins: Matthew 9:6; Mark 2:7. "He was God manifest in the flesh" (1 Timothy 3:16), "for in Him dwells all the fullness of the Godhead bodily" (Colossians 2:9). "God was in Christ" (2 Corinthians 5:19), who is "the brightness of His glory, and the express image of His person"(Hebrews 1:3).
The Genesis account should not be taken literally. . . . The earth is billions of years old. Creation took eight days, it says in Surah 41:9, 10, 12. Surah 10:3, however, states creation took six days.	A literal interpretation of Scripture indicates the earth is only a few thousand years old. God created the universe in six days and rested on the seventh day (Genesis 1:1 to 2:2).

---

1 Student essay by Michael Ross.

The Koran claims divine authorship and inspiration:	The New Testament undeniably declares the inspiration of the Old Testament (the contents of which the Koran denies):
"This is indeed a Qur'an most honorable, a Book well-guarded . . . a Revelation from the Lord of the Worlds" (Koran 56:77–80). "This Qur'an is not such as can be produced by anyone other than God" (10:37).	Matthew 1:22, 2:15, 3:3, 4:14, 8:17, 12:17, 13:35, 21:4, 22:42; Mark 12:36; Acts 1:16, 4:25, 28:25; 1 Peter 1:10–11; 2 Peter 1:21.

Discussion Question

What is your view concerning Islam in America?

12th Century Qur'an in Reza
Abbasi Museum (CCA-SA3.0).

Lesson 3

Militant Islam — One View

By Marvin Olasky, Editor, *World Magazine*

Many newspapers and magazines offered crash courses in the basics of Islam following the destruction of the World Trade Center towers, and *WORLD MAGAZINE* went deeper in a special issue the month after **9/11**. Sadly, newspaper presentation of the basics was generally done in the context of stories that advocated the positive, toleration, without coming to grips with the negative, the existence for centuries of a sizeable war party within Islam. Instead of describing both faces of Islam, reporters displayed superficiality and tried to foster syncretism.

Reporters have frequently labeled Osama bin Laden's pronouncements as deviations from moralistic but peace-loving Islam. For example, the Riverside (Calif.) *Press-Enterprise* contrasted "self-declared 'Islamic militants' " with the "authentic Islam" absorbed by convert Nancy Hadiza Collins: " 'I used to love drinking strawberry margaritas,' she said. 'Now I read Muslim books and avoid sleazy films or music.' "

On the other side of the United States, the *Orlando Sentinel* told readers that "Muslims Strive to Educate," which means that "[w]hen Errol Peterkin says Islam is peace, it's more than just an expression. 'It's how we live, by nature of our religion.' " The *Sentinel* reported that at an open house for the Muslim Academy of Central Florida "kindergartners did finger paintings, some students created collages, and older children wrote essays. 'The terrorists called themselves Muslim, but Muslims do not behave with such violence and evil,' wrote fifth-grader Sufeya Yasin." Sadly, the US press had not delved into the debate about what kind of war and violence the Quran condemns. Let's look at several Arabic words. Saddam Hussein and Saudi members of the Wahhabi sect argue that terrorists are martyrs: They pay $25,000 or more to the surviving families of *mujahideen* (holy warriors) who participate in jihad and become *shahidin* (martyrs). But other Muslims call terrorists *mufsidoon* (evil-doers) engaged in *hirabah* (unholy war against society) and heading not to paradise but to *jahannam* (eternal hellfire).

Muslims originally used the term *hirabah* to condemn vicious attacks by members of barbarian tribes who murdered or enslaved those they fought and defeated. Such barbarians engaged in "war against society," attacking indiscriminately as today's *hirabah mufsidoon* (vicious war evildoers) attack indiscriminately. The TrueSpeak Institute in Washington argues that traditional Islamic law bans "the fomenting of hatred between communities, religions, nations and civilizations; committing and enticing others to commit suicide for the purpose of intimidation; and wanton killing of innocents and noncombatants, even including fellow Muslims."

Even if that is true, Saddam, Bin Laden, and other purveyors of violent hatred have been redefining the classic concepts. Israeli adults are not innocent because many at some point had military training, and Israeli children are future aggressors, Saddam charges. Clerks in the World Trade Center were not noncombatants because they fueled capitalism that makes possible American aggression, bin Laden argues. US forces' attack on Iraq is not to force change in a regime that has violated the peace agreements signed after Gulf War I, but to destroy a center of Islam, many mullahs mutter. . . .

Conversion from any religion to another is a major step, yet reporters — apparently coming from the view that Islam and Christianity are essentially similar religions — have generally made it seem easy. The *Houston Chronicle*, under a "Drawn to Islam" headline, concentrated on food, not faith: "Huevos rancheros for breakfast; fasouliye for dinner. . . . For El-Kassir, a Mexican-American convert to Islam, starting the day with the Mexican egg breakfast and ending it with a Lebanese meat-and-bean dinner meant nothing more than the merging of cultures easily found in Islam." Nothing more than the merging of cultures? . . .

Major theological differences tended to be reported in an "oh, by the way" manner: The *Florida Times-Union* (Jacksonville) stated that "Muslims believe in all of God's prophets, including Jesus Christ. However, they believe Muhammad was the last and final prophet." Oh, that's it? But Christianity is based on the belief not that Christ is one among many prophets, but that He is the Son of God. Many newspapers have reported variations on this theme: "Same God: Muslims accept the teachings of the Jewish Torah and the Christian Gospels." That's not true; Muslims accept those teachings only when they conform to the teachings of the Quran, and often they do not. . . .

It is neither wise nor compassionate to remain uninformed about those fiery religious rulings, and whether they have a basis in the Quran. Nor is it wise, when one culture may be threatening another, to settle for the most superficial coverage of that culture's belief, or to assume that both cultures have essentially the same understanding of who God is.[2]

Discussion Question

Summarize Olasky's arguments.

Lesson 4

A Touch of TLC — Tammy L. Carter

To onlookers, it may have looked like just another tree planting. To 11-year-old Mia Dawson, however, planting 16 southern live oaks in Winter Park Tuesday morning was symbolic of planting world peace.

The plantings must be watered, fertilized and handled with care if they are to become 80-foot sprawling providers of shade. Planting peace works in a similar way, says Mia, a Hebrew Day School student. If peace is planted and nurtured long enough to take root, it will spread around the world — even in the Middle East.

"I am already working with others for peace . . . by spending time with Christian and Muslim students from other schools," Mia wrote in an essay that won her a two-week trip to the Holy Land to plant olive trees in June. "This may seem unimportant, but in reality it is crucial.

"By getting to know and like them, and realizing how alike we really are, I know that I will not grow up to hate them and they will not grow up to hate me," she added. "By becoming friends with Christians and Muslims, I am the change that I want to see."

That's heady stuff for a sixth-grader to grasp, but all it took was for Mia and about 85 students from the Muslim Academy of Central Florida, the Hebrew Day School, and Orangewood Christian School to make a connection. They know that peace is possible among them, so why can't it be possible around the world?

For most of their young lives, these Jewish, Muslim, and Christian students have been immersed in their own faiths. They have had few opportunities to mingle with children who have different religious beliefs. That changed this school year.

---

2 http://www.worldmag.com/2003/03/coverage_of_islam.

The students have gathered throughout the year to learn about each religion and to find common ground. Last year, the Jewish and Muslim students participated in a similar program sponsored by the Olive Trees Foundation for Peace. This year, the foundation added Christian students to the mix.

"It has been great to get to know people outside of our little bubble," says Orangewood eighth-grader Rachel Good, who turns 14 Saturday. "We are in a sheltered environment and don't experience a lot of other cultures. It's really nice to get out there and meet others who are different from us.

"It was a little awkward at first," Rachel adds, "because we didn't know one another."

By the end of the first meeting at the Hebrew Day School, however, the students had warmed toward one another. After similar meetings at the Muslim Academy and Orangewood, and now the tree planting, the students have built bonds that should endure.

"I think we really connected and were able to share, and not just about our religions, " Rachel says. "I think we could share personal things, too."

Students have exchanged screen names to chat online. "We're not going to lose touch with anyone over the summer," Rachel adds.

At Shady Park in Winter Park's Hannibal Square Tuesday, it took Rachel, 13-year-old Emily Longden of Orangewood, and 13-year-old Farah Nawaz of Muslim Academy about 20 minutes to plant their tree.

"I think it's cool that everyone's getting together and everyone is trying to bring peace with all these different religions," Farah says. "We're actually more alike than I thought."

To close the program, organizer Louise Franklin Sheehy told the students that they have been doing God's work in a special way.

They have planted peace. Now, we must nurture it to make it grow.[3]

Discussion Questions

Do you agree with Ms. Carter's assessment of Islam? Will these efforts bring world peace?

3 http://articles.orlandosentinel.com/2005-05-05/news/0505040498_1_christian-students-tree-planting-rachel.

Lesson 5

Militant Islam

After Muhammad's death, the Muslim Empire continued to expand until the 17th century, when Muslims were unquestionably the world's greatest military force, having conquered extensive territory and converted millions throughout the Middle East and southern Europe. Islam had also achieved unmatched advances in architecture, art, law, mathematics, and science.

With the exception of battling Christian Crusaders, most Muslims had little to do with the West. In fact, Ottoman Turkey, the dominant Islamic power in the 16th century, viewed the Christian West with indifference and scorn.

However, after initial successes, in the 15th century, all over Europe, in parts of Africa, and even in the Middle East, Islam was defeated by Western Christian armies. First, Hungary fell. Then Islamic forces were driven from Spain. Eventually, even in Egypt and portions of North Africa, Islamic forces retreated.

In subsequent years, while many Muslims adapted to the fast-paced changes common to Western industrialization and modernization, some Muslims rejected them. Instead, they created a rigid ideology imbedded in the traditional values and laws of the Koran. This is the phenomenon known today as **Islamic fundamentalism**, or Islamism.

Islamism came to be seen as a struggle to return to the glorious days when Islam reigned supreme. It represents a yearning for the "pure" Islam as practiced by the prophet. Not unlike the American Quakers, the movement rejects much that is innovative. Islamists, however, take the rejection of **modernity** a step further. They perceive those who have introduced these innovations (the West) as their enemy and seek to destroy them.

Discussion Question

What are the roots of Islamic militancy?

United Airlines Flight 175 crashes into the south tower of the World Trade Center complex in New York City during the September 11 attacks (CCA-SA2.0).

Chapter 25

Islam Spreads: The Sword of Allah

First Thoughts

In the centuries after the life of Muhammad, Muslim armies poured out into all surrounding areas, bringing the lands from Persia to Spain under their control. With this huge amount of land under their control, the Umayyad (and latter, the Abbasid) Caliphates allowed merchants and scholars to travel through western Eurasia, bringing goods and knowledge through their conquered territories outward to less advanced regions, such as western Europe. In the Middle East, the success of Islam meant that culture would be changed forever. Indeed, the world would be changed forever!

Chapter Learning Objectives

Chapter 25 explores the genesis of militant Islam and its impact on the Middle East and Europe. We first examine the Umayyad and then the Abbasid Dynasties. We learn why Islamic armies were so successful. Next, we watch the Ottoman Empire conquer all of the Middle East and much of eastern Europe. Finally, we look more closely at the Islamic family.

As a result of this chapter you should be able to:

1. Discuss the genesis of the Sunni and Shiites.
2. Analyze why the Islamic Army was such a formidable enemy.
3. Describe who the Abbasid were and what contributions to world culture they made.
4. Compare how the Ottoman campaigns were very different from the Umayyad campaigns.
5. Delineate in what ways Islamic families were different from Christian families.

CONCEPTS

Caliphs

Umayyad

Sunni

Shiites

Battle of Tours

Horse Archer

Abu al-Qasin

Arabesque

Ottoman Empire

Sacrament

The Caliphs

After Muhammad died, leadership passed to sacred men called **caliphs**. These religious leaders were also political leaders. In Christianity, the pope was an important ecclesiological leader but in fact had very little political power. From the beginning, this was not the case in Islam.

In **Islam**, the religious leaders enjoyed political control too. An Islamic caliph wielded far more control than a Christian king.

These men were called "The Rightly Guided Caliphs" because of their political acumen and religious fervor. Under their rule, the Islamic State of Arabia expanded to the rest of the Middle East, including Persia, Iraq, and into Africa, including Egypt and North Africa.

An important Caliph was Uthman. When he died in A.D. 656, Muhammad's extended family claimed leadership of the Islamic world. Later, a new leader named Muawiyah, unrelated to Muhammad, became caliph and greatly expanded the Islamic state. A majority of Islamic people accepted his rule, and this marked the beginning of the **Umayyad Dynasty**. This group referred to themselves as the **Sunni**. They comprised the majority of Islamic people.

A very vocal and powerful, if small in number, minority also emerged. They called themselves **Shiites**.

The Umayyad were not around long, but in a very short time they spread Islam over most of the known world. Sensing that Mecca was too isolated from the rest of the world to be the geo-political capital, the Umayyad moved the capital to Damascus. In the latter stages of the dynasty the Islamic faith was spread to Europe via the Iberian Peninsula. It appeared that the Islamic forces were unstoppable. They were until Charles Martel stopped them at the **Battle of Tours**.

The Umayyad then turned east and almost conquered Constantinople. They were a militant people looking for a campaign!

Charles de Steuben's *Bataille de Poitiers en octobre 732* depicts a triumphant Charles Martel (mounted) facing 'Abdul Rahman Al Ghafiqi (right) at the Battle of Tours.

Discussion Question

Discuss the genesis of the Sunni and Shiites.

The Islamic Army

The main military threat of the Islamic army was the **horse archer**. As a light cavalry, the horse archers that made up the bulk of the Islamic armies were highly mobile. This mobility was used in four ways, which gave the Umayyads an advantage over their enemies. High mobility allowed the Islamic army to maintain a distance from the enemy and choose the moment at which they would close with them. Significant casualties could be unleashed on its enemies without a loss of a man. The English long bow, developed by England, later had a similar effect.

The predominance of the horse archer generally allowed the Islamic Army to control the place and timing of the major confrontations. The second use of this mobility was the feigned retreat, which allowed Islamic forces to lead their enemies into ambushes or to cause a fake retreat to last for some days to tire the enemy. Good mobility allowed them to attack the weakest points in the enemy's army. The rear and the flanks made ideal targets against their enemies since the commander would travel in the vanguard at the front of the column while traveling. This caused chaos while traveling, and in a battle it allowed the Islamic army to attack their enemies without ever coming into a pitched battle with their enemies until they were worn down and had lost all support from the flanks of the attack in battle. The last way in which this mobility helped the Islamic Army was in attacking the enemy and forcing him to fight on the march. Instead of sitting in a defensive circle and gradually being killed by arrows, the Islamic Army marched toward either safety or where they supposed the enemy to be.

The horse archers themselves could loose their arrows from the saddle without halting or dismounting, and even shoot backward while in retreat. Islamic archers, moving and shooting, would often, with great success, kill their opponents' horses.

Islamic armies introduced military innovations like the horse archer, which allowed Islamic armies to be extremely mobile. The introduction of the horse archer is comparable to the introduction of the tank in World War I.

Mounted rider on a floor fresco from Syria, circa 730.

Discussion Question

Why was the Islamic Army such a formidable enemy?

Lesson 3

The Abbasids

A manuscript written during the Abbasid Era, 13th century (CCA-SA3.0).

By A.D. 747, some of the Shiite Islamic people groups were disenchanted with the Sunni Umayyad rule and broke away, settling in Iran. The Abbasid family were descendents of Muhammad, and eventually they replaced the Umayyad family as the major Islamic group in the Middle East. During the Abbasid Dynasty, specifically during the rule of Harun al-Rashad (A.D. 786–809), Islamic culture experienced a Golden Age. The empire became a global empire and the Shiite Abbasids showed a great deal of tolerance of other faiths.

Islamic culture flourished. For instance, the Arab surgeon **Abu al-Qasim** pioneered surgical techniques that were used until the 20th century. He wrote the first illustrated surgical textbook. Thousands of decorative scrolls, beautifully illustrated with calligraphy, were written by Islamic scholars. They developed the art of **arabesque**, in which intricate geometric designs were created for religious decoration.

Discussion Question

Who were the Abbasid and what contributions to world culture did they make?

Lesson 4

Ottoman Empire

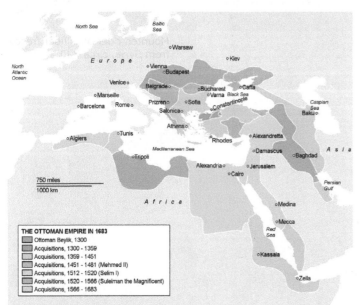

Map depicting the Ottoman Empire at its greatest extent, in 1683.

The Ottomans were not one of the original Turkish peoples involved in Middle Eastern affairs. They moved into the region later, primarily as a result of a vacuum created by the Mongol Empire.

The Ottoman dynasty was named after a tribal leader called Osman, the leader of a small band of nomadic Oguz Turks in northwestern Anatolia, on the Byzantine border.

The history of the birth of the **Ottoman Empire** is also the history of the death of Byzantium. Throughout the Middle Ages, Byzantium was the defender of an economic, political, and civil model opposed to other Christian lands. While lands of the western Roman Empire evolved into a decentralized order called feudalism and the cities declined, in the east the economy and culture was based on a network of cities and non-feudal pastoral communities. The western feudal states had marginal, insignificant navies, whereas Byzantium maintained a vigorous navy.

By the 1300s, however, the eastern Mediterranean trade was dominated by the Venetian-led Italian city states. It was from Venice that Marco Polo went east to visit the Mongol capital in China.

Islamic Ottoman forces were expanding into its remaining lands. Seeing the danger in 1302, the Byzantium Empire decided to crush the head of the snake while young, and sent an army of two thousand against Osman. Osman thoroughly destroyed the Byzantiums. Osman was replaced as **Bey** (district governor) by his son Orhan, who continued to expand his state against the Byzantines. By 1352, he had taken much of Byzantium.

In 1352, Ottomans entered the European continent in Gallipoli. A few years later, the Ottomans successfully conquered portions of the Balkans.

Their first problem, of course, was to cross the sea to Europe without a navy. This was possible due to an alliance with Genoa, who was at war with Venice at the time. In return for the crossing, Ottomans helped Genoa in Gallipoli, and granted them favorable terms in trade. These were the first capitulations in Ottoman history. Once they were in Gallipoli, the Ottomans managed to stay in Europe.

Ottoman dominance in the Balkans brought them into direct conflict with Hungary, the strongest state bordering the region. While the Ottomans succeeded in defeating their enemies on the battlefield, their 400-year rule over the fratricidal Balkans, populated completely by people of different cultures and religions, would have been impossible without draconian measures. The Ottomans were ruthless.

It is also important to acknowledge that both in the east and in the west, Ottoman foreign policy was never determined by religion. Never in their history were the Ottomans a crusading state or a theocracy. Relationship of the Ottoman state with Islam was essentially the same as any other empire's relationship with its official ideology. For the Ottomans, Islam was always the way to justify their policies, both foreign and domestic. They were never exclusively an Islamic state.

Battle of Nicopolis, 1396; painting from 1523 (PD-Art).

Discussion Question

Both the Umayyad and the Ottoman were able to make significant territory acquisitions in Europe for Islam. Yet, the Ottoman campaigns were very different from the Umayyad. How?

Sociology: The Islamic Family

According to the Koran, Muslim men were allowed to have as many as four wives if they were rich enough to take care of them all, but most men in the Islamic world still had only one wife. Family life was one of the most important institutions in Islamic society.

Among Muslims, the selection of a marriage partner was a very different process than in the Western world. Because Islam emphasizes chastity and modesty so strongly, there was very little contact between young men and young women in most parts of the Muslim world, hence between potential spouses, before the actual marriage ceremony. It was not uncommon for husbands and wives to meet one another for the first time the day of the marriage.

In Islam, marriage is not a **sacrament**, as it is in Roman Catholicism, but rather a legal, binding contract between a man and a woman which establishes the legality of their relationship, as well as an acceptance of one another as spouses with a mutual commitment to live together according to the teachings of Islam. Both are to be mindful of their duty to God and their responsibilities to one another. The Koran teaches, "O mankind, be careful of your duty to your Lord Who created you from a single soul and from it created its mate, and from them twain hath spread abroad a multitude of men and women. Be careful of your duty toward Allah in Whom ye claim (your rights) of one another, and toward the wombs (that bare you). Lo! Allah hath been a watcher over you"[1] (4:1).

Islam is a very male-centered and male-dominated religion. "Men are responsible for women because God has given the one more than the other, and because they spend of their property (for the support of women). Virtuous women are therefore obedient, guarding in their (husband) absence that which God has guarding"[2] (4:34).

In Islam a woman, married or single, is seen as a person in her own right, not merely as an adjunct to her husband. However, women were required to be completely clothed while in public and were completely subservient to the husband.

Children in the Islamic empire were treated like little adults. They were clothed the same as adults and expected to perform helpful functions in the home. Play was not encouraged.

Females never went to school, but rather worked at home taking care of their brothers and sisters and cooking. Often women did most of the domestic work. Females carried water from the well and went out to look for fuel for the fire. Young men usually worked in the fields, plowing or weeding. Wealthier male children went to school where they learned to recite the Koran, and also learned how to live an Islamic life. When they got older, if they were hardworking and their families had enough money, they might go to a Koran college for more education. Education was entirely connected to the Koran.

Discussion Question

In what ways were Islamic families different from Christian families?

---

1 M.M. Pickthall, http://www.islamawakened.com/quran/4/1/.
2 www.islamic-world.net/parenting

Chapter 26

Ancient Spain: Inferiority Complex

First Thoughts

Throughout its history, Spain has suffered from a sort of identity crisis. The Pyrenees and Moorish Conquests isolated Spain from the rest of Europe. Madrid is much closer to Casablanca than to Paris. Spain has historically looked beyond the Pyrenees with mixed emotions — admiring their neighbors, but fearing the loss of their own identity should the European influence gain the upper hand. From the 16th to the early 18th century, Spain was the world's most powerful nation, dominant in Europe and with authority over immense territories in America and the Pacific. Yet, within a generation, Spain lost its New World Empire and prestige in Europe. Why? How?

Chapter Learning Objectives

We explore the history of Spain. Central in that history, until the end of the 15th century, were the Moors. We will see that the Islamic Moors controlled Spain for more than 700 years. Next, we will examine the life of Charles Martel, a Frankish ruler who stopped the Moors from conquering western Europe. Finally, we will examine a controversial and influential essay that discusses Roman Catholicism in Spain.

As a result of this chapter you should be able to:

1. Discuss Spanish history.

2. Analyze the impact of the Moorish invasion on Spain and western Europe.

3. Study the life of Charles Martel.

4. Evaluate the impact of Roman Catholicism on Spain.

CONCEPTS

Pyrenees Mountains

Strait of Gibraltar

Bay of Biscay

Iberians

Basques

Charles Martel

Philip II

Armada

Moorish Spain

Lesson 1

Geography: Iberian Peninsula

Only in Greece and the British Isles did geography determine the development of a nation as much as the seashores, mountains, and Spain's proximity to Africa determine its history.

Geography has had a great impact on Spanish history. The **Pyrenees Mountains** in the north have been an impediment to European involvement. The close proximity to Africa across the **Strait of Gibraltar** drew Spain into African politics. Its deep-water warm ports encouraged Spain to be a seafaring nation.

The Spanish mainland is bordered to the south and east almost entirely by the Mediterranean Sea (except for a small land boundary with Gibraltar); to the north by France, Andorra, and the Bay of Biscay; and to the west by the Atlantic Ocean and Portugal. Spain is the second largest country in western Europe (behind France) and the second highest country in Europe (behind Switzerland).

The Pyrenees mountain range extends to the **Bay of Biscay**. In the extreme south of Spain lie the Straits of Gibraltar, which separate Spain and the rest of Europe from Ceuta and Morocco in North Africa; at its narrowest extent, Spain and Morocco are separated by only eight miles.

18th century hand-colored engraved map of the Iberian peninsula depicting various topographical features of the land, as published in Robert Wilkinson's *General Atlas*, circa 1794, (Volume 2, page 666).

Most of Spain's boundaries are water: the Mediterranean Sea on the south and east from Gibraltar to the French border, and the Atlantic Ocean on the northwest and southwest (in the south as the Golfo de Cádiz and in the north as the Bay of Biscay). Spain also shares land boundaries with France and Andorra along the Pyrenees in the northeast, with Portugal on the west, and with the small British overseas territory of Gibraltar near the southernmost tip. The affiliation of Gibraltar has continued to be a contentious issue between Spain and Britain.

The majority of Spain's peninsular region consists of highland plateaus rimmed and dissected by mountain ranges. There are sea-level coastal regions. The major lowland regions are the Andalusian Plain in the southwest, the Ebro Basin in the northeast, and the coastal plains. The coastal plains regions are narrow strips between the coastal mountains and the seas. They are broadest along the Golfo de Cádiz, where the coastal plain adjoins the Andalusian Plain, and along the southern and central eastern coasts. The narrowest coastal plain runs along the Bay of Biscay, where the Cordillera Cantábrica ends close to shore.

Spain also owns several important islands. These include the Balearic and the Canary Islands, the former located in the Mediterranean Sea and the latter in the Atlantic Ocean.

Spanish climate is a Mediterranean climate characterized by dry and warm summers. Only in the Pyrenees would one find harsher, colder climates.

Discussion Question

In what ways did Spanish geography affect Spanish history?

The History of Spain

Spain, originally inhabited by Celts, **Iberians**, and **Basques**, became a part of the Roman Empire in 206 B.C. In A.D. 412, the barbarians crossed the Pyrenees and ruled Spain, first in the name of the Roman emperor and then independently. In 711, the Muslims under Tariq entered Spain from Africa and within a few years completed the subjugation of the country. In 732, the Franks, led by **Charles Martel**, defeated the Muslims near Poitiers, thus preventing the further expansion of Islam in southern Europe. Internal dissension of Spanish Islam invited a steady Christian conquest from the north.

Aragon and Castile were the most important Spanish states from the 12th to the 15th century, consolidated by the marriage of Ferdinand II and Isabella I in 1469. In 1478, they established the Inquisition, to root out heresy and uncover Jews and Muslims who had not sincerely converted to Christianity. Torquemada, the most notorious of the grand inquisitors, epitomized the Inquisition's harshness and cruelty. The last Muslim stronghold, Granada, was captured in 1492. Roman Catholicism was established as the official state religion and most Jews (1492) and Muslims (1502) were expelled.

In the era of exploration, discovery, and colonization, Spain accumulated tremendous wealth and a vast colonial empire through the conquest of Mexico by several conquistadors. The Spanish monarchy became, for a time, the most powerful in the world. In 1588, **Philip II** sent his Armada to invade England, but its destruction paved the way for the English empire to emerge. Spain then sank rapidly to the status of a second-rate power, and it never again played a major role in European politics.

The Spanish Armada off the English coast by Cornelis Claesz van Wieringen, 1620–1625 (PD-Art).

Why? The decline began with the destruction of the **Armada**. Then it continued with defeats in expensive foreign wars. The War of the Spanish Succession (1701–1714) resulted in Spain's loss of Belgium, Luxembourg, Milan, Sardinia, and Naples. Its colonial empire in the Americas vanished, too, lost as a result of English invasions of Spanish territory. By the end of the 17th century, Spain was a second-rate European power.

Discussion Question

Why did Spain emerge, at the end of the 17th century, as a second-rate European power?

The Moors in Spain

Christian and Moor playing chess. From the *Book of Games* by King Alfonso X, 1283 (PD).

The Islamic African Moors ruled in most of Spain from A.D. 710 until the late 1400s. The Moors had a significant impact on European cultural, socio economic, and political institutions.

In 46 B.C., the Roman army entered West Africa where they encountered black Africans whom they called "Maures" from the Greek adjective *mauros*, meaning dark or black. The Moors were the African people who occupied northwest Africa, or present-day Morocco and Mauritania. These same African people became converts to Islam in the seventh century.

Spain was conquered not by Arabs, but by armies of Moors led by Arabs. The truth is that the conquest of the Iberian Peninsula, Spain, and Portugal was an African, not an Arab, conquest.

While Berlin, Paris, and London were barely more than large villages, the Moors built magnificent cities in Spain. Cordoba, in the tenth century, was much like a modern metropolis. The streets were paved and there were sidewalks for pedestrians. At night it was said that one could travel for ten miles by the light of lamps along a continuous strip of buildings. This was several hundred years before there was a paved street in Paris or a street lamp in London. The population of the city was more than one million. There were 200,000 homes, 800 public schools, a number of colleges and universities, and many royal places surrounded by beautiful gardens. Public baths numbered in the hundreds. This amenity was present at a time when cleanliness in Christian Europe was regarded as a sin.

Education was universal in **Moorish Spain**, available to the most humble, while 99 percent of Christian Europe was illiterate — not even the kings could read or write. In the 10th and 11th centuries, public libraries did not exist in Christian Europe, while Moorish Spain had more than 70, of which the one in Cordoba contained more than 600,000 manuscripts. There were more than 17 great universities in Moorish Spain, while Christian Europe had only two universities.

Gibraltar, at the tip of the Spanish peninsula, continued under Moorish dominion for more than seven centuries, but was taken by Spain for a period of 24 years in the early 14th century. It was not until 1472 that the Spaniards finally recaptured the Rock. It remained a Spanish possession until the beginning of the 18th century, when it fell to a combined Anglo-Dutch force. The Treaty of Utrecht ceded the Rock to the "Crown of Great Britain" in perpetuity.

Some scholars argue that the Moorish civilization enlightened Europe and brought it out of the dark ages to usher in the Renaissance period.[1]

Discussion Question

Who were the Moors, and what impact did they have on European history?

---

1 http://www.essortment.com/were-moors-spain-tarik-ibn-zeyad-63937.html.

Charles Martel

Charles Martel was the son of Pippin II, an early ruler of a Frankish kingdom (in what is now France). Martel (the name means "hammer") succeeded in reuniting the Frankish realm, eventually acquiring Aquitaine and Burgundy. He supported the missionary efforts of Saint Boniface and others like him in the hopes of consolidating his military victories. In 732, he achieved one of the most significant victories in early Europe at the Battle of Tours, which stemmed the tide of Muslim advancement from Spain into Frankish territory. This battle was arguably the most important battle of European history.

In 721, the Moors invaded France. They fought a battle with Charles Martel at Tours. It was on this ground that they were defeated and left Europe forever. In another generation they were driven from Spain as well. Charles Martel's victory at the Battle of Tours saved western Europe from the Muslim invasions and was a turning point in European history.

Although Martel was in practice king of the Franks, he never took the title. When he died, he divided his lands between his two legitimate sons: Pippin III (father of Charlemagne) and Carloman.

Charles Martel in battle.

Discussion Question

Martel was able to stop the Moors from conquering western Europe. What if the Moors were not stopped and they did indeed conquer western Europe?

A Historical Essay

Analyze the following 1840 essay concerning Roman Catholicism in Spain.

As to Roman Catholicism in Spain: we see thrown in its face its cruel intolerance, its puerile practices, its profane language, its blind submission, or rather the absolute slavery in which it places the believer with respect to the priest. There is much truth in these charges; but all of them are accounted for by an observance of history, and by a knowledge of the natural character and circumstances which have contributed to foster and strengthen religious sentiments in Spain.

The intolerance of Roman Catholicism in the Peninsula, carried to tyranny, and, frequently, even to ferocity, has been a consequence of the religious wars of six centuries — wars which the Goths sustained with unwearied perseverance against the Moors of Africa. The Goths had embraced the Christian religion with all the ardor and sincerity

Vazco Nunez de Balboa claims Pacific Ocean for Spain.

peculiar to a nation but recently delivered from a violent and savage state; for, although a generous race, they were ignorant and coarse in their habits. Their conversion to Christianity not only entirely modified their moral and religious notions, and introduced among them a greater elevation of feeling and an amplitude of ideas, but associated, intimately, the religious with the poetical sentiment, in such a manner that, in their eyes, every enemy of Christ was the enemy of the whole nation; difference of creed, therefore, according to their rude code of international laws, was a legitimate cause of war. In their eyes the unbeliever was a political enemy. Mere contact with an unbaptized person was considered a pollution. They believed that all who did not worship Christ were worshippers of the devil, and that Mahomet and the Moses of the Jews were nothing more than the representatives and agents of the fallen angel. Whilst those ideas were gaining ascendancy, the clergy, the only depositaries of letters and of knowledge, were rapidly possessing themselves of power, riches, and influence, and endeavoring to conserve and confirm those advantages by all possible means. Of those means none was so convenient, in times of continual violence and warfare, to the habits of a nation just emerging from a savage state, and which recognized no other merit than physical force and warlike valor, as that of encouraging those sanguinary and ruthless propensities, sanctifying them in some way or other by religious sentiment, and stirring up and inflaming the passions of the nation, with a view of exterminating all persons who did not acknowledge the jurisdiction of the church and the power of its ministers. Thus it happened that Christianity, from a very early period after its introduction to Spain, was deprived of that spirit of meekness, suavity, and tolerance, impressed upon it by its Divine Founder, and became possessed of a spirit of the most implacable resentment against every person who had not gone through the baptismal ceremony; and thus, also, it was that the religion of the country degenerated into a violent and revengeful sentiment, and took part in all the excesses and all the aberrations of the human passions; thus it was, in fine, that the national spirit became predisposed to the persecution of the Jews and Protestants, by means of that execrable tribunal, the Inquisition.

Immediately after the conquest of Granada, in which these cruel and destructive habits were openly displayed, an occasion presented itself for giving still greater scope to their exercise. The subjugation of the Continent discovered by Columbus was a war of religion no less than of ambition and of conquest. The mere circumstance that the aborigines of America had not received the light of the gospel was sufficient to induce Spaniards to regard them as so many enemies of God, and as slaves and worshippers of the devil. In the various forms of religious worship which prevailed in those vast territories were embodied certain principles which might, if carried out, have been of great service to the conquered nation. In nearly all of those forms, the unity of God was acknowledged, and also, in many of them, the necessity of a spiritual regeneration. In Mexico, and that part of the country now called Central America, was preserved a traditional remembrance of a severe chastisement inflicted by the Supreme Creator on rebellious humanity, but accompanied with a promise that the species should not be annihilated. . . . Many thousands of that unhappy people were exterminated, for they did not even understand the language in which doctrines the most sublime and marvelous in history were attempted to be enforced.[2]

Discussion Question

Offer evidence that the author is obviously anti-Roman Catholic.

---

2 Anonymous, *Roman Catholicism in Spain* (Edinburgh: Johnstone & Hunter, 1855), p. 10–14, http://www.gutenberg.org/files/29025/29025-h/29025-h.htm.

Chapter 27

The Middle Ages: A People Under Stress

First Thoughts

In A.D. 500, Europe was under great stress. Kings found themselves vast lands with declining populations and no government. Wolves, canines, and humans roamed the land. The first plague came through and promised even more havoc. The barbarians were no longer at the gates of Rome — they were in everyone's backyard! The Vikings destroyed whatever nascent trade there was. The Europeans fell further and further behind everyone else. When the Chinese thought about opening trade routes with Marco Polo they sincerely asked themselves, "What in the world do we want from the Europeans?" This was a nadir point in Western civilization. Yet there was reason for hope. Charlemagne brought stability. He drove out the Vikings and re-established the Church as a viable institution. The disintegration of central power, the rise of a landed aristocracy, and the increased reliance on feudalism marked this most amazing of millennia in world history.

Chapter Learning Objectives

Chapter 27 is an overview of the Middle Ages. Was it a "dark age"? We will understand why knights were indeed a key element of medieval feudalism. Next, we will examine the Charter of Liberties signed by King Henry I, second in importance only to the Magna Carta. Finally we will look more closely at medieval feudalism.

As a result of this chapter you should be able to:

1. Discuss whether or not the Middle Ages were the "Dark Ages" .
2. Understand why knights were a key element of medieval society.
3. Evaluate why the Charter of Liberties was uniquely a medieval European document.
4. Analyze what advantages and disadvantages feudalism brought to the medieval world.
5. Write a 300-word fictional narrative describing a Viking attack.

CONCEPTS

Teutonic Tribes

Franks

Code of Chivalry

Pages

Squires

Charter of Liberties

Barons

Peasants

Serfs

Norsemen

Viking Age

Middle Ages: The Dark Ages?

Medieval French manuscript illustration of the three classes of medieval society: those who prayed—the clergy, those who fought—the knights, and those who worked—the peasantry(Li Livres dou Sante, 13th century).

The so-called Middle Ages extended, more or less, from A.D. 500 to 1500. It has been called the "Dark Ages" because of the paucity of cultural offerings. However, such an appellation is at best ungenerous, at worst, inaccurate.

During the decline of the Roman Empire, the migrations of German barbarians — or **Teutonic tribes** — swept across the Rhine and the Danube into the Roman Empire. They indelibly changed the course of history. They ended the greatest and longest empire to date: the Roman Empire.

However, if the barbarians conquered the Romans, the Roman Christians conquered the barbarians. Most German tribes became Christian. The union of barbarian military ardor and religious spirit is a trademark of the Middle Ages.

As I have stated, the Middle Ages cover about one thousand years — from about A.D. 500 to about 1500. This millennium marked a transition from the ancient, dynasty regimes to the early modern nationalist era. It heralded a technological revolution. The Middle Ages began with chariots and horses and ended with caravel ships plying the Spanish Main. These changes came so gradually, however, that it was difficult to tell exactly when the Middle Ages began and when it ended. Some historians say that the Middle Ages began in A.D. 476, when the barbarian Odoacer overthrew the emperor Romulus Augustulus, ending the western Roman Empire. Other historians give the year 410, when Alaric, king of the Visigoths, sacked Rome. Still others say about 500 or even later. Historians say variously that the Middle Ages ended with the fall of Constantinople in 1453; with the discovery of America in 1492; or with the beginning of the Reformation in 1517.

The first dominant kingdom to emerge from the decentralization of the early Middle Ages was that of the Germanic tribe of the **Franks**. From 714 to 814, the Carolingian House of the Franks brought stability and progress to northern Europe. A large portion of the west enjoyed military and political security as well as religious unity. The most notable king in this era was Charlemagne.

The Frankish Empire did not endure, partly because it lacked the strong economic bases, namely world markets, that had supported the Romans. By the ninth century, Muslim conquests and commercial activity successfully competed with the Franks; inland trade declined sharply and urban life almost disappeared in the north. In addition, the Empire had no strong administrative machinery to compensate for the weak rulers who followed the dominating leadership of the emperor Charlemagne; the Empire disintegrated and if there was a dark age, it descended now, and would last until the Renaissance jarred the harassed European civilization out of its sleep.

Discussion Question

Were the Middle Ages the "Dark Ages"? Why or why not?

Knights

Perhaps no symbol of the Middle Ages is more pervasive than the image of knights, jousting, and ladies in distress. And, the truth is, there were a lot of armor-clad knights!

Knights were, first and foremost, soldiers — mean, lean, killing machines! They were the best warriors and soldiers in the world. Their armor made them practically immortal fighters.

The duty of a Middle Ages knight was to learn how to fight and so serve their liege lord according to the Code of Chivalry. The **Code of Chivalry** dictated that knights must be fearless in battle, but also cultured and generous in character. Knights must be ambidextrous and able to wield a two-handed sword, battle axe, mace, dagger, and lance. A knight guarded the castle and supported his liege lord. Indeed, chivalry also demanded that the knight guard the Church and, in general, the innocent and helpless.

To gain knighthood in the Middle Ages was a long and arduous task. It began when young noble boys were only 5 or 6 years of age. They were put under the tutelage of feudal scholars and were called **pages**. Next, by age 12 or 14, they became esquires (shortened to **squires**), and their soldier training began in earnest.

Every son of a nobleman either became a knight or joined the clergy. There was no other choice.

The armor of a Middle Ages knight was very pricey. It had to be tailor-made to fit the knight exactly or the knight ran the risk of an ill-fitting suit of armor hampering him in battle. A Middle Ages knight's armor was not merely a forged empty covering of flat metal. It was a complex series of garments, chain mail and iron plate.

Jousting tournaments were serious business. They were not merely shows to impress the ladies! Knights practiced their knightly skills at the tournaments. The joust roughly simulated a calvary charge that was often employed in medieval warfare. Truthfully, most knights lived and died by using the lance — very few actually engaged on foot, in hand-to-hand combat against the enemy. Various forms of combat were practiced at the tournaments including jousting, archery, and hand-to-hand combat using swords and other weapons.

If knights survived to old age, they were always generously rewarded by their liege lord and lived in handsome estate manors where they no doubt relived and exaggerated their exploits to their grandchildren!

> The knight was a peace officer, soldier, and diplomat.

Konrad von Limpurg as a knight being armed by his lady in the Codex Manesse (early 14th century).

Discussion Question

Why were knights a key element of medieval society?

Primary Source: The Charter of Liberties

The Charter of Liberties was written by English King Henry I on his crowning (August 5, 1100). It included many principles from the laws of Edward the Confessor and became the basis for the Magna Carta of 1215. This was also the first document in the world where the king bound himself with laws. Nothing like this appeared anywhere in the world in the Middle Ages! The Rule of Law reigned supreme in medieval Europe.

The Charter of Liberties

Miniature from illuminated Chronicle of Matthew Paris (1236–1259), from Cotton Claudius showing Henry I of England enthroned (PD).

Henry, king of the English, to Bishop Samson and Urso de Abetot and all his barons and faithful, both French and English, of Worcestershire, [copies were sent to all the shires] greetings.

1. Know that by the mercy of God and the common counsel of the barons of the whole kingdom of England I have been crowned king of said kingdom; and because the kingdom had been oppressed by unjust exactions, I, through fear of God and the love which I have toward you all, in the first place make the holy church of God free, so that I will neither sell nor put to farm, nor on the death of archbishop or bishop or abbot will I take anything from the church's demesne or from its men until the successor shall enter it. And I take away all the bad customs by which the kingdom of England was unjustly oppressed; which bad customs I here set down in part:

2. If any of my barons, earls, or others who hold of me shall have died, his heir shall not buy back his land as he used to do in the time of my brother, but he shall relieve it by a just and lawful relief. Likewise, also the men of my barons shall relieve their lands from their lords by a just and lawful relief.

3. And if any of my barons or other men should wish to give his daughter, sister, niece, or kinswoman in marriage, let him speak with me about it; but I will neither take anything from him for this permission nor prevent his giving her unless he should be minded to join her to my enemy. And if, upon the death of a baron or other of my men, a daughter is left as heir, I will give her with her land by the advice of my barons. And if, on the death of her husband, the wife is left and without children, she shall have her dowry and right of marriage, and I will not give her to a husband unless according to her will.

4. But if a wife be left with children, she shall indeed have her dowry and right of marriage so long as she shall keep her body lawfully, and I will not give her unless according to her will. And the guardian of the land and children shall be either the wife or another of the relatives who more justly ought to be. And I command that my barons restrain themselves similarly in dealing with the sons and daughters or wives of their men.

5. The common seigniorage, which has been taken through the cities and counties, but which was not taken in the time of King Edward I absolutely forbid henceforth. If any one, whether a moneyer or other, be taken with false money, let due justice be done for it.

6. I remit all pleas and all debts, which were owing to my brother, except my lawful fixed revenues and except those amounts, which had been agreed upon for the inheritances of others or for things which more justly concerned others. And if any one had pledged anything for his own inheritance, I remit it; also all reliefs which had been agreed upon for just inheritances.

7. And if any of my barons or men shall grow feeble, as he shall give or arrange to give his money, I grant that it be so given. But if, prevented by arms or sickness, he shall not have given or arranged to give his money, his wife, children, relatives, or lawful men shall distribute it for the good of his soul as shall seem best to them.

Bayeux Tapestry with King Edward the Confessor and Harold Godwinson at Winchester, 1070s (PD).

8. If any of my barons or men commit a crime, he shall not bind himself to a payment at the king's mercy as he has been doing in the time of my father or my brother; but he shall make amends according to the extent of the crime as he would have done before the time of my father in the time of my other predecessors. But if he be convicted of treachery or heinous crime, he shall make amends as is just.

9. I forgive all murders committed before the day I was crowned king; and those, which shall be committed in the future, shall be justly compensated according to the law of King Edward.

10. By the common consent of my barons I have kept in my hands forests as my father had them.

11. To those knights who render military service for their lands I grant of my own gift that the lands of their demesne ploughs be free from all payments and all labor, so that, having been released from so great a burden, they may equip themselves well with horses and arms and be fully prepared for my service and the defense of my kingdom.

Henry's royal seal, showing the king on horseback (r) and seated on his throne (l).

12. I impose a strict peace upon my whole kingdom and command that it be maintained henceforth.

13. I restore to you the law of King Edward with those amendments introduced into it by my father with the advice of his barons.

14. If any one, since the death of King William my brother, has taken anything belonging to me or to any one else, the whole is to be quickly restored without fine; but if any one keep anything of it, he upon whom it shall be found shall pay me a heavy fine.

Witnesses Maurice Bishop of London, and William Bishop-elect of Winchester, and Gerard Bishop of Hereford, and Earl Henry, and Earl Simon, and Walter Giffard, and Robert de Montfort, and Roger Bigot, and Eudo the Steward, and Robert, son of Hamo, and Robert Malet. At London when I was crowned. Farewell.[1]

Discussion Question

Nothing like this document appeared in Islamic countries, nor in the Far East. Why?

Feudalism

> During the period of history known as the Middle Ages, feudalism was the way order was maintained in the Medieval English world.

During the period of history known as the Middle Ages, feudalism was the way order was maintained in the Medieval English world. It was the law of the land. But it was much more. It was the basis by which the upper nobility class maintained control over the lower classes. It maintained the moral integrity and social fabric of the medieval world. Feudalism was a worldview that dominated Europe for more than one thousand years.

This rigid structure of government consisted of kings, lords, and peasants. Other crucial contributors to this structure were the leaders of the church. Feudalism emerged and remained for so long because order could not be maintained in large kingdoms. Kings, who were at the top of the feudal hierarchy, held their domain by what they claimed was "divine right," the right to rule granted by God and then passed on through heredity. They did not see themselves as "gods," but they did see themselves as "anointed by God."

However, there was no physical way for a king to govern all the land effectively, because there was no quick communication system, and it often took several days to travel from one part of the country to the other, even in a relatively small country such as England. The king needed a way to maintain control over his lands, even if indirectly. Feudalism, then, developed from the top down, not vice versa.

By necessity, a king created a contract with his **barons**. The barons were given a large portion of the king's land, known as fiefs or manors. In turn, they had to pay "homage and fealty" to the king. They did this by giving their support to the king at all times, governing the land that was given them, offering some tax revenue, and protecting their lord and his possessions and family with their lives if necessary.

However, the barons had the same problem the king had. The problem had merely been passed down the line. Because barons governed large tracts of land, they, too, had to divide their land. They made the same type of agreement the king made with their trusted knights.

---

1 http://www.fordham.edu/halsall/source/hcoronation.asp.

The class of lords solidified into an upper nobility class. They felt that they were much superior to the "common" **peasants**, or **serfs**. Medieval European society was as stratified and structured as any society or group in South Asia!

The church was immune to this process and more or less stood outside of it. Or it was more feudal than feudalism!

It was divided into spheres of influence, much like fiefs. Each "fief" was a diocese headed by a bishop. In addition to spiritual fiefs, many bishops were given real manors to govern. In this way, the church was firmly entrenched in the spiritual and practical lives of the medieval peasant. The church had a great influence over many of the common people.[2]

Discussion Question

What advantages and disadvantages did feudalism bring to the medieval world? Is there a societal structure that would have worked better?

Vikings

Late in the eighth century strange, long ships with one mast and a sail appeared along the coasts of England and continental Europe. They were obviously well-built ships with 50 or so men doubling up as oarsmen. They seemed to be volunteers — but after the ships came to shore, the oarsmen became fierce warriors!

Bright shields overlapped along the gunwale. The ships were pointed at each end so that they could go forward or backward without turning around. They had tall curved prows, usually carved in the shapes of dragons. They were truly awful things!

These dragon ships, as they were often called, usually appeared in a bay at about dawn. As soon as the ships reached the beach, tall blond men jumped out, shouting battle cries. Armed with swords and battle-axes, they attacked the sleeping villagers. They killed most of the villagers, captured some of the young people and many of the women, but took all of the loot that their ships could carry. Then they sailed away just as quickly.

These medieval terrorists were from Scandinavia — what is now Denmark, Norway, and Sweden. The people who lived there were **Norsemen**, or Vikings. Their expression

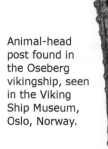

Animal-head post found in the Oseberg vikingship, seen in the Viking Ship Museum, Oslo, Norway.

2 http://history-world.org/middle_ages.htm.

for this type of warfare was to "go a-viking." *Vik* in Norse means "harbor" or "bay." The Vikings came to be the most feared raiders of their time and were the only Norsemen with whom most Europeans came in contact. Their name was given to the era that dated from about 740 to about 1050 — **the Viking Age**.

The ferocious Viking attacks destabilized the fragile political development and stability of Europe. Many of the functioning components in medieval society, like the church, suffered more heavily than many other sectors of European society. Despite the notoriety the Vikings attracted, within a century or two many converted to Christianity and some settled in the lands they had raided. At the same time, the Vikings were developing new outposts of settlement in Iceland, Greenland, North America, and the North Atlantic, and establishing kingdoms in Scandinavia along the lines of the European kingdoms to the south.[3]

Discussion Question

Write a 300-word fictional narrative describing a Viking attack. Write the narrative from the perspective of a young person in the community that was attacked.

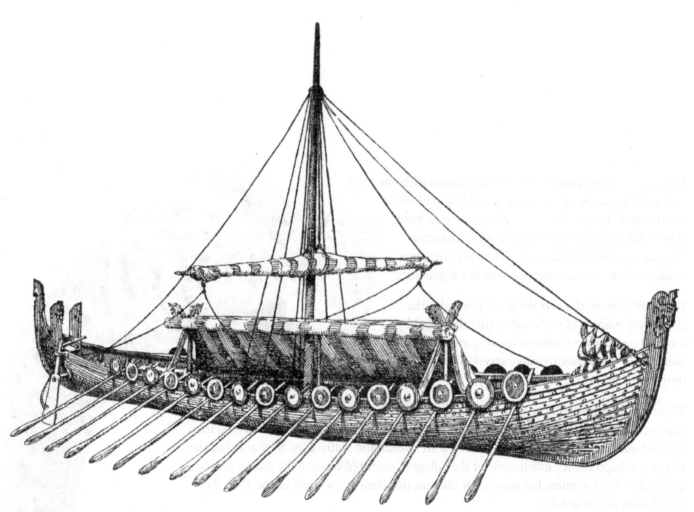

The Drakkar description of a Viking longship, circa 1870 (PD).

---

3 http://history-world.org/vikings.htm.

Chapter 28

Life in the Middle Ages: Emotive Legends

First Thoughts

More than one thousand years after the close of the Middle Ages, the Middle Ages continues to exercise a unique emotive power over western culture. We have a love/hate relationship with the Middle Ages. A governmental system we dislike is termed 'medieval,' yet we continue to be drawn to tales of King Arthur and Robin Hood. We consider the Middle Ages a ferocious time, yet the Middle Ages furnish some of our most enduring icons: the knight in shining armor, the damsel in distress, the pillaging and raping Vikings. We do not remember the Renaissance, for example, or the Enlightenment, but the Middle Ages somehow remain with us in a way that other historical periods do not.

Chapter Learning Objectives

We will explore medieval occupations and choose one for ourselves! Next, we will study the harsh life of medieval women. We will examine the rise of medieval, walled cities. Using a primary source, we will generalize about life in medieval Europe. Finally, we will create a synthesis of medieval life based upon an analysis of a world map.

As a result of this chapter you should be able to:

1. Explore medieval occupations.

2. Study the life of medieval women.

3. Analyze medieval cities.

4. Evaluate a primary source medieval document.

5. Synthesize an analysis of the medieval worldview by examining a medieval world map.

CONCEPTS

Cottage Industries

Wimple

Boroughs

Epic

Song of Roland

Poema del Cid

Divine Comedy

Canterbury Tales

Lesson 1

Medieval Occupations

Medieval life was hard, but mercifully short. Most people never saw their fortieth birthday. Plagues wiped out whole communities. Wars ravaged and destroyed. But medieval Europeans persevered.

They worked hard. Basically, society was divided into two classes — those who had status and those who did not. Nevertheless, while the lord and members of his entourage had status, they could not survive without the support of the peasants. The common peasant made possible the life of the gentry. No one was willing to admit it.

As villages developed alongside the castle, a professional class appeared. This class of professionals was mostly freemen, with no obligation to any feudal barons and knights. However, this class clearly relied on the gentry lords for their business. Indeed, the growth of many towns directly resulted from the introduction of commercial endeavors, which were necessary to sustain the castle or the manor, as well as the local populace. Urban centers, then, grew as support structures to castles and monasteries. This was exactly opposite from the way urban centers had emerged in other civilizations! In other civilizations, the agricultural food producers and the professional class had grown by supporting urban centers. Now, in medieval Europe, the rural gentry and farmers were sustained by the city!

A merchant class quickly developed to feed the commercial needs of feudal Europe. As Europe grew more stable, the merchants began to export goods, with limited success. European goods were generally inferior to Asia products. Also, no European nation had a substantial merchant marine that could transport products. This was to change, but only after the 16th century.

The following lists many occupations that prevailed during the Middle Ages. Their legacy is still very visible in modern surnames.

- Almoners: a worker who ensured the poor received alms

- Atilliator: a skilled castle worker who made crossbows

- Baliff: a worker in charge of allotting jobs to the peasants, building repair, and repair of tools used by the peasants

- Barber: someone who cut hair; also served as dentist, surgeon, and blood-letter

- Blacksmith: someone who forged and sharpened tools and weapons, beat out dents in armor, made hinges for doors and window grills. Also referred to as smiths.

- Bottler: a person in charge of the buttery or bottlery

- Butler: a worker who cared for the cellar and was in charge of large butts and little butts (bottles) of wine and beer. Under him a staff of people might consist of brewers, tapsters, cellarers, dispensers, cupbearers, and dapifers.

- Carder: someone who brushed cloth during its manufacture

Detail of two falconers circa 1240, from De arte venandi cum avibus. Biblioteca Apostolica Vaticana.

- Carpenter: a worker who built flooring, roofing, siege engines, furniture, paneling for rooms, and scaffolding for buildings

- Carters: workmen who brought wood and stone to the site of a castle under construction

- Castellan: a resident owner or person in charge of a castle (custodian)

- Chamberlain: a worker responsible for the great chamber and for the personal finances of the castellan

- Chaplain: someone who provided spirtual welfare for laborers and the castle garrison. The duties might also include supervising building operations, acting as a clerk and keeping accounts. He also tended to the chapel.

- Clerk: a person who checked material costs and wages, and kept accounts

- Constable: a person who took care (the governor or warden) of a castle in the absence of the owner. This was sometimes bestowed upon a great baron as an honor and some royal castles had hereditary constables.

- Cook: someone who roasted, broiled, and baked food in the fireplaces and ovens

- Cottars: a person who was the lowest of the peasantry; worked as swine-herds, prison guards, and did odd jobs

- Ditcher: a worker who dug moats, vaults, foundations, and mines

- Dyer: someone who dyed cloth in huge heated vats during its manufacture

- Ewerer: a worker who brought and heated water for the nobles

- Falconer: a highly skilled expert responsible for the care and training of hawks for the sport of falconry

- Fuller: a worker who shrinks and thickens cloth fibers through wetting and beating the material

- Glazier: a person who cut and shaped glass

- Gong Farmer: a latrine pit emptier

- Hayward: someone who tended the hedges

- Herald: a knights' assistant and an expert advisor on heraldry

- Keeper of the Wardrobe: a person in charge of the tailors and laundresses

- Knight: a professional soldier. This was achieved only after long and arduous training that began in infancy.

- Laird: a minor baron or small landlord

- Marshal: an officer in charge of a household's horses, carts, wagons, and containers. His staff included farriers, grooms, carters, smiths, and clerks. He also oversaw the transporting of goods.

- Master Mason: a person responsible for designing and overseeing the building of a structure

Miniature of Richard of Wallingford, Abbot of St. Albans, who was a mathematician and inventor of a mechanical astronomical clock (14th century).

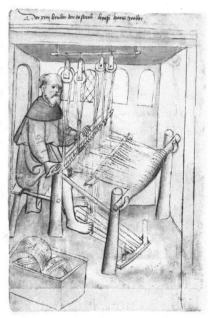

Weaver from Nuremberg Chronicles, c. 1425.

- Messengers: servants of the lord who carried receipts, letters, and commodities

- Miner: a skilled professional who dug tunnels for the purpose of undermining a castle

- Minstrels: part of the castle staff who provided entertainment in the form of singing and playing musical instruments

- Porter: someone who took care of the doors (janitor), particularly the main entrance. Responsible for the guardrooms. This person also insured that no one entered or left the castle without permission. Also known as the door-ward.

- Reeve: a person who supervised the work on the lord's property. He checked that everyone began and stopped work on time, and insured nothing was stolen. Senior officer of a borough.

- Sapper: an unskilled person who dug a mine or approach tunnel

- Scullions: someone responsible for washing and cleaning in the kitchen

- Shearmen: a person who trimmed the cloth during its manufacture

- Shoemaker: a craftsman who made shoes. Known also as Cordwainers.

- Spinster: a name given to a woman who earned her living spinning yarn. Later this was expanded and any unmarried woman was called a spinster.

- Steward: a person who took care of the estate and domestic administration. Supervised the household and events in the great hall. Also referred to as a seneschal.

- Squire: a title someone attained at the age of 14 while training as a knight. He would be assigned to a knight to carry and care for the weapons and horse.

- Watchman: an official at the castle responsible for security. Assisted by lookouts (the garrison).

- Weaver: someone who cleaned and compacted cloth, in association with the walker and fuller

- Woodworkers: tradesmen called board-hewers who worked in the forest, producing joists and beams[1]

Discussion Question

If you had to choose one medieval occupation, which of the above would you choose? Why?

---

1 http://hkcarms.tripod.com/occ.html.

Medieval Women

Medieval women had absolutely no status; however, medieval women had a lot of responsibility and were vital to medieval society. Many toiled alongside their families in the fields, some were employed in workshops, and some were even tradeswomen. Women would have successful **cottage industries** in their homes. They would run home laundries and sewing shops, sometimes hiring other women to work as extra help. Women sometimes had the responsibility of running large estates due to the death of a husband. They often, informally, settled local disputes and arranged estate finances.

Unmarried women holding lands were powerful and had the same rights as men. However, when a woman married, she forfeited her lands and rights to her husband. Upon her husband's death, she was entitled to a third of the lands so that she might support herself.

Some unmarried women entered convents. This afforded them the chance to obtain an education or lead a devout life. Many nuns cared for the sick and were also much-loved figures in the community.

Young single women often wore their hair loose, but once married almost all medieval women wore a linen **wimple** (wrap up) to cover their hair. This was a sign of modesty. Other items worn by medieval women included hairpins, prayer beads, leather purses, woolen knee stockings, and leather shoes.

Anna Jagiellon, Queen regnant of Poland, wearing a wimple, c. 1595 (PD).

Discussion Question

Contrast medieval European women with women in Mesopotamia, Greece, India, and China, places you have studied earlier this year.

East Germanic woman's brooch or pin, goldfoil on silver with inlaid garnet, glass, and enamel, from the Untersiebenbrunn grave, early 5th century.

Paris, France

Medieval roots can be found in all of today's major European cities. When Julius Caesar conquered western Europe, there were few places that could have been called cities. Paris was the exception. It was the earliest and probably the largest of the early cities. By the 13th century, cities were flourishing along the coast but not in the interior. Viking conquests were quelled by this time and urban centers sprang up on the coast. Antwerp, Marseille, and Calais all emerged at this time. Paris, though, was the exception. It was an interior river town.

Viking invasions were a major factor in the development of cities during the early Middle Ages. To protect themselves from marauding Vikings, villages erected walls; this led to the great medieval walled cities. These walled cities became known as "bourgs," "burghs," and later, **boroughs**. Inhabitants were known as bourgeois. By the mid-900s, these fortified towns filled the European landscape from the Mediterranean as far north as Hamburg, Germany.

In the 11th and 12th centuries, the borough of Paris in particular experienced a renaissance.

The importance of the supply route provided by the Seine River gave power to the commercial sector of the city. At the same time, Paris was far enough from French enemies — England, in particular — that it could enjoy some peaceful prosperity.

Discussion Question

Why were European cities fortified?

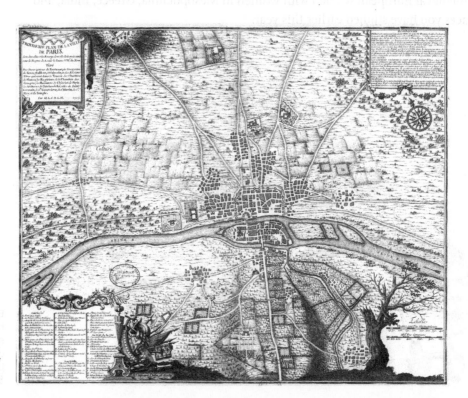

Third plan of the city of Paris, extent and towns with which it was surrounded in the reign of Louis VII, 1705 (PD).

Primary Source Material

The Abbot of Battle's Court at Brithwaltham

Although the primary function of a manor court was to hear cases involving property and inter-tenant disputes, manorial court rolls are especially useful to social historians who wish to study daily medieval life.

Lawday. Court of Brightwaltham holden on Monday next after Ascension Day in the twenty-first year of King Edward (AD 1293)

The tithingman of Conholt with his whole tithing present that all is well save that William of Mescombe has stopped up a . . . [the word is indecipherable in the manuscript, but Maitland thinks it is a water-course] wrongfully. Therefore he is in mercy (12 d.). Also they say that Edith of Upton has cut down trees in the enclosure and the seisin of the lord contrary to a prohibition, and they say that she has no property and has fled into foreign parts, (amercement, 12 d.).

Adam Scot is made tithingman and sworn to a faithful exercize of his office.

Gate House at the Battle Abbey.

(b) John son of Hugh Poleyn enters on the land which Randolph Tailor held saving the right of everyone and gives for entry-money 4 marks and will pay 1 mark at Michaelmas in the twenty-second year of King Edward, 1 mark at Christmas next following, 1 mark at Easter, and 1 mark at Mechaelmas next following, and for the due making of all these payments the said Hugh Poleyn finds sureties, to wit, Adam Scot, John Gosselyn, William of Mescombe, Jhn Gyote. And because the said John is a minor the wardship of the said lands and tenements is delivered to his father the said Hugh Poleyn until he be of full age, on the terms of his performing the services due and accustomed for the same. Also there is granted to teh said Hugh the crop now growing on the sown land, and the heriot due on this entry, for a half-mark payable at Michaelmas next on the security of the above-named sureties.

(a) Hugh Poleyn gives the lord 2 s. that he may have the judgment of the court as to his right in a certain tenement in Upton which J. son of Randolph Tailor claims as his right. And upon this the whole township of Brightwaltham sworn along with the whole township of Conholt say upon their oath that Hugh Poleyn has better right to hold the said tenement than anyone else has, and that he is the next heir by right of blood.

(The Conholt case as to the tenure of Edith wife of Robert Tailor according to the inquest made by the jurors. One Alan Poleyn held a tenement in Conholt upon servile terms and had a wife Cristina by name. The said Alan died when Richard was the farmer [of the manor]. Thereupon came the friends of the said Cristina and procured for her a part of the land by way of dower making a false suggestion and as though [the land] were of free condition, and this was to the great prejudice of the lord Abbot. Upon this came one Richard Aleyn and espoused the said Cristina and begot upon her one Randolph. Then Richard died, and the said Cristina of her own motion enfeoffed Randolph her son of the said tenement. Then Cristina died, and Randolph being in seisin of the said tenement espoused Edith the present demandant; and after Randolph's death Edith married Robert Tailor. Now you can see and give your counsel about the right of the said Edith. And know this, that if I had at hand the court-rolls of the time when William of Lewes [was steward] I could certify the facts and I could show you many strange things that were improvidently done.)

The whole tithing of Hartley comes as it ought to come and presents that all is well.

The tithingman of Brightwaltham with his whole tithing present that all is well, save that William of Westwood has made default. They say also that John son of Richard at Cross dwells at Bromham and is not in a tithing. Therefore his father is ordered to produce him at the next court. They say also that Henry Smith struck Sir Robert the chaplain and drew blood and then to conceal his fault raised the hue. Therefore he is in mercy; pledges, John Atgreen, Richard Young and Thomas Smith. They also present that Cristina widow of Ralph Smith has received [a guest] contrary to the assize. Therefore she is in mercy, pledge, Richard Smoker.

Agnes Maud's daughter at the instance of her friends gives the lord 12 d. for permission to marry; she gives no more because she is very poor.

Court of Brightwaltham holden on Wednesday next before the feast of S. Peter at Chains in the twenty-second year of King Edward [Maitland thinks it is the 21st year of Edward's reign, making this A.D. 1294]

Prohibition is made that none of the lord's tenants upon pain of a half-mark do in anywise give any sheaves in the fields to anyone of the township or to any stranger.

Inquest made by the steward on Tuesday the morrow of S. Matthew as to the abduction of sheep and other trespasses committed in the manor of Brightwaltham in the said year: by which inquest it is found that John Sket bought from the reeve three sheep and when a price had been agreed on between them the said John pastured the said sheep in the lord's pasture. Therefore he is in mercy. Pledges, John Parlefrens and Richard Young; [amercement,] 40 d.

Richard Fette in mercy for receiving sheaves in autumn upon the delivery of the reeve against the prohibition of the steward; pledge, the whole .

And the jurors [of the said inquest] further say that the sheep were not abducted nor brought back again by any malice, but owing to the negligence of William Wachel the shepherd many sheep were wandering about the country hither and thither; and therefore the said [William] is inmercy; pledge, the whole.

They say that John Atgreen, John of Southwood, Thomas Smith and Richard Young are the best and most competent men of the whole for the purpose of filling and executing the office of reeve. And of these the steward has chosen Thomas Smith for the office. Afterwards the said Thomas made fine that he might be absolved from the office of reeve and gives the lord 40 s.

They say also that John surnamed Lord is a good man needful to the lord for the keeping of the ewes. And the whole undertook for him that he shall keep them well and truly and with all diligence and will answer for him. They say also that John son of John Atgreen is needful to the lord for keeping the lord's muttons; and he is admitted [to the office] and the whole undertakes for him. They say also that Thomas Bagge is needful for holding one plough and Richard Uhtred for driving it. As to the other teams whether of oxen or of horses, they say that it is well that those men should stay with the lord who were wiht him in the past year.[2]

Discussion Question

Pretend that you are a social historian. Based on this document alone, what can you say about medieval life?

Medieval Art

It is true that most medieval men and women did not have the energy or time to devote to art. However, that does not mean that it was absent. For one thing, monks copied Bibles to be given to other churches. Without a printing press, this was the only way a new church could receive the written Word of God. Monks, however, did not merely copy words. They often decorated the margins!

Sometimes created in fatigue or in boredom, the illustrations were trite, even humorous. Other times, they were absolutely beautiful!

During the entire Middle Ages, Latin served as an international means of communication. This common tongue provided much of the cohesion of the Middle Ages, for virtually all the crucial communications of the Church, governments, and schools were in Latin. Thus, in many ways, Europe was more united in the Middle Ages than it was to be united again until the modern era!

A decorated incipit page
c. 1637–1638 (PD).

2 http://www.fordham.edu/halsall/seth/court-brightwaltham.asp.

A rising tide of literature in the vernacular, or common, tongues began to appear by the 12th century, with the **epic** as the earliest form. The greatest of the French epics was the **Song of Roland**, which describes the valiant deeds and death of this hero in the Pyrenees while defending the rear of Charlemagne's army.[3] Likewise, the great Spanish epic, the **Poema del Cid** was an epic celebration of the departure of the Moorish forces from Spain. Dante Alighieri wrote the **Divine Comedy** in his own language, Italian. It was the first major literary work to be written in this way. Finally, in the **Canterbury Tales**, Geoffrey Chaucer (c. 1343–1400), one of the greatest figures in medieval literature, wrote an earthy compilation of short stories about contemporary English life, customs, and thought.

Discussion Question

In the midst of such traumatic change, the arts flourished in medieval Europe. Why?

Ellesmere manuscript of *Canterbury Tales*; the first page of Knight's Tale, 14th century (PD).

---

3 http://www.sparknotes.com/lit/songofroland/.

Chapter 29

Life in the Middle Ages: Complexity

First thoughts

Most contemporaries romanticize the Middle Ages as a time when things were simpler, but in reality, medieval society was highly complex. Modern societies are structured by documents and constitutions, and many of their pivotal relationships are defined by abstract institutions like governments and corporations. In the Middle Ages, society was shaped by personal relationships like kinship and patronage. These structures were perpetuated not by abstract institutions, but by the personal ties of inheritance. The force of tradition gave these personal relationships some stability, but they were never static. Relationships changed over time in response to changing circumstances, and the actual social structure at any given place and time was an intricate network reflecting a whole history of personal relationships. One peasant might enjoy more rights than his neighbor because one of his forebears had been particularly assertive in his relationship to the manor lord. A baron might be required to provide extra knights for the king's service because his great-grandfather had been a poor negotiator.[1]

Chapter Learning Objectives

We will begin by looking at the typical fare of a medieval family. Next we will look at medieval medicine. We will look at the rise of courtly love in medieval society. We will end by comparing the life of a baron to a peasant.

As a result of this chapter you should be able to:

1. Describe what a typical medieval family would eat for breakfast, lunch, and dinner.
2. Discuss what medieval remedies would be proposed to cure bronchitis.
3. Explain what caused the rise of courtly love in medieval society.
4. Describe a typical day in a castle.
5. Contrast the life of a peasant to a baron.

1   Jeffrey L. Singman, *Daily Life in Medieval Europe* (Westport, CT: Greenwood Press, 1999).

CONCEPTS

Pottage

Humors

Courtly Love

Food and Famine

Preparing and serving cheese; 14th century (PD).

Medieval foods and diets depended much on the class of the individual. For those living in the castle, there might be capons, geese, or chickens. They might also eat beef, bacon, and lamb, and those living close to water may have regularly dined on salmon, herring, eels, and other freshwater fish. Fish would either be sold fresh or smoked and salted. Wealthy society could afford large quantities of milled flour and other meals made from grain. Dairy products such as cheese and butter could be seen on the manor table. In any event, wealthy medieval families inevitably ate a protein meat-rich meal. Vegetables were absent or eaten in small quantities. Most medieval cooks found them to be indelectable, if not downright unhealthy!

Medieval peasants, on the other hand, ate mostly bread. It was their main staple. The best harvested wheat went exclusively to the market or to the castle. Peasant breads were made from barley and rye, baked into dark heavy loaves. No doubt, bad breath was the standard fare for most medieval peasants!

Rich gentry drank wine; peasants drank beer. No one wanted to drink water — it was generally unhealthy and no one knew to boil it first.

Pottage, a thick soup, was often favored over bread for any meal, because it required grains that were not very valuable. Pottage is very similar to what my Scottish in-laws call "mince," which is ground meat cooked in its juices, with carrots and other vegetables added. This is poured over potatoes or bread.

A group of travelers sharing a simple meal of bread and drink; 14th century.

Soups were popular with all. Onions, cabbage, garlic, nuts, berries, leeks, spinach, parsley, and carrots were some of the foods that were combined to make thick soup. Fortunate families might have added salt pork or fatty bacon for flavor and protein. Ironically, after the Black Death, food was abundantly available for all.

Medieval diets lacked vitamins A, C, and D, and were not high in calories, making the regular drinking of beer a necessity for most. The only positive part of these diets was that they were somewhat "heart-smart" — low in fat and high in fiber.

In spite of long periods of relative surpluses, medieval societies always feared famines.

Adequate quantities did not assure nutritious meals. Malnutrition had always been present, but few actually died. But the cold and wet springs and summers of 1315–1317 decimated crops, and all classes of society suffered. People resorted to eating their horses and pets. There were even rumors of cannibalism.

Discussion Question

What would a typical medieval family eat for breakfast, lunch, and dinner?

Health

There was no health industry in medieval Europe. No one thought about it. Health was controlled by the stars, and affliction was a sign of impurity of the soul — a curse from God. Certainly health could not be tied to diet.

Disease was a constant concern, as was infection from injuries. Barbers doubled as surgeons, and a good bleeding was often the cure prescribed. Medieval doctors practiced medicinal practices championed by the Greeks. For physicians, it was an unquestioned fact that the healthy human body consisted of four different substances or **humors**. Sickness was nothing more than an imbalance of these humors.

Hospitals existed but superstition remained, and medieval science was undoubtedly primitive. Medieval doctors did more witch-doctoring than anything else. Doctors often consulted with **astrology** and **numerology**. Constellations and the alignment of the planets were assumed to have direct influence on the human body.

A dentist with silver forceps and a necklace of large teeth, extracting the tooth of a seated man. c. 1360–1375 (PD).

Physicians were recognized as a professional class in 1215 and soon began to form their own **guilds**. Guilds were professional organizations formed to facilitate communication and fellowship. They were not labor unions.

Medical textbooks in the Middle Ages were rare. These writings wound their way from the Middle East to Spain. Arabic anatomical and pharmaceutical knowledge, far greater in scope than that of medieval Europe's learning, was quickly assimilated. However, practical anatomy, viewed best through dissection of corpses, was rarely studied.

As intimated, bleeding and the use of leeches to draw "bad blood" from the patient were the preferred treatments. Some surgeries were performed without the benefit of anesthetics to cure patients of hernias and cataracts, or for the removal of gallstones.

When doctors' treatments failed, the church was often called to exorcise demons and say prayers and incantations over the patient.

> Medieval medicine was virtually the same as it was practiced by the Greeks two thousand years before.

Mental illness was not uncommon. Injuries received to babies during the birthing process often led to brain trauma. Often women delivered their babies by standing and the infants would fall and hurt themselves. Little could be done for these people, but there were no institutions for them and many were accepted into society. Others, however, would have crosses shaved into the backs of their heads, or be tied to pews in the church in hopes that mass would bring them relief.

Leprosy remained the most feared disease of the Middle Ages, until the Black Death, that is. This disease was rampant throughout western Europe, and leper colonies could be found everywhere. In France alone, from the 11th to 13th centuries, there were two thousand such colonies.[2]

Discussion Question

What medieval remedies would be proposed to cure bronchitis?

---

2 http://www.omnibusol.com/medieval.html.

Lesson 3

Romance

Romantic stories of courtly love were spread throughout medieval Europe by troubadours and minstrels.

Women in the Middle Ages were, quite literally, property. Of course, most men honored their wives and daughters, but in fact women had very few rights.

While medieval country marriages were often the result of mutual affection — after all, virtually nothing was to be gained anyway between a poor miller's daughter and a farmer — marriage among the gentry was more a business transaction than anything else.

Something very strange emerged, however: **courtly love**. Among knights and gentry, which were hungry for intrigue, romance and love became an imagined vocation. Courtly love became the subject of some of the most famous medieval poems and early paintings.

Woodcut of St. George slaying the dragon from *Life of Saint George*, 1515 (PD).

A knight would choose a lady as the object of his unrequited love. For a knight, this could mean any lady other than his wife. According to the "rules" of courtly love, a knight had to promise to be ardent, secretive, and above all, courteous. No matter how long the love was unrequited, a knight had to be true. He could never violate the honor of the lady.

Rules evolved — such as, chosen women given a ring should wear it "on the little finger of their left hand, and always keep the stone hidden inside her hand." When writing letters, they refrained from using their proper names so their identities could never be revealed.

With good reason, church leaders publicly opposed courtly love, fearing that knights would succumb to temptation. However, some of the best songs of courtly love were being written by monks and nuns!

A double standard existed within these rituals as well, for where knights might boast of their chosen lady, women, especially those who were married, had to be quite cautious who learned of this relationship. Married women, while they might be the objects of this affection, could not encourage it in anyway or return even the slightest bit of affection in return.

Romantic stories of courtly love were spread throughout medieval Europe by troubadours and minstrels. The language used by this new poetry was intended to be sung, played on musical instruments brought back from the crusades. This was a new style of expressive writing.

Courtly love rituals, in one form or another, remain with us today.[3]

Discussion Question

What caused the rise of courtly love in medieval society?

_____
3 http://www.medieval-life.net/history_main.htm.

Life in a Medieval Castle

Supported by the brawn and taxes of the peasants, and with no reason whatsoever to work, the feudal baron and his wife had a comfortable life.

Many barons lived in castles. Some of these, with their great outer walls and courtyard buildings, covered perhaps 15 acres and were built for defensive warfare.

An early 13th-century drawing by Matthew Paris showing contemporary warfare, including the use of castles, crossbowmen, and mounted knights.

Ironically, though, castles were generally far more uncomfortable than the most modest thatched room dwellings enjoyed by peasants. The winters were dreary and cold. Even in summer, dampness clung to the stone rooms, and the lord and his retinue spent as much time as possible outside of the castle! At dawn, the watchman blew a blast on his bugle to awaken the castle. After a Spartan breakfast of bread and wine or beer, the nobles attended mass in the castle chapel.

The lord then would hold court, functioning as judge, advocate, general, and counselor for all his fiefdom.

The lady of the castle inspected the work of her large staff of servants. She saw that her spinners, weavers, and embroiderers furnished clothes for the castle, and rich vestments for the clergy. She and her ladies also helped to train the pages.

Sometime between 9 a.m. and noon, a trumpet summoned the lord's household to the great hall for what they called dinner and what we would call lunch. They gustily ate huge quantities of rich food. In winter, the ill-preserved meat smacked fierily of East Indian spices, bought at enormous cost to hide the rank taste. Great, flat pieces of bread called trenchers served as plates and, after the meal, were flung to the dogs around the table or given to the poor. Huge pies, or pasties, filled with several kinds of fowl or fish, were relished. Metal or wood cups or leather "jacks" held cider, beer, or wine. Coffee and tea were not used in Europe until after the Middle Ages.

Tournaments during this time were serious business. Barons would wager bets on the outcome. They were also occasion to weave intrigue and to nurture networking among competing or friendly barons in the kingdom.

Bodiam Castle, East Sussex, England; a 14th century castle (CCCA-SA3.0).

Finally, unless it was a very special affair, supper was served soon after dark. Lack of lighting made this difficult, so it was a simple affair. Shortly after sunset, most of the household was in bed and fast asleep.[4]

Discussion Question

Describe a typical day in a castle.

---

4 http://history-world.org/castle_life.htm.

Lesson 5

Peasant Life

About 90 percent of the people were peasants — farmers or village laborers. Only a few of these were freemen — peasants who were not bound to a lord and who paid only a fixed rent for their land.

Most peasants lived in villages in the shadow of the castle. A peasant village housed perhaps 10 to 60 families. Each family lived in a dark, dank hut made of wood or wicker daubed with mud and thatched with straw or rushes. Layers of straw or reeds covered the floor, fouled by the pigs, chickens, and other animals housed with the family. The one bed was a pile of dried leaves or straw. All slept in their rough garb, with skins of animals for cover. Whole families shared one bed.

Peasant Dance in a Tavern, attributed to Marten van Cleve, 1581 (PD-Art).

A cooking fire of peat or wood burned drearily day and night in a clearing on the dirt floor. The smoke seeped out through a hole in the roof or the open half of a two-piece door. Nobody built chimneys.

The only furniture was a plank table on trestles, a few stools, perhaps a chest, and a loom for the women to make their own cloth. Every hut had a vegetable patch.

All the peasants worked to support their lord. They gave about half their time to work in his fields, cut timber, haul water, spin and weave, repair his buildings, and wait upon his household. In war, the men had to fight at his side. Besides labor, peasants had to pay taxes to their lord in money or produce. They had to give a tithe to the church — every tenth egg, sheaf of wheat, lamb, chicken, and all other animals.

Life was hard, but there were respites. Because of the many holidays, or holy days, in the Middle Ages, peasants actually labored only about 260 days a year. They spent their holidays in church festivals, journeying to mystery or miracle plays, or engaging in wrestling, bowling, cockfights, apple bobs, or dancing.

Discussion Question

Discuss the life of a peasant.

Chapter 30

Age of Charlemagne: A Man Creates an Era

First Thoughts

By the sword and the cross, Charlemagne (Charles the Great) became master of western Europe. It was falling into decay when Charlemagne became joint king of the Franks in 768. Except in the monasteries, people had all but forgotten education and the arts. Boldly, Charlemagne conquered barbarians and kings alike. By restoring the roots of learning and order, he preserved many political rights and revived culture. Charlemagne's grandfather was Charles Martel, the warrior who crushed the Saracens. Charlemagne was the elder son of Bertrade ("Bertha Greatfoot") and Pepin the Short, first "mayor of the palace," to become king of the Franks. Although schools had almost disappeared in the eighth century, historians believe that Bertrade gave young Charles some education and that he learned to read. His devotion to the Church motivated him throughout life.

Chapter Learning Objectives

We begin by talking about Charlemagne in general, his contributions, and triumph, in medieval history. We grasp the importance of the Holy Roman Empire and its entrance on the world stage. Charlemagne greatly improved education in his empire. We examine what that looked like. Next, we are blessed with a reading of Charlemagne's friend and advisor Eihnard's description of Charlemagne's walk with God, and we'll decide if it is a reliable source.

As a result of this chapter you should be able to:

1. Summarize some of the accomplishments of the reign of Charlemagne.
2. Discuss why the Holy Roman Empire was created and what advantages and potential problems it brought.
3. Compare medieval education to earlier Greek and Roman education.
4. Describe Charlemagne's Christian life, based on Einhard's description of Charlemagne.
5. Understand what advantages primary sources bring to historical studies.
6. Evaluate if Einhard is a reliable source.

CONCEPTS

Carolingians

Frankish Kingdom

Charlemagne

Einhard

Pope Leo III

Holy Roman Empire

Eusebius

Overview

Central Europe at the beginning of the Middle Ages was an inhospitable place. Onto this chaotic stage walked the **Carolingians**. The main political power was the **Frankish Kingdom,** which was more of a compilation of warring warlords than a nation.

Window of the Cathedral Basilica of Our Lady of the Annunciation of Moulins from the late 15th century.

The first Carolingian was Charles Martel. He stopped the Islamic invasion of Europe at the Battle of Tours. Pepin the Short was Martel's son. He was a competent king and made ample progress in consolidating royal power. However, it was Charles, the son of Pepin the Short, later known as **Charlemagne** (776–814), who really created a nation that would last for more than one thousand years.

Einhard, Charlemagne's friend, wrote an account of the life of Charlemagne which gives much insight to this great leader. Einhard not only told about the lifelong accomplishments of his friend, but also gave a physical description and a feel for his personality.

When Pepin the Short died, he foolishly divided his kingdom between his two sons. By the time the brothers took over the kingdom, it was fast declining into decay. The Franks were falling back into their barbarian ways, neglecting their education and religion, the German Saxons were still pagans, and the Roman Catholic Church was trying to regain land confiscated by Italy. Charlemagne had many challenges.

Charlemagne was a smart and ambitious king, aggressive and ruthless. He was not a great military tactician, but he was a stubborn campaigner and was often able to wear the enemy down through sheer force. Indeed, one of his more important attributes was his physical energy.

During his reign he sent out more than 50 military expeditions. He rode as commander at the head of at least half of them. He moved his armies over wide reaches of country with unbelievable speed, but every move was planned in advance.

Schools had all but disappeared in the eighth century under the rule of Charles Martel, Charlemagne's grandfather. Charlemagne, in spite of his illiteracy, valued education and promoted it through his reign. Most of all, though, Charlemagne was a very committed Christian believer. His devotion to the church became the great driving force of his remarkable life.

Discussion Question

Summarize some of the accomplishments of the reign of Charlemagne.

The Holy Roman Empire

The Roman Catholic Church during the Middle Ages had no significant army, so it relied on secular rulers to protect it. For instance, in 799, for the third time in half a century, **Pope Leo III** was in need of help from the Frankish king. After being physically attacked by his enemies in the streets of Rome, Pope Leo III made his way through the Alps to visit Charlemagne at Paderborn.

Charlemagne traveled to Rome in 800 to support the pope. In a ceremony in St. Peter's on Christmas Day, Leo was due to anoint Charlemagne's son as his heir. But in a stirring ceremony, Pope Leo III crowned Charlemagne as the new Roman emperor, the king of the **Holy Roman Empire**.

Charlemagne reluctantly accepted the honor. Charlemagne knew that the legal emperor was undoubtedly in Byzantium, Constantinople. Nevertheless, this public alliance between the pope and the ruler of a confederation of Germanic tribes now reflected the reality of political power in the West. And it launched the **concept** of the new Holy Roman Empire, which would play an important role throughout the Middle Ages.

The confusion between ecclesiological and secular authority would continue for several centuries, but at that time, the Holy Roman Empire brought much needed stability and peace to central Europe.[1]

Discussion Question

Why was the Holy Roman Empire created, and what advantages and potential problems did it bring?

The Imperial Crown of Western Germany from the second half of the 10th century. The cross is an addition from the early 11th century; the arch dates from the reign of Emperor Conrad II (ruled 1024–1039); the red velvet cap is from the 18th century. Made of gold, cloisonné enamel, precious stones, and pearls.

1 http://www.historyworld.net/wrldhis/PlainTextHistories.asp?historyid=aa35.

Lesson 3

Education

Of course in all cultures, in all times, home schooling was practiced, especially in the very poor families where no other kind of education was affordable, and in the very rich families, where any kind of education could be bought.

One significant reform measure that Charlemagne instituted was improvements in education.

At the end of the Roman Empire, the invading Germanic tribes that moved into the civilized world of the West and all but destroyed ancient culture provided virtually no formal education for their young. In the early Middle Ages, the elaborate Roman school system had disappeared. Only the Church remained as a formal educating institution in western society.

Of course in all cultures, in all times, home schooling was practiced, especially in the very poor families where no other kind of education was affordable, and in the very rich families, where any kind of education could be bought. The difference was that in poor families, the mother typically taught the students. In rich families, famous tutors were hired — Aristotle, for instance, tutored Alexander the Great.

Coronation of Charlemagne.

Medieval cathedral, monastic, and palace schools were operated by the clergy in parts of western Europe. Most students were future or present members of the clergy, though a few lay students were trained to be clerks. Unlike Greek and Roman schools, which sought to prepare men (but not women) for public service, church schools had a decidedly spiritual agenda. The schools taught students to read Latin so they could copy and thereby preserve and perpetuate the writings of the church fathers. Students learned the rudiments of mathematics so they could calculate the dates of religious festivals, and they practiced singing so they could take part in church services.

Unlike the Greeks, who considered physical health a part of education, the church had no physical component of their education at all.

Schools were ungraded — a 6-year-old and a 16-year-old (or an adult for that matter) sat side by side in the same classroom.

Historian Robert Guisepi argues that "medieval education can be understood better if one realizes that for thousands of years childhood, as it is known today, literally did not exist. No psychological distinction was made between child and adult. The medieval school was not really intended for children. Rather, it was a kind of vocational school for clerks and clergymen. A 7-year-old in the Middle Ages became an integral part of the adult world, absorbing adult knowledge and doing a man's work as best he could during what today would be the middle years of elementary education. It was not until the 18th century that childhood was recognized; not until the 20th that it began to be understood."[2]

Discussion Question

Compare medieval education to earlier Greek and Roman education. Which would you prefer? Why?

2 http://history-world.org/history_of_education.htm.

Primary Source: The Life of Charlemagne

by Einhard

He cherished with the greatest fervor and devotion the principles of the Christian religion, which had been instilled into him from infancy. Hence it was that he built the beautiful basilica at Aix-la-Chapelle, which he adorned with gold and silver and lamps, and with rails and doors of solid brass. He had the columns and marbles for this structure brought from Rome and Ravenna, for he could not find such as were suitable elsewhere. He was a constant worshipper at this church as long as his health permitted, going morning and evening, even after nightfall, besides attending mass; and he took care that all the services there conducted should be administered with the utmost possible propriety, very often warning the sextons not to let any improper or unclean thing be brought into the building or remain in it. He provided it with a great number of sacred vessels of gold and silver and with such a quantity of clerical robes that not even the doorkeepers who fill the humblest office in the church were obliged to wear their everyday clothes when in the exercise of their duties. He was at great pains to improve the church reading and psalmody, for he was well skilled in both although he neither read in public nor sang, except in a low tone and with others.

> Charlemagne was a capable ruler—warrior, politician, humanitarian, Christian.

He was very forward in succoring the poor, and in that gratuitous generosity which the Greeks call alms, so much so that he not only made a point of giving in his own country and his own kingdom, but when he discovered that there were Christians living in poverty in Syria, Egypt, and Africa, at Jerusalem, Alexandria, and Carthage, he had compassion on their wants, and used to send money over the seas to them. The reason that he zealously strove to make friends with the kings beyond seas was that he might get help and relief to the Christians living under their rule.

He cherished the Church of St. Peter the Apostle at Rome above all other holy and sacred places, and heaped its treasury with a vast wealth of gold, silver, and precious stones. He sent great and count-less gifts to the popes; and throughout his whole reign the wish that he had nearest at heart was to reestablish the ancient authority of the city of Rome under his care and by his influence, and to defend and protect the Church of St. Peter, and to beautify and enrich it out of his own store above all other churches. Although he held it in such veneration, he only repaired to Rome to pay his vows and make his supplications four times during the whole 47 years that he reigned.[3]

Equestrian statue of Charlemagne, by Agostino Cornacchini (1725) at St. Peter's Basilica, Vatican.

Discussion Question

Based on Einhard's description of Charlemagne, describe Charlemagne's Christian life.

---

3 http://www.fordham.edu/halsall/basis/einhard.asp.

Lesson 5

Why Study History Through Primary Sources

It is clear that all our information in regard to past events and conditions must be derived from evidence of some kind. This evidence is called the source. Sometimes there are a number of good and reliable sources for an event as, for example, for the decapitation of King Charles I of England in 1649, or for the march of Napoleon into Russia. Sometimes there is but a single, unreliable source as, for instance, in the case of the burial of King Alaric in a riverbed. For a great many important matters about which we should like to know there are, unfortunately, no written sources at all, and we can only guess how things were. For example, we do not know what the Germans were doing before Julius Caesar came into contact with them and took the trouble to give a brief account of them. We can learn but little about the bishops of Rome (or popes) before the time of the Emperor Constantine, for few references to them have come down to us.

Few, however, of those who read and study history ever come into contact with the primary, or firsthand sources; they get their information second hand. It is much more convenient to read what the modern historian Edward Gibbon has to say of Constantine than to refer to **Eusebius**, and other ancient writers from whom he gained knowledge. Moreover, Gibbon carefully studied and compared all the primary sources, and it may be urged that he has given a truer, fuller, and more attractive account of the period than can be found in any one of them. His *Decline and Fall of the Roman Empire* is certainly a work of the highest rank; but, nevertheless, it is only a report of others' reports. It is therefore not a primary but a secondary source.

Most of the historical knowledge today is not derived from even a secondary source such as Gibbon and similar authoritative writers; rather, it comes from the reading of textbooks, encyclopedia stories, dramas, and magazine articles. Popular manuals and articles are commonly written by those who know little or nothing of the primary sources; they are consequently at least third-hand, even when based upon the best secondary accounts. As a matter of fact, they are usually patched together from older manuals and articles and may be four, five, or six removes from the original source of knowledge.

It is well known that the oftener a report passes from mouth to mouth the less trustworthy and accurate it tends to become. Unimportant details which appeal to the imagination will be magnified, while fundamental considerations are easily forgotten if they happen to be prosaic and commonplace. Historians, like other people, are sometimes fond of good stories and may be led astray by some false rumor which, once started into circulation, gets further and further from the truth with each repetition.

For example, a distinguished historian of the Church, Cardinal Baronius, writing about 1600, made the statement, upon very insufficient evidence, that as the year 1000 approached, the people of Europe generally believed that the world was about to come to an end. Robertson, a very popular Scotch historian of the 18th century, repeated the statement and went on to describe the terrible panic which seized upon sinful men as the awful year drew on. Succeeding writers, including some very distinguished ones,

A Charlemagne denier coined in Frankfurt from 812 to 814 (PD).

accepted and even elaborated Robertson's account. About thirty years ago, however, a French scholar pointed out that there was really no adequate basis for this strange tale. To the chroniclers of the time the year 1000 was clearly no more portentous than 997 or 1003. This story of the panic, which passed current as historical fact for some three hundred years, offers an excellent illustration of the danger of relying upon secondary sources.

One of the first questions then to ask upon taking up an historical work is, where did the writer obtain the information? Has the writer simply copied his statements from the more easily accessible works in a familiar language, however unreliable and out of date they may be; or, dissatisfied with such uncertain sources, has the writer become familiar with the most recent research of the distinguished scholars in the field, in whatever language they may have been written; or, still better, has the historian made a personal study of the original evidence which has come down to us of the events and conditions which are under discussion?

No improvement in the methods of historical instruction in our high schools and colleges bids fair to produce better results than the plan of bringing the student into contact with the firsthand accounts of events or, as they are technically termed, the primary sources.

This term may perhaps call up in the minds of some the vision of a solitary stoop shouldered, spectacled enthusiast, engaged in painfully deciphering obscure Latin abbreviations on yellow parchment. But it is a mistake to conclude that the primary sources are always difficult to get at, dull, and hard to read. On the contrary, they are sometimes ready to hand, and are often more vivid and entertaining than even the most striking descriptions by the pen of gifted writers like Gibbon or Macaulay.

The best secondary authorities stand to the sources somewhat as the description of a work of art or of a masterpiece of literature stands to the original. Just as we cannot afford to ignore the picture itself, or the great poem or drama, and confine ourselves to someone else's account of it, so in our historical work we ought to grasp every opportunity of examining for ourselves the foundations upon which history rests.

It may, of course, be urged that the trained historians, after acquainting themselves with the people and the circumstances of a particular period, can make better use of the

Conquest of Jerusalem by Charlemagne.

sources than any relatively unskilled student. But, admitting the force of this argument, there is, nevertheless, so much to be learned from a study of the original accounts that cannot be reproduced by the most skilled hand, that no earnest student or reader should be content with secondhand descriptions when primary sources are available.

The sources are unconsciously molded by the spirit of the time in which they were written. Every line gives some hint of the period in which the author lived and makes an impression upon us which volumes of secondhand accounts can never produce. The mere information, too, comes to us in a form which we do not easily forget. The facts sink into our memory. One who actually talked with Attila, or who witnessed the capture of Jerusalem by the crusaders, is clearly more likely to excite our interest than a writer of our own day, however much the modern may know of the king of the Huns or of the first crusade. It makes no great impression upon us to be told that the scholars of Dante's time had begun to be interested once more in the ancient learning of the Greeks and Romans; but no one can forget Dante's own poetic account of his kindly reception in the lower regions by the august representatives of pagan literature, — Homer, Horace, Ovid, and Lucan, —people "with eyes slow and grave, of great authority in their looks," who "spake seldom and with soft voices."

Moreover, the study of the sources enables us to some extent to form our own opinions of the past, so that we need not rely entirely upon mere manuals, which are always one, and generally two or three, removes from the sources themselves. When we get at the sources themselves we no longer merely read and memorize; we begin to consider what may be safely inferred from the statements before us and so develop the all-important faculty of criticism. We are not simply accumulating facts but are attempting to determine their true nature and meaning.

The power to do this is not alone necessary to scholarly work; it is of the utmost importance as well in dealing with the affairs of everyday life. To take a single illustration: one cannot fail to see from a study of the sources that Luther was exceedingly unfair to his enemies and ascribed their conduct to evil motives when they were acting quite consistently and according to what they considered the truth. His opponents, on the other hand, treated him with equal unfairness and proclaimed him a wicked and profligate man only because he refused to accept their views.

We meet precisely the same unfairness nowadays as, for instance, in the case of a municipal election, where each party speaks only evil of the other. It is, however, not so hard to look impartially at the motives and conduct of people who lived long ago as it is to be fair-minded in matters which interest us personally very deeply. By cultivating sympathy and impartiality in dealing with the past we may hope to reach a point where we can view the present coolly and temperately. In this way, really thoughtful, historical study serves to develop the very fundamental virtues of sympathy, fairness, and caution in forming our judgments.[4]

Discussion Question

According to Robinson, what advantages do primary sources bring to historical studies?

---

4 Adapted from James Harvey Robinson, "The Historical point of View," in *Readings in European History*, Vol I (Boston, MA: Ginn, 1904), p. 1–13.

Chapter 31

Church Life in the Middle Ages

First Thoughts

Until the Reformation, the only Christian churches were the Roman Catholic Church and the Eastern Orthodox Church. Quite literally, life for all revolved around the church. From birth to death, whether you were a peasant, a serf, a noble, a lord, or a King — life was dominated by the church.

Chapter Learning Objectives

We will examine the role of the church in medieval Europe. We will look closely at the successful missionary approach taken by the church during these turbulent times. We will see how the clergy preserved learning and were a vital part of the medieval world.

As a result of this chapter you should be able to:

1. Discuss how the Roman Catholic Church became so powerful during the Middle Ages.

2. Offer a missionary strategy you would employ if you were a medieval pope.

3. Analyze why *all* scholarship and learning was so important to the medieval church.

4. Compare the role of medieval clergy with that of modern clergy.

5. Evaluate the importance of cathedrals to medieval society.

6. Summarize the description of a parson (local priest), in Middle English, by English poet Geoffrey Chaucer.

CONCEPTS

Gregory the Great

Parousia

Benedictine Monk

Papal States

Bishops

Archbishops

Ulfilas

Visigoths

Boniface

Beothius

Ostrogothic

Theodoric

Cassidorous

Scriptoria

Venerable Bede

Mass

Monk

The Early Medieval Papacy (600–1000)

Engraving depicting Saint Gregory the Great Maimbourg, 1686, France (CCA-SA3.0).

As Europe gradually emerged from the destruction of the Roman Empire, the Church became one of the mainstays of civilization. The medieval papacy asserted its authority during the leadership of **Gregory I the Great** (590–604). Gregory's achievement was to go beyond the claim of papal primacy in the Church by beginning to establish the secular power of the papacy. In other words, under the rule of Pope Gregory I, the papacy moved from the spiritual to the secular realm.

A Roman aristocrat by birth, Gregory witnessed and commented on the devastation of Rome as the city changed hands three times during Justinian's long struggle to retake Italy from the Ostrogoths:

Ruins on ruins. . . . Where is the senate? Where are the people? All the pomp of secular dignities has been destroyed. . . . And we, the few that we are who remain, every day we are menaced by scourges and innumerable trials.[1]

Concluding that the world was coming to an end and the **Parousia** was near, Gregory became a **Benedictine monk**. After Gregory was elected pope in 590, he assumed the task of protecting Rome and its surrounding territory from the barbarian threat. Thus, Gregory was the first pope to act as temporal ruler of a part of what later became the **Papal States**.

Gregory took the first step toward papal control of the church outside of Italy by sending a mission of Benedictine monks to convert the pagan Anglo-Saxons. The pattern of church government Gregory established in England — **bishops** supervised by **archbishops**, and archbishops by the pope — became standard in the church.

Under Pope Gregory, Roman Catholicism became even more hierarchical. Not until 900 did the papacy fall more and more under the control of the state, instead of vice versa.

With its own laws, lands, and taxes, the Catholic Church was a very powerful, wealthy institution. The Catholic Church also imposed taxes. Furthermore, opposition to the Catholic Church would result in excommunication. The person who was excommunicated could not attend any church services or receive the sacraments, and they would presumably go straight to hell when they died. This was a very ominous threat to all medieval people.[2]

Discussion Question

How did the Roman Catholic Church become so powerful during the Middle Ages?

---

1 R.H.C. Davis, *A History of Medieval Europe: From Constantine to Saint Louis* (London: Longmans, Green & Co., Ltd., 1957), p. 80.

2 http://history-world.org/midchurch.htm.

Missionary Activities of the Church

The early Middle Ages was a period of widespread missionary activity. By spreading Christianity, missionaries aided in the fusion of barbarian and Roman cultures. Monasteries served as havens for those seeking a contemplative life, as repositories of learning for scholars, and often as progressive farming centers.

One of the earliest Christian missionaries to the Germans was **Ulfilas** (311–383), who spent 40 years among the **Visigoths** and translated most of the Bible into the Gothic language.

Another great missionary, Patrick, was born in England about 389 and later fled to Ireland to escape the Anglo-Saxon invaders. As a result of his missionary activities in Ireland, Christianity became the dominant religion. In the late sixth and seventh centuries a large number of monks from the Irish monasteries went to Scotland, northern England, the kingdom of the Franks, and even Italy. The Irish monks eagerly pursued scholarship, and their monasteries became storehouses for priceless manuscripts.

Pope Gregory was a missionary pope and encouraged vigorous missionary activity. Gregory sent a Benedictine mission to England in 596. Ultimately the Benedictine mission, with a slightly different view of Christianity than Patrick, supplanted this mission.

Boniface, the greatest missionary from England in the eighth century, spent years among the Germanic tribes. Known as "the Apostle to the Germans," he established several works in Germany. Boniface even shared the Gospel with Scandinavians.[3]

Discussion Question

If you were a pope in the Middle Ages, what sort of missionary strategy would you develop?

> The Roman Catholic Church effectively spread the Gospel over the known world.

Martyrdom of St. Boniface, 1903 (PD-Art).

---

3 http://history-world.org/churchmiddleages.htm.

Preservation of Learning

One of the great contributions of the monasteries was the preservation of the learning of the classical world and that of the church. Learning did not entirely die out in western Europe, of course. Seeing that the ability to read Greek was quickly disappearing, and knowing that the New Testament was originally written in Greek, the sixth century Roman scholar **Boethius**, an administrator under the barbarian **Ostrogothic** king **Theodoric**, determined to preserve Greek learning by translating all of Plato and Aristotle into Latin. Unjustly accused of treachery by **Theodoric**, Boethius was thrown into prison, where he wrote *The Consolation of Philosophy*. This book became a medieval textbook on philosophy.

Cassiodorus, a contemporary of Boethius who had also served Theodoric, devoted most of his life to the collection and preservation of classical knowledge. He established **scriptoria**, departments concerned exclusively with copying manuscripts. This meant that accurate versions of the Bible were preserved during the worst of the Middle Ages.

The most famous church scholar was the **Venerable Bede**. An outstanding scholar of the early Middle Ages, the Venerable Bede (d.735), followed the Irish tradition of learning in a northern English monastery. Bede's best work, the *Ecclesiastical History of the English People*, with its many original documents and vivid character sketches, is our chief source for early British history.

Discussion Question

Why were all scholarship and learning so important to the medieval church?

A page from a copy of Bede's Lives of St. Cuthbert, showing King Athelstan presenting the work to the saint. This manuscript was given to St. Cuthbert's shrine in 934 (PD-Art).

Cathedrals

Medieval cathedrals dominated the skyline of medieval England. They were the largest man-made structures in the world! Cathedrals were far larger than castles — symbolic of their huge importance to medieval society, where religion dominated the lives of all.

How were such huge buildings constructed? Medieval workers worked with the most basic of tools and in conditions that modern-day health and safety laws would forbid. But for all this, the most common driving force was to build a magnificent building for the greater glory of God. It could take perhaps a decade to build such beautiful buildings!

The most obvious starting point was for an architect to be found who would design a cathedral. An architect would also know who were the best master craftsmen to employ — and many highly skilled men were needed.

Each master of his own trade ran a workshop for his own particular trade — so a master mason would employ a number of masons who were trusted enough to be considered competent to work on a cathedral as they, themselves, worked toward becoming a master. These were skilled men, and they would not do any laboring — unskilled laborers who lived near to where a cathedral was being built would do this. Craftsmen would function as foremen, then, as local serfs and peasants built their own cathedral.

Discussion Question

Why were cathedrals, even in poor areas, built with such care and great expense?

Salisbury Cathedral is an Anglican cathedral in Salisbury, England, and one of the leading examples of early English architecture. The main body was completed in only 38 years, from 1220 to 1258.

Men of God

A Mass at the close of the Middle Ages or early Renaissance, 15th century.

There were many different kinds of clergymen during the Middle Ages. Each one had his own duties and corresponding authority. Some had huge amounts of power politically. They also had vast amounts of spiritual authority. In Roman Catholic theology they were the mediators between man and God, and without the clergy, man could not contact God.

Bishops were the acknowledged leaders of the church. The leader of the bishops, of course, was the pope. Bishops were often very wealthy and had their own castles from which to conduct business. They more or less functioned as feudal lords.

The primary religious and social event was the **Mass**. The priest conducted Mass. Lay attendance was mandatory. The priests conducted Mass for the town in the town church and also said Mass in the castle chapel. They were also responsible for the collection of church taxes and the spreading of alms among the poor. Often these priests were the only people who could write and read in the village. Thus, they were sometimes responsible for village and castle record keeping. They would write letters for peasants and perform other literary tasks.

Monks were a common sight as well. Even though they lived in private monasteries, they often walked among the people. They usually wore brown robes with hoods around their heads. They were also well educated and could usually read and write Latin.

Discussion Question

Compare the role of medieval clergy with that of modern clergy.

Page from *Canterbury Tales* by Chaucer depicting The Monk, his horse standing on a grassy plot and his dogs running free (PD).

Chapter 32

Medieval Saints: History Makers

First Thoughts

The universality and power of the Church rested not only upon a systematized, uniform theology, but also upon the most highly organized administrative system in western Europe. All of this was irrelevant without people. It was the saints, the unselfish, godly women who lived and spoke the Gospel in the midst of people, who really made a difference. History, especially medieval history, is about people. The people who really make a difference are those who serve God with all their hearts! They change history. They are history makers!

Chapter Learning Objectives

We will examine five men and women of God who changed the world for Christ. They not only served Him, they served His people. We could use some folks like those around here today!

As a result of this chapter you should be able to:

1. Explain what Francis of Assisi meant when he said, "It is in pardoning that we are pardoned."

2. Explain what Catherine of Sienna meant when she stated, "When she was lifted up in prayer, with great elevation of mind, God was not wont to conceal, from the eye of her intellect, the love which He had for His servants, but rather to manifest it."

3. Analyze what Julian of Norwich meant when she said, "This shewed our good Lord for to make us glad and merry."

4. Discuss what Ignatius meant when he said, "Man is created to praise, reverence, and serve God our Lord, and by this means to save his soul."

CONCEPTS

Franciscans

Cistercian Monastery

Sixteen Revelations of Divine Love

Francis of Assisi (1182–1226)

Praising God in All Circumstances

Francis lived a life devoted to the Lord and founded the Franciscans, a religious order. The **Franciscans** devote themselves to preaching and to caring for the poor and the sick. Francis combined an absolute dedication to poverty with a joyful affirmation of creation. He wrote "Canticle of the Sun" in 1225, while he was in intense physical pain. Francis knew how to praise God in good and bad times!

"The Prayer of Peace" - St. Francis of Assisi

Lord, make me an instrument of Thy peace;
Where there is hatred, let me sow love;
Where there is injury, pardon;
Where there is error, the truth;
Where there is doubt, the faith;
Where there is despair, hope;
Where there is darkness, light;
And where there is sadness, joy.
O Divine Master, Grant that I may not so much seek
To be consoled, as to console;
To be understood, as to understand;
To be loved as to love.
For it is in giving that we receive;
It is in pardoning that we are pardoned;
And it is in dying that we are born to eternal life.

Saint Francis of Assisi and scenes of his life, 1235 (PD).

Discussion Question

What does Francis mean when he says, "It is in pardoning that we are pardoned?"

Mechtild of Magdeburg (c. 1207–1297)

Critic Poet

Mechtild was critical of the clergy of her age. She was the first German woman to write poetry and spiritual texts not in Latin but in German. Little is known about her except that she must have been of noble descent and led her life as a Begine — one of a group of unmarried women who lived together caring for the poor and the sick — in Magdeburg. Mechtild, being rather critical in her writings about the decline of morals amongst the clerics of her time, left Magdeburg and moved into a **Cistercian monastery**.

From *God and the Soul,* by Mechtild (translated by Oliver Davies)

God Speaks to the Soul:
And God said to the soul:
I desired you before the world began.
I desire you now as you desire me.
And where the desires of two come together
There love is perfected.

How the Soul Speaks to the God:
Lord, you are my lover, my longing,
My flowing stream, my sun,
And I am your reflection.

How God Answers the Soul:
It is my nature that makes me love you often,
For I am love itself.
It is my longing that makes me love you intensely,
For I yearn to be loved from the heart.
It is my eternity that makes me love you long,
For I have no end.[1]

Discussion Questions

What does Mechtild mean in these lines?

How God Answers the Soul:
It is my nature that makes me love you often,
For I am love itself.
It is my longing that makes me love you intensely,
For I yearn to be loved from the heart.
It is my eternity that makes me love you long,
For I have no end.

Sculpture of the Holy Mechtild of Magdeburg by Susan Turcot on the Fürstenwall in Magdeburg-Altstadt (PD).

---

1 http://seekingauthenticvoice.blogspot.com/2008/08/god-speaks-to-soul-mechtild-of.html.

Catherine of Siena (1347–1380)

Believing in Prayer

Catherine really believed that God answered her prayers. She was a contemplative who devoted herself to prayer. She was also a nurse who undertook to alleviate the suffering of the poor and the sick. Moreover, she was a strong Christian social activist who took a strong stand on the issues affecting society in her day.

Passage From *Dialogues,* by Catherine of Siena

Saint Catherine of Siena by Sano di Pietro, circa 1442 (PD-Art).

The soul, who is lifted by a very great and yearning desire for the honor of God and the salvation of souls, begins by exercising herself, for a certain space of time, in the ordinary virtues, remaining in the cell of self-knowledge, in order to know better the goodness of God towards her. This she does because knowledge must precede love, and only when she has attained love, can she strive to follow and to clothe herself with the truth. But, in no way, does the creature receive such a taste of the truth, or so brilliant a light therefrom, as by means of humble and continuous prayer, founded on knowledge of herself and of God; because prayer, exercising her in the above way, unites with God the soul that follows the footprints of Christ Crucified, and thus, by desire and affection, and union of love, makes her another Himself. Christ would seem to have meant this, when He said: *To him who will love Me and will observe My commandment, will I manifest Myself; and he shall be one thing with Me and I with him.* In several places we find similar words, by which we can see that it is, indeed, through the effect of love, that the soul becomes another Himself. That this may be seen more clearly, I will mention what I remember having heard from a handmaid of God, namely, that, when she was lifted up in prayer, with great elevation of mind, God was not wont to conceal, from the eye of her intellect, the love which He had for His servants, but rather to manifest it; and, that among other things, He used to say: "Open the eye of your intellect, and gaze into Me, and you shall see the beauty of My rational creature. . . . adorned with many virtues, by which they are united with Me through love. And yet I tell you, if you should ask Me, who these are, I should reply" (said the sweet and amorous Word of God) "they are another Myself, inasmuch as they have lost and denied their own will, and are clothed with Mine, are united to Mine, are conformed to Mine." It is therefore true, indeed, that the soul unites herself with God by the affection of love.[2]

Discussion Questions

Catherine states that "when she was lifted up in prayer, with great elevation of mind, God was not wont to conceal, from the eye of her intellect, the love which He had for His servants, but rather to manifest it." What does Catherine mean? What is she arguing?

Are you maintaining a balance between your prayer/devotional life and your praxis, or life of action? Why or why not? How does one do that?

2 http://www.ccel.org/ccel/catherine/dialog.iv.ii.i.html.

Julian of Norwich (1342–1413)

Touching the Divine

Julian was a 14th-century prophet who claimed to have knowledge or awareness of things beyond ordinary human experience. She is famous for her book *Sixteen Revelations of Divine Love,* in which she described 16 religious visions. She is also known as Juliana of Norwich. She spent most of her life alone, intentionally seeking the Lord as a hermit.

Passage From *Sixteen Revelations of Divine Love* Tenth Revelation, by Julian of Norwich

Then with a glad cheer our Lord looked unto His Side and beheld, rejoicing. With His sweet looking He led forth the understanding of His creature by the same wound into His Side within. And then he shewed a fair, delectable place, and large enough for all mankind that shall be saved to rest in peace and in love. And therewith He brought to mind His dearworthy blood and precious water which he let pour all out for love. And with the sweet beholding He shewed His blessed heart even cloven in two.

And with this sweet enjoying, He shewed unto mine understanding, in part, the blessed Godhead, stirring then the poor soul to understand, as it may be said, that is, to think on, the *endless* Love that was without beginning, and is, and shall be ever. And with this our good Lord said full blissfully: *Lo, how that I loved thee, as if He had said: My darling, behold and see thy Lord, thy God that is thy Maker and thine endless joy, see what satisfying and bliss I have in thy salvation; and for my love rejoice [thou] with me.*

And also, for more understanding, this blessed word was said: *Lo, how I loved thee! Behold and see that I loved thee so much ere I died for thee that I would die for thee; and now I have died for thee and suffered willingly that which I may. And now is all my bitter pain and all my hard travail turned to endless joy and bliss to me and to thee. How should it now be that thou shouldst anything pray that pleaseth me but that I should full gladly grant it thee? For my pleasing is thy holiness and thine endless joy and bliss with me.*

This is the understanding, simply as I can say it, of this blessed word: *Lo, how I loved thee.* This shewed our good Lord for to make us glad and merry.[3]

Discussion Questions

To Julian, the supernatural was natural, the presence of God normal. She lived there, so to speak, and walked and talked with God. Are you comfortable with God's supernatural presence in your life? Why or why not?

Statue of Julian of Norwich by David Holgate, Norwich Cathedral.

---

3 http://www.ccel.org/ccel/julian/revelations.xi.i.html.

Lesson 5

Ignatius (1491–1556)

Focused Purpose

Ignatius was a very pious Christian and an enthusiastic missionary.

Ignatius was a great evangelist whose followers evangelized North America. He had thousands of followers in Spain and France. In fact, most of the French and Spanish priests and monks who came to the New World were a part of Ignatius' order, the Jesuits or Society of Jesus, a religious order of men in the Roman Catholic Church. The motto of the order was "to the greater glory of God," and its object was the spread of Roman Catholicism. Unfortunately, this included supporting almost any activity that advanced the Gospel. As often happens, Ignatius' zealous followers took his admonitions too far and committed many cruel acts in his name. Ignatius, though, was really a godly man who loved Christ with all his heart. Many pious Jesuits led many unbelievers to Christ. In fact, millions of Roman Catholics, and some Protestants, have found their lives transformed by Ignatius' words.

St. Ignatius of Loyola by Peter Paul Rubens. 1600s. (PD-Art).

Passage From *Spiritual Exercise*, by Ignatius

Man is created to praise, reverence, and serve God our Lord, and by this means to save his soul. And the other things on the face of the earth are created for man and that they may help him in prosecuting the end for which he is created. From this it follows that man is to use them as much as they help him on to his end, and ought to rid himself of them so far as they hinder him as to it. For this it is necessary to make ourselves indifferent to all created things in all that is allowed to the choice of our free will and is not prohibited to it; so that, on our part, we want not health rather than sickness, riches rather than poverty, honor rather than dishonor, long rather than short life, and so in all the rest; desiring and choosing only what is most conducive for us to the end for which we are created.[4]

Discussion Questions

Ignatius called his Jesuit priesthood to a committed life of constant meditation and hard work. This was a winsome combination.

If anyone comes to me and does not hate his father and mother, wife and children, brothers and sisters — yes, even their own life — such a person cannot be my disciple (Luke 14:26).

Do you have any personal habits that do not bring glory to God?

---

4 http://www.companionofjesus.com/animaignatiana/ai-theendofman.html.

Chapter 33

The Crusades: Changing World History

First Thoughts

The most dramatic expression of chauvinistic Europe in the Middle Ages was the Crusades. In 1095, Pope Urban II proclaimed the First Crusade to regain the Holy Land. Preaching at the Council of Clermont in that year, he exhorted Christians to take up the cross and strive for a cause that promised not only spiritual rewards but material gain as well. At the end of his impassioned oration, the crowd shouted, "God wills it" — the expression the crusaders later used in battle. Even though the Crusades failed to achieve their specific objective, they cannot be written off as mere adventures. On the contrary, their influence extended over a much wider geographical field than just the Holy Land. Much of the crusading fervor carried over to the fight against the Moors in Spain and the Slavs in eastern Europe. Politically, the Crusades weakened the Byzantine Empire and accelerated its fall. And even today, in the Middle East, the word "crusades" has a negative connotation.

Chapter Learning Objectives

Chapter 33 discusses the impact of the Crusades on world history. Along the way, we will examine the story of the Holy Grail. We will look specifically at a special group, the Teutonic Knights.

As a result of this chapter you should be able to:

1. Explain the causes of the Crusades.

2. Discuss if there was really a Holy Grail.

3. Evaluate what medieval audiences preferred in heroes.

4. Analyze what dangers ultimately occur when a mercenary, warlike organization allies itself with the church.

5. Discuss how the Crusades changed world history.

Lesson 1

Overview

> The Crusades were much more than a zealous attempt to destroy the enemies of God and take back the Holy Land. They were an opportunity for the pent-up energy of the medieval world to be deposited into a new realm.

The Crusades that were launched on the Holy Land, from Pope Urban II's speech at the council of Clermont in 1095 to the siege and conquest of Jerusalem by the Crusaders in 1099, initiated a new phase of relationship between the West and Islamic peoples. There is no doubt that the brutality of the Crusades, with no less than nine major attacks initiated on the Middle East, left the Islamic world in such a shock that, even today, any Western intrusion to the region is considered a "crusade."

From the end of the 11th century to the end of the 13th, there were seven major Crusades as well as various small expeditions which warred against Islamic kingdoms in the Middle East, whom the crusaders called **Saracens**.

The Crusades were much more than a zealous attempt to destroy the enemies of God and take back the Holy Land. They were an opportunity for the pent-up energy of the medieval world to be deposited into a new realm. The absence of permanent influence of the crusaders on the Holy Land can be attributed to its comparatively short reign over the area east of the Mediterranean, and to the return of most European inhabitants of the Holy land to Europe.

Saladin and Guy de Lusignan after battle of Hattin in 1187 (PD).

The economic impact on Europe, which resulted from the Holy Land Crusade, was considerable and permanent. The European economy emerged as a world economy. New permanent markets were opened in the Middle East; old ones with China were strengthened. At the end of the Crusades, the Italian city-states, like Venice and Naples, were powerful, rich entities. They were more powerful than many European nations. They grew extremely rich, selling both to the European Crusaders and to their Islamic enemies! Remember, it is from the Italian states that Christopher Columbus emerged. The **Italian city-states** were bold, sassy, and innovative.

For the large expeditions of crusaders to the Holy Land, financing was always an issue. Because of that demand, European kingdoms and states were forced to develop and improve their system of administration, including the taxing system. Borrowing money for such expeditions became another source.

Discussion Question

What were the causes of the Crusades?

The Holy Grail

In today's society, **the Holy Grail** has been portrayed by movies and by Grail legends to be a Sacred Cup that bestowed special powers upon the individual who drank from it. That person had to be noble enough and possess a true heart to be worthy of finding the Grail. However, while this is the most commonly known and accepted theory, it is only one of many possible explanations as to what the Grail actually is.

In typical Grail stories and legends, there are many recurring **motifs**. One of them is the unknown vessel or object that sustains life: the grail, which is usually found in a mysterious castle. In this castle there is usually a king who sends the knight out on a quest. There will be many attempts in this quest, and not every knight is eligible to stand before this vessel. Also, there is always a beautiful girl who is holding the vessel. The knight also has to be familiar with chivalry and act accordingly. The vessel can be characterized in a procession with many jewels adorning it, or it can simply be made of gold. Or, in Stephen Spielberg's *The Last Crusader*, it was merely a wooden chalice.

The Damsel of the Sanct Grael or Holy Grail by Dante Gabriel Rossetti, 1874 (PD-Art).

The Holy Grail was the dish, plate, or cup used by Jesus at the Last Supper, said to possess miraculous powers. The connection of Joseph of Arimathea with the Grail legend dates from Robert de Boron's *Joseph d'Arimathie* (late 12th century) in which Joseph receives the Grail from Jesus and sends it with his followers to Great Britain. Building upon this theme, later writers recounted how Joseph used the Grail to catch Christ's blood while interring him and that in Britain he founded a line of guardians to keep it safe.

The quest for the Holy Grail shows up in other legends — like the Arthurian legend.

Was there a Holy Grail? Almost all historians agree that there was not. And if there was, it was lost or destroyed. However, the story itself celebrated much of the spirit of the age.

Discussion Question

Was there really a Holy Grail?

Heroes of Myth and Legend (1903)

Illustration from page 278 of The Boy's King Arthur: Launcelot and Guenevere - "He rode his way with the queen unto Joyous Gard," 1922, N.C. Wyeth (PD-US).

by Baron Thomas Babington Macaulay

For many days after he had left the hermitage, Sir Lancelot rode through the forest, but there came to him no such adventures as had befallen him on other quests to the increase of his fame. At last, one night-tide, he came to the shores of a great water and there he lay down to sleep; but as he slept, a voice called on him: "Lancelot, arise, put on thine amour and go on thy way until thou comest to a ship. Into that thou shalt enter." Immediately, Sir Lancelot started from his sleep to obey and, riding along the shore, came presently to a ship beached on the strand; no sooner had he entered it, than the ship was launched — how, he might not know. So the ship sailed before the wind for many a day. No mortal was on it, save only Sir Lancelot, yet were all his needs supplied. Then, at last, the ship ran ashore at the foot of a great castle; and it was midnight. Sir Lancelot waited not for the dawn, but, his sword gripped in his hand, sprang ashore, and then, right before him, he saw a postern where the gate stood open indeed, but two grisly lions kept the way. And when Sir Lancelot would have rushed upon the great beasts with his sword, it was struck from his hand, and a voice said: "Ah! Lancelot, ever is thy trust in thy might rather than thy Maker!"

Sore ashamed, Sir Lancelot took his sword and thrust it back into the sheath, and going forward, he passed unhurt through the gateway, the lions that kept it falling back from his path. So without more adventure, Lancelot entered into the castle; and there he saw how every door stood open, save only one, and that was fast barred, nor, with all his force, might he open it. Presently from the chamber within came the sound of a sweet voice in a holy chant, and then in his heart Lancelot knew that he was come to the Holy Grail. So, kneeling humbly, he prayed that to him might be shown some vision of that he sought. Forthwith the door flew open and from the chamber blazed a light such as he had never known before; but when he made to enter, a voice cried: "Lancelot, forbear," and sorrowfully he withdrew. Then where he knelt, far even from the threshold of the wondrous room, he saw a silver table and, on it, covered with red samite, the Holy Grail. At sight of that which he had sought so long, his joy became so great that, unmindful of the warning, he advanced into the room and drew nigh even to the Table itself. Then on the instant there burst between him and it a blaze of light, and he fell to the ground. There he lay, nor might he move nor utter any sound; only he was aware of hands busy about him which bore him away from the chamber.

For four-and-twenty days, Sir Lancelot lay as in a trance. At the end of that time, he came to himself, and found those about him that had tended him in his swoon. These, when they had given him fresh raiment, brought him to the aged King — Pelles was his name — that owned that castle. The King entertained him right royally, for he knew of the fame of Sir Lancelot; and long he talked with him of his quest and of the other knights who followed it, for he was of a great age and knew much of men. At the end of four days, he spoke to Sir Lancelot, bidding him return to Arthur's court; "For," said he, "your quest is ended here, and all that ye shall see of the Holy Grail, ye have seen." So Lancelot rode on his way, grieving for the sin that hindered him from the perfect vision of the Holy Grail, but thanking God for that which he had seen. So in time he came to Camelot, and told to Arthur all that had befallen him.

After he had rescued Sir Percivale from the twenty knights who beset him, Sir Galahad rode on his way till night-fall, when he sought shelter at a little hermitage. Thither there came in the night a damsel who desired to speak with Sir Galahad; so he arose and went to her. "Galahad," said she, "arm you and mount your horse and follow me, for I am come to guide you in your quest." So they rode together until they had come to the sea-shore, and there the damsel showed Galahad a great ship into which he must enter. Then she bade him farewell, and he, going on to the ship, found there already the good knights Sir Bors and Sir Percivale, who made much joy of the meeting. They abode in that ship until they had come to the castle of King Pelles, who welcomed them right gladly. Then, as they all sat at supper that night, suddenly the hall was filled with a great light, and the holy vessel appeared in their midst, covered all in white samite. While they all rejoiced, there came a voice saying: "My Knights whom I have chosen, ye have seen the holy vessel dimly. Continue your journey to the city of Sarras and there the perfect Vision shall be yours."

Now in the city of Sarras had dwelt long time Joseph of Arimathea, teaching its people the true faith, before ever he came into the land of Britain; but when Sir Galahad and his fellows came there after long voyage, they found it ruled by a heathen king named Estorause, who cast them into a deep dungeon. There they were kept a year, but at the end of that time, the tyrant died. Then the great men of the land gathered together to consider who should be their king; and, while they were in council, came a voice bidding them take as their king the youngest of the three knights whom Estorause had thrown into prison.

So in fear and wonder they hastened to the prison, and releasing the three knights, made Galahad king as the voice had bidden them.

King Arthur's knights, gathered at the Round Table to celebrate the Pentecost, see a vision of the Holy Grail. The Grail appears as a veiled ciborium, made of gold and decorated with jewels, held by two angels. From a manuscript of Lancelot and the Holy Grail, 14th century, (PD).

255

Thus Sir Galahad became King of the famous city of Sarras, in far Babylon. He had reigned a year when, one morning early, he and the other two knights, his fellows, went into the chapel, and there they saw, kneeling in prayer, an aged man, robed as a bishop, and round him hovered many angels. The knights fell on their knees in awe and reverence, whereupon he that seemed a bishop turned to them and said: "I am Joseph of Arimathea, and I am come to show you the perfect Vision of the Holy Grail." On the instant there appeared before them, without veil or cover, the holy vessel, in a radiance of light such as almost blinded them. Sir Bors and Sir Percivale, when at length they were recovered from the brightness of that glory, looked up to find that the holy Joseph and the wondrous vessel had passed from their sight. Then they went to Sir Galahad where he still knelt as in prayer, and behold, he was dead; for it had been with him even as he had prayed; in the moment when he had seen the vision, his soul had gone back to God.

So the two knights buried him in that far city, themselves mourning and all the people with them. And immediately after, Sir Percivale put off his arms and took the habit of a monk, living a devout and holy life until, a year and two months later, he also died and was buried near Sir Galahad. Then Sir Bors armed him, and bidding farewell to the city, sailed away until, after many weeks, he came again to the land of Britain. There he took horse, and stayed not till he had come to Camelot. Great was the rejoicing of Arthur and all his knights when Sir Bors was once more among them. When he had told all the adventures which had befallen him and the good knights, his companions, all who heard were filled with amaze. But the King, he caused the wisest clerks in the land to write in great hooks this Quest of the Holy Grail, that the fame of it should endure unto all time.[1]

Discussion Question

What does this legend about the Holy Grail tell the reader about what medieval audiences preferred in heroes?

Statue of King Arthur, Innsbruck, designed by Albrecht Dürer and cast by Peter Vischer the Elder, 1520s.

1 Baron Thomas Babington Macaulay, *Heroes of Myth and Legend* (New York: P.F. Collier & Son, 1903), p. 648–653, *books.google.com/books?id=NGYAAAAAMAAJ*.

The Teutonic Order

The Teutonic Order was a special group of knights from Germany. They were, literally, a band of brothers. Formed in 1143 by Pope Celestine II, they operated at first in Palestine as nurses in a hospital, but soon turned into a military order, and ended up playing an important role in the Crusades. The Teutonic Order served as personal guards at some of the holy shrines in Palestine. After Christian forces were defeated in the Middle East, the Order moved north in 1211 to help defend Hungary against Ottoman invaders. They settled there for a while, but were expelled in 1225 after attempting to place themselves directly under papal instead of Hungarian rule. The Teutonic Order, then, was a sort of mercenary force that embraced moral causes in Europe.

> The Teutonic Order was a zealous group of Christian knights who sought to preserve western culture and to advance the influence of the Church.

Although the Order had their roots in the Middle East, their most famous exploits took place in Lithuania and the Baltic in the Northern Crusades. In 1226, Kuonrad I, Duke of a small state in Poland, appealed to the knights to defend his borders and to subdue the pagans in nearby Lithuania, allowing the Teutonic knights to use Poland as a base for their campaign. They were also granted lands by the Holy Roman Empire. The conquest of the Baltic pagans was accomplished with much bloodshed over more than 50 years, during which natives who remained unbaptized were killed.

In 1410 at the Battle of Tannenberg, a combined Polish-Lithuanian army, led by Władysław II and Vytautas, decisively defeated the Order.

In 1929, the Teutonic knights were converted to a purely spiritual Roman Catholic religious order. After Austria's annexation by Nazi Germany, the Teutonic Order was suppressed throughout the Reich from 1938–1945, although the Nazis used imagery of the medieval Teutonic knights for propaganda purposes. The Order survived in Italy, however, and was reconstituted in Germany and Austria in 1945. By the end of the 1990s, the Order had developed into a charitable organization.

Tannhäuser in the habit of the Teutonic knights, from the Codex Manesse, between 1305 and 1315 (PD).

Discussion Question

What dangers ultimately occur when a mercenary, warlike organization allies itself with the Church?

Consequences and Conclusion

The Crusades kept all Europe in a fever for two centuries, and directly and indirectly cost Europe several millions of lives (from 2 million to 6 million, according to different estimates), besides incalculable expenditures in suffering. They were, moreover, attended by cruelty and excesses. However, the Holy Wars formed a most important factor in the history of the progress of civilization.

The Crusades could not fail to affect in many ways the life of western Europe. For instance, they helped to undermine feudalism. Thousands of barons and knights mortgaged or sold their lands in order to raise money for a crusading expedition. Thousands more perished in Syria, and their estates often reverted to the crown. Of course, it was also hard to keep the peasants down on the farm after they had seen Damascus! With declining feudalism, kings gained more power.

Detail of a miniature of Philip Augustus arriving in Palestine, sometime after 1332, before 1350 (PD-Art).

At the same time, the cities also gained many political advantages at the expense of the crusading barons and princes. Real money was transferred from feudal lords to towns and merchants.

Even though the Crusades failed to achieve their specific objective permanently, they permanently changed the complexion of world history. On the contrary, their influence extended over a much wider geographical field than just the Holy Land. Much of the crusading fervor carried over to the fight against the Moors in Spain and the Slavs in eastern Europe. Politically, the Crusades weakened the Byzantine Empire and accelerated its fall. Although the early Crusades strengthened the authority of the papacy in Europe, the bad performance of the later crusades weakened both the crusading ideal and society's respect for the papacy. Contact with the East widened the Europeans' scope, ended their isolation, and exposed them to an admirable civilization. Although it is easy to exaggerate the negative economic effects of the crusades, they did influence the reopening of the eastern Mediterranean to Western commerce, which itself had an effect on the rise of cities and the emergence of a hard money economy in the West.

Discussion Question

How did the Crusades change world history?

Chapter 34

1492:
The New World

First Thoughts

Columbus. 1492. The name and the date provoke many questions related to the linking of very different parts of the world, the western hemisphere and the Mediterranean. What was life like in those areas before 1492? What spurred European expansion? How did European, African, and American peoples react to each other? What were some of the immediate results of these contacts?

Chapter Learning Objectives

We explore the life of Ferdinand and Isabella and their interest in overseas expansion. Next, we will look, in general, at the world in 1492. We will look in particular at the voyages of Christopher Columbus. Finally, we will examine a contemporary account of Columbus' voyages.

As a result of this chapter you should be able to:

1. Analyze Spain's interest in overseas expansion.

2. Discuss what the world was like in 1492.

3. Review the voyages of Christopher Columbus.

4. Study a contemporary account of Columbus' voyages.

CONCEPTS

Ferdinand of Aragon

Isabella of Castile

October 12, 1492

Bartolome de las Casas

Columbus
Quincentenary of 1992

Ferdinand and Isabella

The marriage in 1469 of cousins **Ferdinand of Aragon** (1452–1516) and **Isabella of Castile** (1451–1504), eventually unified all of Spain. Both Isabella and Ferdinand understood the importance of unity; together they achieved needed reform and left Spain one of the most powerful countries in Europe.

Ferdinand and Isabella resumed the wars to remove the Moors from Spain, a campaign that had been dormant for more than 200 years, and in 1492 removed the last Moorish strongholds. The first of many self-defeating purges also removed thousands of Islamic settlers.

Everyone in Europe believed that religious unity was necessary for political unity, but only in Spain was it actually tried. In the next generation, all Spanish Jewish and Islamic peoples were converted or killed.

In the exploration and exploitation of the New World, Spain found an outlet for the crusading energies that the war against the Muslims had stimulated. New discoveries and conquests came in quick succession. Vasco Nunez de Balboa reached the Pacific in 1513, and the survivors of Ferdinand Magellan's expedition completed the circumnavigation of the globe in 1522. In 1519, the conquistador Hernando Cortes subdued the Aztecs in Mexico with a handful of followers, and between 1531 and 1533 Francisco Pizzaro overthrew the empire of the Incas and established Spanish dominion over Peru.

By the end of the reign of Ferdinand and Isabella, Spain was a first-rate power in the European world.

Discussion Question

Why did Spain show such interest in overseas exploration?

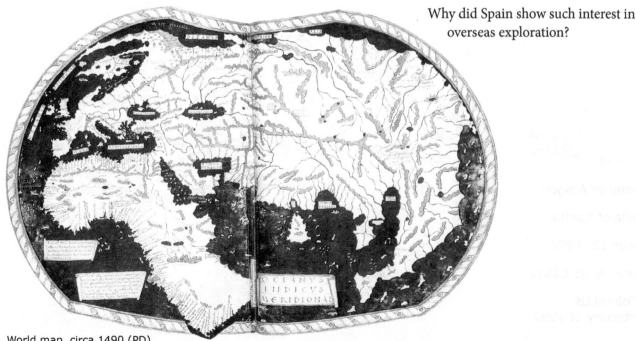

World map, circa 1490 (PD).

The World in 1492

Columbus was part of the Mediterranean world. The peoples who inhabited the semi-arid shores of the Mediterranean saw themselves as living at the center of the world. Prosperous city-states were on the rise amidst the decline of medieval feudal society. Renewed interest in Greek and Roman cultures fostered studies in art and science. New, stimulating ideas were spread with the advent of printing. Out of the doomsday mentality caused by the Black Death, civil wars, and economic uncertainties, emerged expansionism, cohesion, and a sense of prosperity. As the eastern Mediterranean struggled before the expanding Ottoman Islamic Empire, and Muslim rule ended in Iberia, western Mediterranean traders and sailors looked beyond the Straits of Gibraltar for alternative routes to the riches of the East.

> Two worlds collided in the Columbus expeditions to the new world.

Meanwhile, in Africa, was Timbuktu. In 1492, Timbuktu was the legendary city of gold. It was a transit point and a financial and trading center used for trade across the Sahara Desert in North Africa. Timbuktu was founded in 1080, and within 300 years had become one of the era's most important trading points. Timbuktu was an influential Islamic intellectual center. When much of Europe was struggling out of the Dark Ages, the emperor of Timbuktu was having stunning mosques built, and thousands of scholars from as far as Islamic India and Moorish Spain were studying in the city. At that time, it was a city of one hundred thousand, and so rich that even the slaves were decorated with gold.

As recently as 1963, a famous British historian, Hugh Trevor-Roper said: "Perhaps, in the future, there will be some African history to teach. But at present there is none, or very little: there is only the history of the Europeans in Africa. The rest is largely darkness. . . ."[1] Indeed!

In America, there was Cahokia. One mound, located across the Mississippi River from St. Louis, is larger than the Great Pyramid in Egypt. Its base covered 14 acres, and it rose in four terraces to 100 feet. Nearly a thousand years ago, when many European cities were little more than villages, the people living at Cahokia built a wooden barricade surrounding their most important buildings. Almost two miles long and enclosing more than 120 acres, the fence required felling twenty thousand trees. Cahokia, the largest settlement north of central Mexico, flourished for three centuries before it was abandoned. Estimates of

Cahokia and outlying villages.

its peak population run from ten thousand to twenty thousand. Cahokia's merchants traded across much of North America, from the Gulf Coast northward to the Great Lakes, eastward to the Atlantic coast and westward to Oklahoma. Cahokia spread the Mississippian culture across much of North America.

Discussion Question

Describe Native American building projects in North America.

---

1 http://davidderrick.wordpress.com/2010/06/09/there-is-no-african-history/.

Christopher Columbus

On October 12, 1492, two worlds unknown to each other met for the first time on a small island in the Caribbean Sea. While on a voyage for Spain in search of a direct sea route from Europe to Asia, Christopher Columbus was absolutely convinced that he had found the Spice Islands of the East Indies (around present-day Indonesia). In Columbus' mind, China was just over the horizon.

Columbus was not the first European to reach the Americas, of course — Vikings from Scandinavia had briefly settled on the North American coast in what is now Newfoundland and Labrador, Canada, in the late 10th or early 11th century. However, Columbus' explorations brought European explorations and colonizations, which made all the difference in the world.

Columbus' idea of sailing west to get to the east was not original with him, nor did he ever claim that it was. Columbus drew upon science and knowledge accumulated over thousands of years. Columbus' ideas of the distance between Europe and Asia were based on the descriptions contained in several reputable geographic works. In fact, most educated Europeans were sure that the world was much smaller than it really is.

With the end of the Moorish Wars, King Ferdinand and Queen Isabella were eager to finance new ventures, especially something like what Columbus proposed.

At daybreak on August 3, 1492, three small ships left Spain and headed into the foreboding ocean. After a trip to the Canary Islands, where the rudder of the *Pinta* was repaired, the voyagers departed the known world on September 6, 1492. Throughout the voyage, the ships traveled primarily westward.

Two hours past midnight on the morning of **October 12, 1492** a lookout named Rodrigo de Triana (sometimes called Juan Rodríguez Bermejo) on the *Pinta* cried out,

American neoclassicist painter John Vanderlyn (1775–1852) was commissioned by Congress in June 1836 to paint the *Landing of Columbus* for the Capitol Rotunda (PD).

"Tierra! Tierra!" ("Land! Land!"). A reward of a pension of ten thousand maravedis per year (an able seaman could earn about twelve thousand maravedis per year) was to go to he who saw land first. Rather cruelly, Columbus pocketed the money himself, claiming that he had seen several lights the night before.

On October 12, 1492, Columbus and a handful of the excited, but weary, voyagers set foot on land after 36 days of sailing. Columbus raised the royal standard, claiming the island for Spain, and two of the captains carried banners decorated with green crosses and letters representing Ferdinand and Isabella. Soon the curious islanders, with some fear, came out of their hiding places and greeted the visitors.

Columbus was to return three more times to the New World, and died without fully understanding that he had not discovered a western route to the East Indies.

Discussion Question

Why did Columbus sail west to reach the East Indies? Why did that seem logical?

Lesson 4

Contemporary Account

Columbus' Voyages

Columbus' journal of his first voyage to America has been lost. However, we do have an accurate abstract of the journal written by **Bartolome de las Casas** in the 1530s. Las Casas was a historian and Columbus' biographer who had access to the original journal of the voyage. We join Columbus' account as his expedition approaches the islands of the Bahamas. Throughout the account, Columbus refers to himself in the third person as the "Admiral":

Thursday, October 11

The course was W.S.W., and there was more sea than there had been during the whole of the voyage. They saw sand-pipers, and a green reed near the ship. Those of the caravel Pinta saw a cane and a pole, and they took up another small pole which appeared to have been worked with iron; also another bit of cane, a land-plant, and a small board. The crew of the caravel Niña also saw signs of land, and a small branch covered with berries. Everyone breathed afresh and rejoiced at these signs. The run until sunset was 27 leagues.

Christopher Columbus, engraving by Johann Theodor De Bry, circa 1590 (LOC).

After sunset the Admiral returned to his original west course, and they went along at the rate of 12 miles an hour. Up to two hours after midnight they had gone 90 miles, equal to 22 1/2 leagues. As the caravel Pinta was a better sailor, and went ahead of the Admiral, she found the land, and made the signals ordered by the Admiral. The land was first seen by a sailor named Rodrigo de Triana. But the Admiral, at ten o'clock, being on the castle of the poop, saw a light, though it was so uncertain that he could not affirm it was land. He called Pero Gutierrez, a gentleman of the King's bedchamber, and said that there seemed to be a light, and that he should look at it. He did so, and saw it. The Admiral said the same to Rodrigo Sanchez of Segovia, whom the King and Queen had sent with the fleet as inspector, but he could see nothing, because he was not in a place whence anything could be seen.

Repilca of Santa María, 1904 (PD).

After the Admiral had spoken he saw the light once or twice, and it was like a wax candle rising and failing. It seemed to few to be an indication of land; but the Admiral made certain that land was close. When they said the Salve, (Salve Regina) which all the sailors were accustomed to sing in their way, the Admiral asked and admonished the men to keep a good look-out on the forecastle, and to watch well for land; and to him who should first cry out that he saw land, he would give a silk doublet, besides the other rewards promised by the Sovereigns, which were ten thousand maravedis to him who should first saw it. At two hours after midnight the land was sighted at a distance of two leagues.

Columbus ordered the three ships to halt and wait for daylight before venturing further. His journal continues:

Friday, October 12

The vessels were hove to, waiting for daylight; and on Friday they arrived at a small island of the Lucayos, called, in the language of the Indians, Guanahani. The Admiral went on shore in the armed boat, and Martin Alonso Pinzon, and Vicente Yanez, his brother, who was captain of the Niña. The Admiral took the royal standard, and the captains went with two banners of the green cross, which the Admiral took in all the ships as a sign, with an F and a Y and a crown over each letter, one on one side of the cross and the other on the other.

Having landed, they saw trees very green, and much water, and fruits of diverse kinds. The Admiral called to the two captains, and to the others who leaped on shore, and to Rodrigo Escovedo, secretary of the whole fleet, and to Rodrigo Sanchez of Segovia, and said that they should bear faithful testimony that he, in presence of all, had taken, as he now took, possession of the said island for the King and for the Queen his Lords, making the declarations that are required, as is now largely set forth in the testimonies which were then made in writing.

Shortly after landing, many of the island's inhabitants assembled on the beach and Columbus gave them gifts of red hats and beads. The natives reciprocated with gifts of parrots, cotton and other goods. In describing the natives,

Columbus wrote: "They go as naked as when their mothers bore them, and so do the women, although I did not see more than one girl. They are very well made, with very handsome bodies, and very good countenances."[2]

Discussion Question

Columbus reports on his voyage to King Ferdinand and Queen Isabella of Spain:

> These people in the Caribbean have no creed and they are not idolaters, but they are very gentle and do not know what it is to be wicked, or to kill others, or to steal . . . and they are sure that we come from Heaven. . . . So your Highnesses should resolve to make them Christians, for I believe that if you begin, in a little while you will achieve the conversion of a great number of peoples to our holy faith, with the acquisition of great lordships and riches and all their inhabitants for Spain. For without doubt there is a very great amount of gold in these lands. . . .

> The people of this island [Hispaniola], and of all the others that I have found and seen . . . have no iron or steel, nor any weapons. . . . They have no other weapons than the stems of reeds . . . on the end of which they fix little sharpened stakes. Even these they dare not use. . . . they are incurably timid. . . .

> I have not found, nor had any information of monsters, except of an island which is here the second in the approach of the Indies, which is inhabited by a people whom, in all the islands, they regard as very ferocious, who eat human flesh. . . .

> They brought us parrots and balls of cotton and spears and many other things, which they exchanged for the glass beads and hawks' bells. They willingly traded everything they owned. They do not bear arms, and do not know them, for I showed them a sword, they took it by the edge and cut themselves out of ignorance. With fifty men we could subjugate them all and make them do whatever we want.[3]

Why, according to Columbus, should Spain be interested in the New World?

The statue features Christopher Columbus and was built in 1893 by Frédéric Auguste Bartholdi.

---

2 "Christopher Columbus Discovers America, 1492," EyeWitness to History, www.eyewitnesstohistory.com (2004).
3 http://www.digitalhistory.uh.edu/historyonline/us1.cfm.

Lesson 5

Summary

> Columbus was a godly man, but he was also a 15th century man with all the prejudices that that entails.

Under monarchs such as Ferdinand and Isabella, Charles V, and Philip II, the newly united nation had other concerns, namely launching the greatest colonial venture in history — the Spanish Empire.

That first voyage of Columbus in the year 1492 marked the birth of a new world . . . but it also helped push a somewhat bewildered young nation to the pinnacle of power way before it was ready. In a few decades, Spain emerged from behind the Pyrenees like a giant to loom over the European stage for more than a century. It would conquer and colonize most of the Americas, bringing its distinctive language and culture to untold generations. Yet within 150 years after 1492, Spain was already in an advanced state of decay. Political and economic greatness were long gone, and the last embers of the Golden Century were growing cool. Each stunning triumph had been followed by an equally dramatic catastrophe, and in most forms of endeavor, Spain's present seemed forever dwarfed by its past.[4] (Student essay by Mark R. Williams)

"Landing of Columbus" - Christopher Columbus disembarks from the Santa Maria on a plank, greeted by Native Americans. This is the first of four scenes of Spanish conquest. Brumidi's central figure seems to have been inspired by the statue of Columbus by Luigi Persico, which was then at the east central steps of the Capitol. (Architect of the Capitol)

The debate about Columbus' character and achievements began at the court of Ferdinand and Isabella. It has been revived periodically ever since. The **Columbus quincentenary of 1992** rekindled the intensity of this early questioning and redirected its aims, often with insightful results. The word "encounter" is now preferred to "discovery" when describing the contacts between Europe and the Americas, and more attention has been paid to the fate of indigenous Americans and to the perspectives of non-Christians. Enlightening discoveries have been made about the diseases that reached the New World through Columbus' agency as well as those his sailors took back with them to the Old. However, the pendulum may have swung too far. Columbus has been blamed for events far beyond his own reach or knowledge, and too little attention has been paid to the historical circumstances that conditioned him. His obsessions with lineage and imperialism, his zealous religious beliefs, his enslaving of indigenous people, and his execution of colonial subjects come from a world remote from that of modern democratic ideas, but it was the world to which he belonged. The forces of European expansion, with their slaving and search for gold, had been unleashed before him and were quite beyond his control; he simply decided to be in their vanguard. He succeeded. Columbus' towering stature as a seaman and navigator, the sheer power of his religious convictions (self-deluding as they sometimes were), his personal magnetism, his courage, his endurance, his determination, and, above all, his achievements as an explorer should continue to be recognized.

Discussion Question

Who was Columbus? A self-seeking opportunist? Or a sincere believer trying to advance the Kingdom of God on earth as it is in heaven?

---

4 See http://www.goldenerabooks.com/SOSIntro.html.

Abu-Lughod, Janet. *Before European Hegemony: The World System A.D. 1250–1350*. New York: Oxford University Press, 1989.

Adams, Brooks. *The Law of Civilization and Decay: An Essay on History*. New York: Alfred A. Knopf, 1943.

Adelson, Howard L. *Medieval Commerce*. Princeton, NJ: Van Nostrand, 1962.

Amin, S., G. Arrighi, A.G. Frank, & I. Wallerstein. *Dynamics of the World Economy*. New York: Monthly Review Press, and London: Macmillan Press, 1982.

Anderson, Perry. *Lineages of the Absolutist State*. London: New Left Books, 1974.

Arrighi, Giovanni, and Jessica Drangel. "The Stratification of the World-Economy: An Exploration of the Semiperipheral Zone." *Review X*, 1 (Summer 1986).

Asad, Talal, ed.. *Anthropology and the Colonial Encounter*. London: Ithaca Press, 1973.

Azzaroli, A.. *An Early History of Horsemanship*. Leiden: Brill, 1985.

Baechler, Jean, John A. Hall, and Michael Mann, eds. *Europe and the Rise of Capitalism*. Oxford: Basil Blackwell, 1988.

Blaut, J.. "Where was Capitalism Born?" in R. Peet, ed. *Radical Geography*. Chicago, IL: Maasoufa Press, 1977, p. 95–110.

_____. "Fourteen Ninety-Two." *Political Geography*, XI,4, July 1992, reprinted in J.M. Blaut et al. *1492: The Debate on Colonialism, Eurocentrism and History*. Trenton, NJ: Africa World Press, 1992.

Bosworth, Andrew. "World Cities and World Systems: A Test of A.G. Frank and B. Gills' 'A' and 'B' Cycles." Paper presented at the Canadian Association of Geographers Conference, Vancouver, May 21, 1992.

Braudel, Fernand. *Civilization and Capitalism*. 3 vols. New York: Harper & Row, 1981–84.

Cantor, Norman F.. *Perspectives on the European Past. Conversations with Historians*. New York: Macmillan Co, 1971.

Chandler, Tertius. *Four Thousand Years of Urban Growth: An Historical Census*. Lewiston/Queenston: St. David's University Press, 1987.

Cox, Oliver. *The Foundations of Capitalism*. New York: Monthly Review Press, 1959.

Cox, Robert W. "Social Forces, States and World Orders: Beyond International Relations Theory," *Millennium: Journal of International Studies*. vol. 10, no. 2, 1981.

Curtin, Philip D. *Cross-Cultural Trade in World History*. Cambridge, MA: Cambridge University Press, 1984.

Dobb, Maurice. *Studies in the Development of Capitalism*. London: Routledge & Keagan Paul, 1963 [original 1946].

Dodgshon, Robert A. *The European Past: Social Evolution and Spatial Order.* New York: Macmillan, 1987.

Duojie, Caidan. "An Initial Study of the Relationship between the Tupo Kingdom and the Silk Road." Urumqi Seminar paper, 1990.

Eisenstadt, S.N. *The Political Systems of Empires.* Glencoe, IL: The Free Press, 1963.

Eisler, Riane. *The Chalice and the Blade. Our History, Our Future.* San Francisco, CA: Harper & Row, 1987.

Ekholm, Kajsa. "On the Limitations of Civilization: The Structure and Dynamics of Global Systems." *Dialectical Anthropology,* vol. 5, 1980, p. 155–166.

Featherstone, Michael, ed. *Global Culture: Nationalism, Globalization and Modernity.* London: Sage, 1991.

Gills, Barry K., and A.G. Frank. "The Cumulation of Accumulation: Theses and Research Agenda for 5000 Years of World System History." *Dialectical Anthropology* (New York/Amsterdam) vol.15, no.1, July 1990, p. 19–42. Expanded version published as "5000 years of World System History: The Cumulation of Accumulation" in C. Chase-Dunn & T. Hall, eds. *Precapitalist Core-Periphery Relations.* Boulder, CO: Westview Press, 1991, p. 67–111.

_____ "World System Cycles, Crises, and Hegemonial Shifts 1700 B.C. to 1700 A.D." *Review,* XV,4, Fall 1992, p. 621–687.

Gilpin, Robert. *War and Change in World Politics.* Cambridge, MA: Cambridge University Press, 1981.

_____. *The Political Economy of International Relations.* Princeton, NJ: Princeton University Press, 1987.

Gimbutas, Marija. *The Early Civilization of Europe.* Los Angeles, CA: UCLA Indo-European Studies Center, 1980.

_____. *The Goddesses and Gods of Old Europe, 7000–3500 B.C.* Los Angeles, CA: University of California Press, 1981.

Gladney, Dru. C. "The Ethnogenisis of the Uighur." *Central Asian Survey,* vol. 9, no. 1, 1990.

Glazer, Nathan, and Daniel P. Moynihan. *Ethnicity: Theory and Experience.* Cambridge, MA: Harvard University Press, 1975.

Gledhill, J., and M. Larsen. "The Polanyian Paradigm and a Dynamic Analysis of Archaic States." In *Theory and Explanation in Archaeology.* A.C. Renfew, M.J. Rowalnds, and B. Seagraces, eds. New York: Academic Press, 1982.

Glover, Ian C. "The Southern Silk Road: Archaeological Evidence for Early Trade between India and Southeast Asia." UNESCO Silk Roads Maritime Route Seminar, Bangkok, 1991.

Going, C.J. "Economic 'Long Waves' in the Roman Period? A Reconnaisance of the Romano-British Ceramic Evidence." *Oxford Journal of Archaeology,* vol. 11, no. 1, March 1992, p. 93–118.

Goldstein, Joshua S. *Long Cycles: Prosperity and War in the Modern Age.* New Haven, CT: Yale University Press, 1988.

Goldstone, Jack A. "Theories of Revolution: The Third Generation," *World Politics,* 32 (1980), p. 425–453; "The Comparative and Historical Study of Revolutions," *Annual Review of Sociology* 8 (1982) p. 187–207.

Goldstone, Jack A. *Revolutions and Rebellions in the Early Modern World.* Berkeley, CA: University of California Press, 1991.

Gouldner, Alvin. *The Two Marxisms.* London: Macmillan Press, 1982

Grousset, Rene. *The Empire of the Steppes. A History of Central Asia.* New Brunswick, NJ: Rutgers University Press, 1970.

Gutman, Herbert G. *The Black Family in Slavery and Freedom, 1750–1925.* New York: Vintage Books, 1977.

Hall, John A. *Powers and Liberties: The Causes and Consequences of the Rise of the West.* London/ Oxford: Penguin with Basil Blackwell, 1985.

Hilton, R. H., ed. *The Transition from Feudalism to Capitalism.* London: New Left Books, 1976.

Hirth, F. *China and the Roman Orient.* Chicago, IL: Ares Publishers, 1885.

Hudson, G.F. *Europe and China.* London: Edward Arnold, 1931. Reprinted by Boston: Beacon Press, l961.

Hunter, James Davison. *Culture Wars: The Struggle to Define America.* New York: Basic-Books, 1991.

James, Peter, et al. *Centuries of Darkness.* London: Jonathan Cape, 1991.

Jameson, F. "Postmodernism, or the Cultural Logic of Late Capitalism." *New Left Review,* 146 (July–August 1984) p. 53–92.

Jaspers, Karl. *The Perennial Scope of Philosophy.* New York: Philosophical Library, 1949.

Jewett, Paul K. *Man as Male and Female.* Grand Rapids, MI: Eerdmans, 1975.

_____. *Reason and Existence. Five Lectures.* New York: Noonday Press, 1955.

Kennedy, Paul. *The Rise and Fall of the Great Powers.* New York: Random House, 1987.

Kwanten, Luc. *Imperial Nomads.* Leicester: Leicester University Press, l979.

Langer, William L. *An Encyclopedia of World History.* Boston, MA: Houghton Mifflin, 1972.

Levine, Lawrence. *Black Culture and Black Consciousness: Afro-American Folk Thought from Slavery to Freedom.* Oxford; New York: Oxford University Press, 2007.

Lin Zhichun. "The Silk Roads before Zhang Opened the Way." Urumqui Seminar paper, 1990.

Lombard, Maurice. *The Golden Age of Islam.* Amsterdam: North Holland, 1975.

Mann, Michael. *The Sources of Social Power. Vol. I. A History of Power from the Beginning to A.D. 1760.* Cambridge, MA: Cambridge University Press, 1986.

McEvedy, Colin. *The Penguin Atlas of Ancient History.* London: Penguin Books, 1967.

McNeill, William H. *The Rise of the West: A History of the Human Community.* Chicago, IL: University of Chicago Press, 1963.

_____. *Europe's Steppe Frontier, 1500–1800.* Chicago, IL: University of Chicago Press, 1964.

_____. *Plagues and Peoples.* New York: Anchor Doubleday, 1977.

_____. *The Pursuit of Power: Technology, Armed Force and Society since AD 1000.* Oxford: Blackwell, l983.

_____. "The Rise of the West After Twenty Five Years." *Journal of World History,* vol. I, no. 1, 1990.

Murray, Charles A. *Losing Ground.* New York: BasicBooks, 1994.

Needham, Joseph. *Civilization in China.* 4 vols. Cambridge, MA: Cambridge University Press, 1961.

North, Douglass C., and Robert Paul Thomas. *The Rise of the Western World: A New Economic History.* Cambridge, MA: Cambridge University Press, 1973

Novak, Lezek. *Property and Power: Towards a Non-Marxian Historical Materialism.* Dordrecht/Boston/Lancaster: D. Reidel Publishing Company of the Kluver Group, 1983.

Oates, Joan. [Comment on Philip Kohl] "The Balance of Trade in Southwestern Asia in the Mid-Third Millennium." *Current Anthropology,* 19:3 (September 1978), p. 480–481.

O'Connor, James. "Capitalism, Nature, Socialism: A Theoretical Introduction." *A Journal of Socialist Ecology.* no. 1 (Fall l988), p. 11–38.

Odani, Nakae. "Some Remarks on the Kushan Coins Found in the Western Chinese Regions." Urumqui Seminar paper, 1990.

Oppenheim, A. Leo. "The Seafaring Merchants of Ur." *Journal of the American Oriental Society,* 74 (1954): p. 6–17.

Oppenheim, A. Leo, and Erica Reiner. *Ancient Mesopotamia.* Chicago, IL: University of Chicago Press, 1977.

Palat, Ravi Arvind, and Immanuel Wallerstein. "Of What World System was pre-1500 'India' a Part?" Paper presented at the International Colloquium on "Merchants, Companies and Trade," Maison des Sciences de l'homme, Paris, May 30–June 2,1990. Revision to be published in S. Chaudhuri & M. Morineau, eds. *Merchants, Companies and Trade,* forthcoming.

Parry, J.H. *The Age of Reconaissance.* New York: Mentor, 1963.

Penguin Atlas of World History. Harmondsworth: Penguin Books, 1974.

Phillips, E.D. *The Royal Hordes: Nomadic Peoples of the Steppes.* London: Thames and Hudson, 1965.

Polanyi, Karl. *The Great Transformation — The Political and Economic Origins of our Time.* Boston, MA: The Beacon Press, 1957.

_____. "Traders and Trade." *In Ancient Civilization and Trade.* Jeremy A. Sabloff and C.C. Lamberg-Karlovsky, eds. Albuquerque, NM: University of New Mexico Press, 1975.

_____. *The Livelihood of Man,* H.W. Pearson, ed. New York: Academic Press, 1977.

Reich, Robert. "The Work of Nations: Preparing Ourselves for 21st Century Capitalism." *The Christian Century,* July 14–21, 1993.

Ryan, Mary P. *Cradle of the Middle Class: The Family in Oneida County, New York, 1790–1865.* Cambridge, Eng.; New York: Cambridge University Press, 1981.

Shaffer, Lynda. *The Rise of the West: From Gupta India to Renaissance Europe.* Medford, MA: Tufts University History Department, 1989, unpublished manuscript.

Stavarianos, L.S. *The World to 1500. A Global History.* Englewood Cliffs, NJ: Prentice Hall, 1970.

Steensgaard, Niels. *Carracks, Caravans and Companies: The Structural Crisis in the European-Asian Trade in the Early 17th Century.* Copenhagen: Studentlitteratur, 1972.

Stein, Mark Aurel. *On Ancient Central Asian Tracks.* Chicago, IL: University of Chicago Press, 1974.

Toynbee, Arnold. *A Study of History.* (Somervell Abridgedment). Oxford: Oxford University Press, 1946.

Wagner, David. "The Family and the Constitution," in *First Things Journal* (August/September 1994).

Wilson, William J. *The Truly Disadvantaged: The Inner City, the Underclass, and Public Policy.* Chicago; London: University of Chicago Press, 2012.

Plowing farmer from the burial chamber of Sennedjem, circa 1200 B.C. (PD).

Concept Words to Know

9/11: Attack on America by Islamic fundamentalists.

Abraham: The father patriarch of Judaism.

Abu al-Qasin: Famous Islamic doctor.

Abyssinia: Ethiopia.

Acropolis: The public square at Athens.

Aegean: A sea surrounding the Greek Peninsula.

Aeneas: The founder of Rome, survivor of Troy.

Aesthetically: Related to art.

Aesthetics: Idea of beauty.

Agape Meal: Love meal.

Agni: Hindu deity.

Agrarian Societies: people groups whose main livelihood is farming.

Ahura Mazda: God of Zoroastrianism.

Alexander: Alexander the Great conquered most of the known world.

Alexandria: Famous Egyptian/Greek city.

Alfred the Great: The greatest Anglo-Saxon king.

Amon Ra: The Egyptian god of the Sun.

Anabaptists: Believed in believer baptism.

Andes Mountains: A mountain range through southern South America.

Anglo-Saxons: German group that invaded and conquered England.

Animalistic: Religion that argues everyone has a soul.

Antediluvian: time before the Great Flood.

Anti-Semites: People who are prejudiced against Jews.

Aphorisms: Pithy truths.

Apocryphal: Debatable inter-testament books of the Bible.

Apologists: Defenders of the Christian faith.

Apostles: The original 12 disciples.

Arabesque: A type of calligraphy.

Archaic: Old.

Archbishops: Part of the Roman Catholic hierarchy.

Archetypal: A type.

Aristotelian Tradition: Tradition of using the Socratic dialogue and the didactic.

Armada: Futile Spanish attempt to conquer England in 1599.

Artha: Hindu deity.

Artisans: Artists and craftsmen.

Aryans: People group that emigrated from Iranian area.

Ascetics: Early Christians who practiced fasting and other disciplines.

Asuka Period: In Japanese history and art, the era from A. D. 552 to 645, which began with the introduction of Buddhism from Korea.

Asura Viviha: Marriage by abduction.

Atheism: A belief that there is no god.

Part of a 15th-century ceramic panel with calligraphy on an arabesque background, first half of 15th century (CCA-SA2.5).

Atonement: Sacrifice for sins.

Attila: Leader of the Huns.

Autocrats: Rulers who are absolutely in control.

Avesta: Sacred texts of Zoroastrianism.

Babylon: a significant city in ancient Mesopotamia.

Bakufu: Shogun commander.

Balkan: Eastern European mountain range.

Barbarians: Germanic people who conquered the western portion of the Roman Empire.

Barons: Nobles in a feudal society.

Barter: To negotiate.

Bartolome de las Casas: Kept a log of Columbus' voyages.

Basques: Northern Spanish tribes near the Pyrenees.

Battle of Hastings: Norman the Conqueror won this battle and England.

Battle of Plataea: Final land battle between Persia and Greece.

Battle of Salamis: Persian fleet was destroyed.

Battle of Thermopylae: Where the Spartan 300 stopped the Persian army for two days.

Battle of Tours: The battle that stopped Islamic expansion into Europe.

Bay of Biscay: North-eastern Bay mostly in France.

Beast Fable: Moral tale whose main characters are animals.

Bedouin: Nomads who were food gatherers.

Benedictine Monk: The Contemplative who founded a monastery order.

Benevolent Autocracy: Good despotism.

Benevolent Totalitarian Ruler: A positive, benign, but autocratic leader.

Bishop of Margus: Roman bishop who negotiated with Attila.

Bishops: Part of the Roman Catholic hierarchy.

Black Land: Fertile loam soil.

Black Sea: The inland sea of Russia.

Blessing of the Cohanim: Ipso facto blessing that belongs to Jewish people.

Boethius: Christian philosophy.

Boniface: Apostle to the Germans.

Boroughs: District of a city.

Bosporus Strait: a short waterway between Asia and Europe.

Brahmins: Highest social strata in India.

Britons: Indigenous group mix of Britons and Celts.

Bubonic Plague: A bacterial infection that devastated Europe.

Buddhism: A religion that espouses a higher consciousness; akin to Hinduism and based on the teachings of Buddha.

Bulgars: Ancestors of Bulgaria.

Bureaucracy: Administrative system.

Burlesque: Parodies of popular characters.

Bushi: Japanese soldiers from traditional warrior families.

Byzantium: The Eastern Roman Empire.

Cahokia Mounds: Spectacular mounds in Middle America.

Caliphs: Islamic head of state.

Saint Ignatius of Antioch, the bishop of the Syrian city of Antioch 10th century (PD).

Calligraphy: Decorative writing.

Cambunian Mountains: Greek mountain range.

Canaan: The Promised Land, the land promised to the Jewish people.

Canon: The officially sanctioned books of the Bible.

Canterbury Tales: A fictional piece written by English poet Geoffrey Chaucer.

Carolingians: First Frankish monarch line.

Caspian Sea: Sea in south Russia.

Cassiodorus: Christian scholar.

Castes: Hindu social class.

Caucasus Mountains: Mountains in southern Russia.

Celsus: An early Christian critic.

Celts: Germanic tribe that occupied England.

Charlemagne: Charles the Great, ruler of the Holy Roman Empire.

Charles Martel: Frankish king who defeated the Moors at Tours.

Charter of Liberties: Written and signed by King Henry I after the Magna Carta.

Christian Worship Assembly: A term for an early church.

Church Fathers: Historical defenders of the faith.

Cicero: Famous Roman orator.

Cistercian Monastery: A Roman Catholic monastic order.

City of Troy: A Greek colony city, in modern Turkey.

City-States: Cities that are also sovereign states.

Civil Law: Law relating to property, not criminal activity.

Civilization: a highly developed, sustaining society.

Clan: Family.

Class System: Division among people groups according to special criteria.

Classical Period: The time before the birth of Christ.

Classical: Traditional.

A Japanese print showing Commodore Matthew Perry, middle, who opened up Japan to the west, circa 1854 (LOC).

Clement: Early Church Father.

Code of Chivalry: An unwritten code of courtesy.

Columbus quincentenary of 1992: 500 year anniversary of Columbus' voyage.

Comedy: Happy endings.

Commodities: Goods and services that have economic value.

Commodore Matthew Perry: The American who opened trade to China.

Composite Bow: Powerful Mongol bow.

Confederation: A loose government composed of voluntary consenting states.

Confucianism: Religion based on a famous Chinese philosopher.

Confucius: Early Chinese philosopher.

Conquistadors: Spanish explorers.

Conscripted: Forced to serve for a purpose.

Constantine the Great: The first Christian emperor.

Constantinople: New name of the capital of Byzantium.

Constitutional Law: Law and legislation based on a written document.

Consuls: Protectors of Rome.

Consumer Driven Society: Prices and supply determined by demand, not by government sanction.

Contiguous: Next to a place.

Conversion: Total change to a new status or allegiance.

Corinth: Greek city.

Cosmology: Study of the supernatural.

Cossacks: Central Asian fierce warriors who lived on the steppes.

Cottage Industries: Industries that occurred in individual homes.

Courage Culture: A culture that mostly emerged in nomadic people groups that emphasized bravery.

Courtly Love: Medieval code for ladies.

Credit: Buy now, by later system.

Crete: Important island off the coast of Greece.

Crossed the Jordan: Expression to describe a conversion and subsequent baptism.

Currency: Money.

Dacians: Ancient Transylvanian people.

Daimyo: Japanese feudal lord.

Daoism: Another word for Taoism.

w: Persian King.

Deacons: A group who serves in the church.

Dead Sea: The lowest in sea level and saltiest body of water in the world.

Deficit: Spending more than one has or can make.

Deforestation: Rapid and total debilitative removal of forests from an area.

Delta: Fertile Lowlands near the mouth of a river.

Democracy: Government by the people.

Desert Fathers: Christians who embraced isolation.

Desert Monasticism: Christians who embraced isolation and to live in the desert.

Despot: A tertiary, omnipotent, usually malevolent leader.

Dharma: Performing the rituals of Hinduism; a follower or convert of Hinduism.

Dhoti: Male loin cloth.

Diaspora: After the destruction of the Temple (AD 70), the Jewish people spread all over the world.

Didache: Writings about the early church that are not sacred.

Didactic: Artistic genres that teach a lesson.

Dionysus: God of the harvest.

Divine Comedy: Written by Dante, the first serious literature written in Italian.

Domesday Book: First Norman census of England.

Domesticated Animals: As opposed to wild animals.

Domicile: Place where one lives.

Donatism: A sect of people who could not forgive apostate repenting Christians.

Dorian: A Greek people group.

Drama: A literary genre.

Detail of Darius III of Persia from the Alexander Mosaic (PD).

Dualistic: A view that good and bad are equal in strength.

Durga: Hindu deity.

Eastern Orthodox Church: The Eastern Catholic Church with a Patriarch at Constantinople.

Eclectic: General.

Einhard: Friend of Charlemagne, who kept a diary which describes Charlemagne.

Elders: The local church leaders.

Emperor Constantine: First Christian Roman Emperor.

Emperor Nero: Roman Emperor who inflicted grievous persecution on the Christian community in the Roman Empire.

Emperor: The supreme leader of a nation. In Japan the Emperor was a god.

Empire: Lands ruled by single authority.

Empress Wu: Female Chinese heroine.

Enculturation Agent: Historical event that causes great cultural changes.

Enculturation: To force, or entice, people or groups to embrace a particular culture.

Entrepreneurship: The art of starting new businesses.

Epic: A long narrative about a hero.

Epistles: Sacred letters in the Church.

Ethics: Morality.

Etruria: A region in Central Italy.

Etruscans: The people group who lived in the area of Rome before the Latins invaded.

European Monarch: Western kings and queens.

Eusebius: Early Church historian.

Excommunication: To be cast out of the Church and its fellowship.

Exegesis: Analysis of Scripture.

Exodus: The liberation of the Jewish people from bondage in Egypt.

Expiation: Complete removal of sins.

Fate: Force determining the future.

Ferdinand of Aragon: King of Spain after the Moors were driven out.

Feudal System: Hierarchical system based on patronage.

Fire Tenders: Ancient peoples who maintained ritual fire.

Four Noble Truths: The four noble truths are the most basic expression of the Buddha's teaching.

Franciscans: A Roman Catholic monastic order.

Frankish Kingdom: First medieval European empire.

Franks: Barbarian tribes that lived in present day France.

Functionality: Operational.

Galilee: Province in Israel.

Galloping Horse Ships: Description of massive Chinese vessels.

Gandharva Vivaha: Love marriage.

Gaugamela: The Battle of Gaugamela took place in 331 BC between Alexander the Great and Darius III of Persia.

Genghis Khan: First major leader of the Mongols.

Geo-Political World: The political aspect of the world.

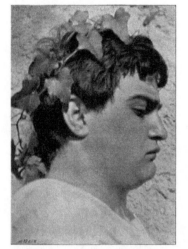

1893 engraving of Nero (PD).

Geometric: The Greek Dark Age.

Germanic Tribes: Central European tribes.

Ghana: Ancient West African nation.

Glaciers: huge layer of ice.

Golden Age of Pericles: Athenian king who brought prosperity and artistic revival.

Gospels: Matthew, Mark, Luke, and John.

Greek Dark Ages: The Greek Dark Age or Ages also known as Geometric or Homeric Age (ca. 1200 BC–800 BC).

Greek Enlightenment: A time of significant artistic production.

Gregory the Great: First medieval pope.

Guilds: Professional organizations.

Guru: Religious teacher.

Guta Empire: Ancient powerful Indian kingdom.

Gypsum: White substance/mineral.

Hammurabi Code: the first written, rule of law, in the world.

Harrappan: First people group to reach India.

Hegemony: Political and cultural control.

Helen: Her kidnapping by Paris precipitated the Trojan War.

Hellas: Greece.

Hellenes: Somebody from Ancient Greece.

Hellenistic: Greek in nature.

Heretical Doctrines: Aberrant Christian theology.

Hindu: Animistic religion.

Hinduism: A polytheistic, animistic religion.

Historical Jesus: The alive, real, historical Jesus.

Holy Roman Empire: The Central European Empire.

Home Meetings: Early church meetings in homes.

Horse Archer: Islamic soldier.

Humanism: A philosophy that places mankind at the center of the discussion.

Humors: Parts of the body temperament.

Huns: Powerful barbarian tribe in Eastern Europe.

Iberians: Spanish tribes.

Icons: Physical representations of Christ that are thought to have spiritual power.

Iliad: Homer's epic classic about the siege of Troy.

Inclusive: Including all persons and genders.

Indigenous: Local people.

Industrial State: Nations whose primary economic prosperity is tied to industries.

Infanticide: Practice of killing young children, usually females.

Ionian Sea: Aegean Sea.

Isabella of Castile: Queen of Spain after the Moors were driven out.

Isis and Osiris: Mother goddess (Isis) and god of the afterlife (Osiris)

Islamic Fundamentalism: Militant Islam.

Island Nation: Japan was an island nation.

Israel: Another name for Jacob, the name of the Jewish state.

Helen is guided by Paris as they leave together for Troy in a 1631 painting by Guido Reni (PD).

Isthmus: Narrow connecting strip of land between two bodies of water.

Jainism Swayamvara: A form of pacifism.

Japanese Feudalism: Japanese hierarchical government based on patronage.

Judges: Leaders of Israel during a period of great stress in Israeli history.

Judicial, Legislative, Executive: Three different branches of government.

Julius Caesar: The last leader of the Republic.

Justinian I: Most famous and capable Byzantium leader.

Kama: Pleasure.

Kamikaze: Divine wind that drove Kublai Kahn's invasion force.

Khan: Mongol chief.

Khazars: A nomadic Turkic-speaking tribal confederation and an offshoot of the Turk kaghanate, the Khazars established one of the earliest and most successful states in medieval eastern Europe.

Kiev: The capital of a 400 year Kevan Rus Empire.

King Arthur: Mythical Briton King.

King Henry I: King who signed the Charter of Liberties.

King John: King when Magna Carta was signed.

King Leonidas: King of the Spartan 300.

King Xerxes: King of the Persians who attacked Greece.

Kinship: To build ties and relationships around family ties.

Koran: The sacred book of Islam.

Korean Peninsula: North and South Korea.

Krishna: Hindu deity.

Kubbutzim: Communal living groups in Israel.

Kublai Khan: Greatest Mongol chief, grandson of Genghis Kahn.

Labor Intensive: An economy that is based on large numbers of labor workers.

Laozi: The founder of Taoism.

Latins: People group who later became the Romans.

Legal Precedence: Civil law procedure enhanced by Justinian reforms.

Liturgies: Worship services.

Local Autonomy: Local control.

Machu Pachacutec: Important Inca ruler.

Magna Carta: Major declaration of the rights of Englishmen.

Magyars: Gothic people who lived in Czechoslovakia.

Mahabharata: Another ancient Hindu Sanskrit epic.

Maize: Native corn.

Mali: Sub-Sahara nation that conquered Ghana.

Mandarins: A Chinese people type.

Manichaeanism: A very popular 5th century religion among intellectuals.

Marathon: A Greek messenger ran approximately 26 miles to Athens to tell his superiors that the Persians were defeated. He died afterwards.

Marco Polo: Italian explorer who opened up trade with China.

Marduk: a significant Babylonian god.

Marketplace: Place where commerce occurs.

Marco Polo wearing a Tartar outfit, 18th century (PD).

Mass: Roman Catholic service.

Mastiff: A large breed dog.

Matrilineal: To find ones identity from ones mother.

Mauritania: West African country.

Meditation: To reflect on life and truth.

Meiji Period: A Japanese era which extended from September 1868 through July 1912.

Menelaus: King of Sparta.

Mennonite: Early, believer baptism, pacifist sect of Christianity.

Merchant Marine: Formal group of ships dedicated to transporting products overseas.

Merchants: Businesses involved in selling and buying, in commerce.

Mesopotamia: the area approximately between and around the Tigris and Euphrates Rivers.

Messiah: The Savior of mankind.

Metaphysical: Reality that originates outside human experience.

Methodist Revival: Intentional meetings to bring new converts into the faith.

Middle Kingdomt: There were several civil wars and King Mentuhotep II united the Kingdom again but he moved the capital to Thebes.

Milan: Italian community.

Militia: Citizen army.

Minoans: Native from Ancient Crete.

Mithraism: A pagan religion with some similarities to Christianity.

Modernity: Movement starting in 1900 that posits that science is most important.

Moksha: Release from rebirth.

Mongol: People group coming from the Mongolian Steppes, conquered China.

Monk's Mound: Spectacular mounds in Middle America.

Monks: Members of a monastery order.

Monotheism: a religion that worships one god.

Monotheistic: To believe in one God.

Montanist: Early heretic who emphasized the supernatural too much.

Moorish Spain: Islamic Spain.

Moscow: Capital of Romanov Russia.

Motif: Theme.

Mound Building: Native American burial mounds and large hills of dirt built, perhaps, to escape high water.

Luxor Temple in Thebes, Egypt (CCA-SA3.0).

Mount Pindus: Greek mountain range.

Muhammad: Founder of Islam.

Mycenaeans: Cultural period in ancient Greece.

Native Americans: Native, indigenous people groups in the Northern hemisphere of the Americas.

Nazareth: The town where Jesus lived.

New Kingdom: It was in the New Kingdom, probably during the reign of Ramses II, that Moses took his people from Egypt to the Promised Land.

Niger: An important West African river.

Nomadic Food Gatherer: People groups who wander and gather food, but do not settle in cities or villages.

Nomadic Societies: people groups whose main livelihood is farming.

Norsemen: Scandinavian peoples.

North Pole: North of Russia.

Novgorod: Russian city.

Octavian: The first Roman emperor.

October 12, 1492: The day Columbus discovered America.

Odyssey: Homer's epic classic about Odysseus' return from Troy.

Old Kingdom: The Old Kingdom, arising after the Great Flood, developed a strong national government--the first in history.

Oligarchy: A government whose leadership is one strong leader.

Omnipotent: Divinely in control everywhere.

Omniscient: Divinely present everywhere.

Oriental Monarch: An Eastern autocrat, monarch, who is usually more despotic than Western types.

Origen: Early Church Father.

Ostrogoths: Gothic people who mostly lived in Germany.

Ottoman Empire: Turkish Islamic Empire.

Ottomans: Turks.

Outlets: Places of commerce.

Pages: Six or seven year old apprentices to be knights.

Panchatantra: Ancient Indian beast fables.

Pandemics: Massive, international outbreaks of disease.

Papal States: Territory that was owned and administered by the Roman Catholic Church.

Papyrus Rolls: Rolls of Scripture written on papyrus.

Papyrus: Paper.

Parchment: High quality paper.

Paris: Trojan noble who kidnapped Helen.

Parousia: The Second Coming of Christ.

Parthenon: The Athenian temple.

Passover: Jewish religious celebration.

Pathos: In literature, pathos is the "heart" or "spirit" of a literary work.

The Jews' Passover from a fifteenth century painting (PD)

Patriarchs of Constantinople: Spiritual leader of the Eastern Orthodox Church.

Patriarchs: Father of a culture.

Patrilineal: Lineage from the father.

Peasants: Poor, landless serfs.

Pelagianism: An emphasis on freewill.

Peloponnesian League: An alliance led by Sparta.

Peloponnesian Peninsula: A peninsula in southern Greece.

Peloponnesian War: Series of wars fought between Athens and Sparta.

Peloponnesus: Southern Greek Peninsula.

Peninsula: land projecting into water.

Pergamon: Or Pergamum was a Greek city in Turkey.

Persepolis: Persepolis was the ceremonial capital of the Achaemenid Empire (ca. 550-330 BCE).

Pharaoh: King/leader of Egypt.

Pharos Island: Island off Alexander. Housed the Pharos light house.

Philip II: Father of Alexander the Great.

Philip II: Spanish king who launched the Armada.

Phoenicians: A sea people in the Middle East.

Picts: Wild Germanic tribe in Scotland.

Plains of Latium: Where the Latins originated.

Poema del Cid: An epic narrative about a Spanish hero.

Poetics: Aristotle's book discussing poetry.

Pogroms: Anti-Semitic actions that destroyed lives and property.

Polis: City.

Polytheism: a religion that worships many gods.

Pope Leo III: Friend and partner with Charlemagne.

Pottage: Thick soup

Prasad: Hindu offerings.

Presbytery: Leadership group in the Church.

Prester John: Imaginary historical figure.

Privatism: Private behavior.

Protocols of the Elders of Zion: Completely spurious theory that Jewish people are conspiratorial.

Ptolemy: Alexander's top general.

Puja: Hindu ritual.

Pyrenees Mountains: Mountains separating Spain from the rest of Europe.

Quakers: Had no clergy and liturgy.

Rabbi: Spiritual leader of the Jewish community.

Rajas: Hindu leader.

Ramayana: An ancient Hindu Sanskrit epic.

Red Land: Arid, dry land, usually rich in iron ore.

Renaissance: Classical revival at the end of the Middle Ages.

Republic: A political entity with elected officials.

Retail: Sale of physical goods to consumers.

Rivedic Period: Ancient Hindu hymns.

Robin Hood: Mythical English hero.

Roger and Hammerstein's Broadway Plays: Musicals popular in the middle of the 20th century.

Roman Empire: The Roman Empire spread all over the Mediterranean world.

Romanov Dynasty: The longest Russian ruling family.

Rome: The city of Rome.

Romulus: One of the legendary founders of Rome.

Rule of Law: law that emanates primarily from written documents or constitutions.

Sacrament: Sacred reenactment of the Eucharist, of the last meal that Christ took with his disciples.

Pharaoh, the king of ancient Egypt, based on New Kingdom tomb paintings (CCA-SA3.0).

Sahara Desert: A desert in northwest Africa.

Sahel: The Sahel is the climate zone of transition between the Sahara desert in the North and the Sudanian Savannahs in the south.

Sakoku: Foreign relations policy that forbid outsiders from entering Japan.

Saris: Woman's garment.

A scribe copying a manuscript in a scriptorium, c. 1478-1480 (PD).

Satyr Plays: Greek tragic comedies.

Savatar: Hindu deity.

Scots: Scottish people groups.

Scriptoria: Room in a monastery devoted to copying Scripture.

Sea of Marmara: An ancient sea connecting Black Sea to Aegean Sea.

Sedentary hunters/gatherers: These are hunters who live in one place.

Senate: The legislators of Rome.

Senegal River: West African river.

Sepphoris: City near Nazareth.

Septuagint: Greek version of the Old Testament.

Serfs: Peasants.

Shaivite: Oldest sect of Hinduism.

Shamans: Native American priests and religious leaders.

Shiites: An Islamic type.

Shimabara: Rebellion by Japanese Christian peasants.

Shiva: Hindu deity.

Shoguns: Japanese leader.

Siddhartha Gautma: The founder of Buddhism.

Sixteen Revelations of Divine Love: Written by Julian of Norwich.

Slavic Tribes: Ancient middle European tribes who settled in Russia.

Solar Monotheism: A pagan religion with some similarities to Christianity.

Song of Roland: An epic narrative about a French hero.

Songhay: A people group who replaced the Malis.

South Asia: India and surrounding countries.

Spiritual Gifts: Gifts of the Holy Spirit were given to the Church, beginning at Pentecost, for the empowering of the Saints, and as an encouragement and helps.

Squires: Twelve to fourteen-year-old apprentices to be knights.

Steppes: Rolling hills of central Asia.

Strait of Gibraltar: The short body of water separating Africa from Spain.

Straits of Artemisium: The Battle of Salamis was fought here.

Subcontinent: Area of Asia; part of a continent.

Sumer: the first significant civilization group in Mesopotamia.

Sundjata: Founder of the Mali Empire.

Sunni: An Islamic type.

Systematic Church Dogma: Comprehensive church doctrine.

Taiho Code: Legal code.

Taikia Reforms: Political and cultural reforms.

Talismans: Religious charms.

Taoism: A philosophy of simplicity and noninterference; the goal of the believer is to establish harmony with the Tao.

Tatar: Mongols.

Tatars: Central Asian Warlike people; absorbed by Mongols.

Temple of Vesta: Roman temple of great importance.

Tertiary Leaders: Leaders who are important, but at the center of the action.

Tertullian: Early Church Father.

Teutonic Tribes: Germanic tribes.

The Concept of Time: the concept of time or mutability.

The Eightfold Path: The way to the end of suffering, as it was laid out by Siddhartha Gautama.

The Gold Coast: West African coastline that sold vast amounts of gold to Europeans.

The Promised Land: Canaan, the land promised to the Jewish people.

Themistocles: Famous Athenian and a politician.

Theodoric: King of Ostrogoth people.

Thermopylae: A narrow isthmus in northeastern Greece.

Three Jewels of the Tao: The goal of Taoism followers.

Three Principles of the People: The 80-20 rule where 80% of the effects comes from 20% of the causes.

Thucydides: Famous Greek historian.

Tiber River: River that runs through Rome.

Tigris and Euphrates Rivers: two ancient rivers in the Middle East; many feel that between or close to these two rivers is the location of the Garden of Eden.

Timbuktu: Famous African city.

Tokugawa Period: Important period of Japanese history where Japan was ruled by shoguns.

Topography: The study of Earth's surface shapes; areas features.

Totalitarian: A government where total control is lodged in one leader.

Tragedy: Unhappy endings.

Turkish: Ottoman Empire.

Two Crop Rotation: To farm with two different crops, rotating each after the other.

Tyre: Palestinian coastal town.

Ukraine: Central Russian province.

Ulfilas: Gothic leader.

Umayyad: Ruling Islamic family.

Untouchables: Lowest Hindu social class.

Ural Mountains: Important mountain range in Russia.

Urban: City.

Utilitarian: Things that are practical and useful.

Utopia: A perfect society or world.

Vassals: Underlings in feudalism whose allegiance was based feudalism.

Vedas: Hindu sacred texts.

Venerable Bede: The Anglo-Saxon author of a history of England.

Viking Age: An age when Vikings conquered most of Europe.

The Turkish Blue Mosque in Istanbul, Turkey. (CCA-SA3.0).

Vikings: Scandinavian Norsemen who ravaged Europe and Russia.

Virtue: Goodness.

Visigoth Alaric: Germanic barbarian tribes.

Visigoths: Gothic barbarians.

Volga Steppes: Rolling hills around the longest river in Europe.

Wadis: Mainly dry water courses.

Wailing Wall: Remaining wall of the destroyed temple.

Wholesale: Sale of physical goods to retailers.

Wimple: A woman's head covering.

Wooden Horse: A trick to get Greek troops in Troy.

Wu Wei: A concept of Taoism: knowing when to act and when not to act.

Xi Shi: One of the famous Four Beauties of Ancient China.

Yagna: A form of intercession to Hindu gods.

Yellow River: The Yellow River or Huang He, formerly known as the Hwang Ho, is the second-longest river in China. It is the location of many ancient Chinese people groups.

Zarathushtra: Founder of Zoroastrianism.

Zhing He: Famous Chinese naval captain.

Zionist: Radical Jewish thought that wishes to form a Jewish state.

Zoroastrianism: Ancient Persian religion.

Western Wall in the Old City of Jerusalem, the most important jewish religious site with the Dome of the Rock (left) on the background. (CCA-SA3.0).